INNOVATION AND TRADITION IN RELIGION

Innovation and Tradition in Religion

Towards an institutional theory

CLAIRE DISBREY PhD
The Open University

Avebury

Aldershot · Brookfield USA · Hong Kong · Singapore · Sydney

Published by
Avebury
Ashgate Publishing Limited
Gower House
Croft Road
Aldershot
Hants GU11 3HR
England

BL
51
.D538
1994

Ashgate Publishing Company
Old Post Road
Brookfield
Vermont 05036
USA

British Library Cataloguing in Publication Data
Disbrey, Claire
  Innovation and Tradition in Religion:
  Towards an Institutional Theory. –
  (Avebury Series in Philosophy)
  I. Title II. Series
  200.1
ISBN 1-85628-852-8

Library of Congress Cataloging-in-Publication Data
Disbrey, Claire, 1942–
    Innovation and tradition in religion : towards an institutional
  theory / Claire Disbrey.
        p.   cm. -- (Avebury series in philosophy)
    Includes bibliographical references.
    ISBN 1-85628-852-8: $59.95 (est.)
    1. Religion--Philosophy. 2. Religion and culture. 3. Language
  and languages--Religious aspects. 4. Experience (Theology)
  I. Title.   II. Series.
  BL51.D538 1994   94-34575
  200'. 1--dc20   CIP
Printed and bound by Athenæum Press Ltd.,
Gateshead, Tyne & Wear.

Contents

Preface

The project that led to the writing of this book began with an attempt to resolve a philosophical problem - the failure of present theories adequately to account for radical innovation in religion. Empiricist theories, which stress the priority of experience in religion, and theories which, following Wittgenstein, stress the priority of language, both face serious problems in this area.

If, as William James claims, religion is based on a kind of private experience, how are such experiences to be recognized prior to cultural institutions such as ritual behaviour and the language of liturgy and belief? If, as the Wittgensteinian tradition claims, religion is an isolated and arbitrary language system, how can such a system be radically changed in ways that seem to be a rational response to factors external to the system?

The pursuit of this problem led me to an innovative analysis of religion - a form, of what I shall call an "institutional" theory of religion.

The philosophy of religion in Britain has in the past tended to be preoccupied with the justification of religious beliefs - with questions about whether the creeds espoused by religious believers can, in any sense of the word, be true, whether they can be rationally assessed and if so how, and with what results. An institutional analysis disconnects understanding and justification. It directs attention away from religions as systems of cognitive beliefs which can or cannot be justified, towards religions as they are practised, within the wider cultures in which they are embedded.

An institutional theory of religion denies that there are any brute facts, that is any property of objects, or quality of experiences, or kinds of activity, attitude or instinct that can be identified as, or used to identify what counts as "religious", independently of, or prior to, cultural institutions. It asserts that it is the historical continuity of these institutions which substantially determines what is, and what is not, to be valued and considered authentic in religion in each community.

Institutional theories have been used in aesthetics. There they seem to run into problems and arouse much criticism. I believe many of these problems and criticisms have been avoided here by including a careful investigation into the nature of institutions. I have, as a result of this investigation and for the purposes of this analysis, defined institutions not in terms of bodies of people (a view which contributed much to the failure of institutional theories of art), but as activities or practices that have acquired special significance and authority within a particular community (like opera, elections or baptism). More specifically they are defined as socially established (rather than natural), repeated, symbolic (i.e. ritual) activities that are shared (rather than being private).

According to an institutional theory, objects, activities and experiences are correctly described as religious by virtue of their position in relation to an institutional framework - a set of culturally established practices - rather than by virtue of any natural property, quality or relationship. People who use the concepts of a religious object, a religious activity and a religious experience, do so (and can only do so) against the background of such sets of practices, even if they do not engage in them themselves.

In general therefore there are no constraints on which activities, objects and experience can be designated religious. But individuals, from within their own social context, are constrained by history - by the activities, objects and experiences which have been so designated by their community (or other communities with which they are familiar) in the past.

The first section of this book explores the subject of radical innovation in religion and offers a critique of current philosophical accounts of it. It considers, as part of the critique, the historical case of George Fox (claimed by both an empiricist and a priority of language theorist to be an exemplar of their theories). It also considers the work of the Alister Hardy Research Centre into religious experience.

the historical case of George Fox (claimed by both an empiricist and a priority of language theorist to be an exemplar of their theories). It also considers the work of the Alister Hardy Research Centre into religious experience.

The second section of the book begins the search for a more adequate account of radical innovation in religion by exploring institutional theories, firstly by surveying some such theories in the field of aesthetics and then by investigating the nature and characteristics of institutions.

In the final section an institutional theory of religion is explored and defended, as the basis for both an adequate account of radical innovation in religion and a sound philosophical analysis of religious belief and behaviour.

A substantial part of Chapters 5-7 has been published as Disbrey, Claire (1989), "George Fox and some Theories of Innovation in Religion", *Religious Studies*, 25, pp. 61-74.

Acknowledgment is due to Professor Stuart C. Brown of the Open University who, as well as teaching me philosophy as an undergraduate, supervised the research and writing of the thesis on which this book was based. Dr. Terry Thomas from the Religious Studies department of the Open University also offered some helpful comments on chapters 16-18.

Every reasonable attempt has been made to obtain appropriate copyright permission.

Aubade by Nuala Ni Dhomhnaill
(trs. Michael Longley)

It's all the same to morning what it dawns on -
On the bickering of jackdaws in leafy trees;
On that dandy from the wetlands, the green mallard's
Stylish glissando among reeds; on the moorhen
Whose white petticoat flickers around the boghole;
On the oystercatcher on tiptoe at low tide.

It's all the same to the sun what it rises on -
On the windows in houses in Georgian squares;
On bees swarming to blitz suburban gardens;
On young couples yawning in unison before
They do it again; on dew like sweat or tears
On lilies and roses; on your bare shoulders.

But it isn't all the same to us that night-time
Runs out; that we must make do with today's
Happenings, and stoop and somehow glue together
The silly little shards of our lives, so that
Our children can drink water from broken bowls,
Not from cupped hands. It isn't the same at all.

Nuala Ni Dhomhnail (1981), *An Dealg Droighinn*,
Mercia Press, Dublin

Part 1
INNOVATION IN RELIGION: A CRITIQUE OF SOME PHILOSOPHICAL THEORIES

1 William James and the priority of experience

Histories of religions involve accounts of innovators - people who rebel against current religious beliefs, who come up with new religious ideas, and whether intentionally or not, start new religious movements. Since the impact of innovators is such a significant factor in the growth and development of religions, theories about the nature of religion need to accommodate them in some way. And most claim they do.

It is, however, surprising to discover that the same historical characters are used to exemplify what appear to be incompatible theories of innovation. William James, who believes, "that feeling is the deeper source of religion and that philosophical and theological formulas are secondary products, like translations of a text into another tongue" [1], claims that no better example can be found for his theories than George Fox, the founder of the Quaker movement [2]. Alasdair MacIntyre, who believes that language is, "prior to... and in a sense formative of," our religious experiences [3], appeals to the same man. George Fox is, he says (with Martin Luther and St. Paul) a good example of how a religious tradition originates in the discovery of a new rule upon which a new system of worship and belief can be built [4].

Both claims can of course only be assessed in the context of the relevant work of the two philosophers. In the case of William James that is mainly his Gifford Lectures of 1901-2 published as *The Varieties of Religious Experience,* although his other writing puts some of the ideas explored in these lectures into a wider context.

William James makes a distinction between two kinds of religious believers. Firstly he describes, "your ordinary religious

3

believer, who follows the conventional observances of his country." His religion has, he says, "been made for him by others, communicated to him by tradition, determined to fixed forms by imitation, and retained by habit" [5]. But, "every imitative phenomenon must once have had its original" [6]. So James goes on to search for the people who have, "the original experiences which are the pattern setters to all this mass of suggested feeling and imitated conduct" [7].

Churches, when once established live at second hand upon tradition, he explains, "but the *founders* of every church owed their power originally to the fact of their direct communion with the divine. Not only the superhuman founders, the Christ, the Buddha, Mahomet, but all the originators of Christian sects have been in this case" [8].

James was clear that religious concepts could be acquired by training and could then have an active role in the interpretation and the formation of experiences [9]. But, he claimed, there was a more fundamental process, whereby people act creatively with regard to religious concepts. When this happens, it takes the form of a response to inner experiences. Experiences are primary in religion because without them, James argues, there would be no need for religious concepts; they constitute both its subject matter and its motivation. "In a world in which no religious feeling had ever existed," he says, "I doubt whether any philosophic theology could ever have been framed" [10]; they produce its energy and its conviction [11]. They are also the source of the idea of God and the very meaning of the word "God" itself:

> These direct experiences of a wider spiritual life...
> form the primary mass of direct religious experience
> on which all hearsay religion rests, and which furnish
> that notion of an ever-present God, out of which
> systematic theology thereupon proceeds to make
> capital in its own unreal pedantic way. What the
> word "God" means is just those passive and active
> experiences of your life... They need not be
> infallible. But they are certainly the originals of the
> God-idea and theology is the translation [12].

These remarks about the priority of experience in the innovatory processes of religion need to be seen in the context of James' empiricist view of the world [13]. James claimed that reality was directly revealed to us in experience and could be transformed into beliefs, knowledge and action without the intervention of conceptual thought.

Ralph Barton Perry says of James: "The notion of pure experience was his deepest insight, his most constructive idea and his favourite solvent for the traditional philosophical difficulties" [14]. James was committed to the view that reality and the field of consciousness were one and the same [15]. For James, "reality is immediately given in experience... *is* experience when the term is properly construed" [16].

James believed that experience, as well as being prior to, and uncontaminated by, thought, could without its intervention flow through a person producing beliefs, knowledge and action [17]. He saw evidence for this in what he perceived as similarities in the feelings and actions prescribed by various religions, compared with the differences in their conceptual systems. He concluded: "The theories which religion generates, being thus variable, are secondary, and if you wish to grasp her essence, you must look to the feelings and the conduct as being the more constant element" [18].

James thought ideas were rather poor instruments, in the service of the will, which could be used to work on our experiences and emotions, to help us capture, remember and understand them, and thus produce more appropriate and effective actions [19].

But conceptual knowledge was for him, "forever inadequate to the fullness of the reality to be known" [20].

> There must always be a discrepancy between concepts and reality because the former are static and discontinuous while the latter is dynamic and flowing... The failure of conception is made good by perception. Concepts are "real" in their "eternal way", they enter into close union with perception, and they play an important role in experience; but they are secondary... imperfect and ministerial [21].

This belief in the priority of perception to conception, which later became known as empiricism, led James to divide religious phenomena into two categories. On the one hand he put what is personal and private in religion - inner experiences, feelings, knowledge and private acts. Language is absent from this category; experiences are ineffable and knowledge is inexpressible. In the other category he put everything that is conceptual, corporate and institutional - ceremonies and theology, creeds, metaphysics and ecclesiastical organization. Here language dominates.

James's first category contains the root and the energy of religion. It represents all that is real, unifying, dynamic and of value; while the phenomena in the second category are derivative, parasitic, divisive and even absurd [22].

The role of religious innovators thus becomes crucial, for these are the people who validate empiricist theory by turning their private experience into theology - by reflecting upon their personal perception of the spiritual aspects of reality and struggling to construct concepts to help themselves and others understand, respond to and discuss them. To James then a religious innovator is someone who experiences strongly, or attends closely to, his perception of one aspect of reality - the unchanging spiritual world. From these special experiences he creates new concepts to name the things he perceives, and goes on to infer new religious ideas and suggest new religious practices. The innovator recognizes these special experiences because he perceives them as communion with what he considers to be divine [23]. He leaves to his followers a new set of concepts which will help them attend more closely to their own religious experiences.

A view opposed to this empiricist account of innovation in religion has been developed by Alasdair MacIntyre.

Notes

1. William James, *The Varieties of Religious Experience*, pp. 414-415.
2. Ibid., p. 30.
3. Alasdair MacIntyre, "The Logical Status of Religious Belief", p. 177.
4. Ibid., p. 200 (fn).
5. William James, *The Varieties of Religious Experience*, p. 29.
6. Ibid., p. 204.
7. Ibid., p. 29.
8. Ibid., p. 49.

9.   E.g. Ibid., p. 416, "The philosophic climate of our time inevitably forces its own clothing on us." And Ibid., pp. 69-70.
10. Ibid., p. 415.
11. Ibid., p. 88, "Our impulsive belief is here always what sets up the original body of truth... The unreasoned argument is but a surface exhibition."
12. William James, "Philosophical Conceptions and Practical Results", p. 357.
13. James is usually characterized as a pragmatist but he is also widely claimed to be the father of empiricism. See e.g. A. J. Ayer, *The Origins of Pragmatism*, p. 183.
14. Ralph Barton Perry, *The Thought and Character of William James*, Vol. II, p. 385.
15. Ibid., p. 589.
16. Ibid., p. 603.
17. William James, *What the Will Effects*, p. 240.
18. William James, *The Varieties of Religious Experience*, p. 481.
19. William James, "The Sentiment of Rationality", p. 57 and *The Varieties of Religious Experience*, pp. 415-6.
20. William James, *The Principles of Psychology*, Vol. 1, p. 78.
21. Ralph Barton Perry, *The Thought and Character of William James*, Vol. II, p. 663.
22. William James, *The Varieties of Religious Experience*, p. 415.
23. Ibid., p. 50.

2 Alasdair MacIntyre and the priority of language

Alasdair MacIntyre refers to the founders of religions in a footnote. He has been attacking the role that empiricist philosophers give to experience in religion. What we say about God is not derived from evidence [1], he says, but grounded in the acceptance of an authoritative rule, that defines a system of worship and belief. The footnote has been added to allay misunderstanding. He is, he says, "merely asserting that in religious practice there are methods of determining which religious utterances are authentic. These methods operate by referring to criteria. The criteria are thus treated as authoritative" [2]. He then explains that the presence of authoritative rules does not, as it might seem, exclude the possibility of radical innovation, for an appeal to personal religious experience can be counted as an appeal to just such a criterion.

MacIntyre continues:

> The rule, "What I came to feel (or see or hear) on such and such an occasion is what I judge theological utterances by," is a common enough criterion. Where one is concerned with the origin of a religious tradition (George Fox, Martin Luther or St Paul) such an appeal to experience is inevitable. For from the original experience the tradition which supplied criteria to later believers is itself defined. I am not of course asserting that those who have pre-eminent religious experiences infer their beliefs from their experiences. If they did their inferences would be

invalid ... What is learnt by the original experience may be used to discriminate between subsequent experiences, some being rejected as non-genuine because discordant with the original. But it is always open to a man to make his own experience his authority and so become the founder of his own religion [2].

Again it is necessary to put these remarks about innovation into the context of MacIntyre's ideas about the nature of religion. These ideas at first seem totally opposed to James. Commenting on the suggestion that religious expressions refer to inner experiences which only some people recognize, he says, "To say this is simply to commit a mistake." This is firstly because many religious expressions are such that according to the normal rules of meaning and syntax in English it is impossible to demonstrate that they refer to inner experiences. Secondly he draws his readers' attention to Wittgenstein's demonstration that this can not be how language is acquired. That theological experiences have private meanings by referring to private experiences is, "ruled out by the fact that no expressions can derive their meaning this way... It is not that we have private experiences and invent words for them". He continues:

But we learn the words and find their application in our experience. The language is in a sense prior to - and even although this could be misleading, in a sense formative of - the experience. This is as true of religious language as of any other. In so far as it refers to private experience, we learn that it does so because the meaning of the expressions can be taught publicly [3].

It would however be wrong to interpret these remarks as a direct contradiction of James. MacIntyre is not claiming that the propositional language of formulated beliefs is primary in religion, rather, that the vocative, performative and metaphorical language of worship is where religion starts. "It is not just that as a matter of historical fact the practice of worship precedes the explicit formulation of belief," he says, "but that we can worship without being able to say clearly what we believe... In formulating doctrine we are trying to say what we do when we

9

pray. So the language of liturgy is at the heart of the matter" [4].

MacIntyre goes on to explain that what is characteristic of religious beliefs is that they are defined by reference to what people accept as authoritative criteria in religious matters.

> The existence of an authoritative rule or set of rules
> is a necessary condition of there being a determinate
> religion. And if we supplement reference to such a
> rule by saying that religion is always concerned with
> how men are to live and with what their fundamental
> attitudes are to be, we produce as near a satisfactory
> definition of religion as we are likely to get [5].

So while James sees religion primarily as a sort of experience - an experience of spiritual reality - that innovators feel particularly strongly, MacIntyre sees religions primarily as sets of attitudes and practices that are governed by an authoritative criterion that innovators question and change.

According to MacIntyre we learn how to use religious concepts by learning their publicly observable criteria of use, particularly by participating in the liturgy of worship. We learn from this training which of our experiences tell us about God. We accept a religion if and when we accept the authority of its criteria on such subjects as what counts as an experience of God or an authentic religious utterance [6]. "We accept authority because we discover some point in the world at which we worship, at which we accept the lordship of something not ourselves... So someone may discover the possibility of worship in the life of the Reformed Churches and accept the Bible as authoritative; or in the Roman Church and accept Papal authority" [7].

MacIntyre does not deny that experiences such as, "awe, intimations of immortality and the like," can be involved in such a decision, but he adds, "They only form a path to religious belief in the full sense when they lead to an acceptance of authority" [8].

"If a man then asks how is he to accept this (the Christian religion), the only possible answer is that he must accept either the Bible itself as authoritative or some other authority such as that of the Church which refers him to the Bible" [9].

We can now see that while James might have problems in explaining the continuity of tradition in religious faith, MacIntyre might have the contrary problem of explaining innovation in religion. For what sort of things could make people want to challenge and change religious authorities? Obviously "experiences", in the Jamesian sense, are prime candidates but, within this theory, there are problems with arguments of this kind. According to MacIntyre a religious system cannot be inferred from, or assessed in relation to, people's experiences because both their experiences and the sort of reasons they use to assess them are determined by the system itself. There is no source of experiences or reasons outside it. There can therefore be no logical relationship between someone's experiences and their subsequent beliefs. "Either a man will find himself brought to say, "My Lord and my God," or he will not" [10]. How then can anyone's experiences lead to the rejection of one religious system based on one set of authoritative criteria and the setting up of another?

MacIntyre's answer to this dilemma is to propose that in the case of innovators, a particular experience can play an unusual role; it can itself become the criterion by which subsequent experiences are judged to be authentic and subsequent claims and utterances are judged to be genuine [11]. Not only is this, in MacIntyre's view, a possible scenario for religious innovation, he claims that, "Where one is concerned with the origin of a religious tradition... such an appeal to experiences is inevitable" [12].

According to MacIntyre's theory we would therefore expect a religious innovator to learn from his religious training, especially from his participation in worship, what God is like and how to know which experiences and utterances are of religious value. Some experience (which might seem to the onlooker, irrelevant [13]) would lead him to reject the authoritative criteria on which this religious tradition is founded and, without inferring anything from his experience, set up some new criteria (the experience itself?) - a different way of deciding which experiences, utterances and practices have religious authenticity and value. Then somehow, although MacIntyre does not suggest how, a new system of worship and belief develops from this new rule. The innovator would leave as a legacy to his followers, a new religious system, based upon a new criteria of authority - the founder's own religious experience.

But *can* experiences play this sort of role in the development of religions? Does it make sense even within the system MacIntyre has set up for himself and can it be shown ever to have happened in this way?

Notes

1. Alasdair MacIntyre's arguments about experience as evidence are enlarged upon in "Visions".   He says, "We could never know from such experiences that they had the character of messages from the divine, unless we already possessed a prior knowledge of the divine and of the way messages from it were to be identified." p. 256.
2. Alasdair MacIntyre, "The Logical Status of Religious Beliefs", p. 200 fn.
3. Alasdair MacIntyre, "The Logical Status of Religious Beliefs", pp. 176-177.
4. Ibid., p. 188.
5. Ibid., p. 201.
6. Ibid., p. 199 "The acceptance or rejection of a religion is thus the acceptance or rejection of such an authority."
7. Ibid., p. 202.
8. Ibid., p. 204.
9.   "
10. Ibid., p. 205.
11. Ibid., p. 200 fn.
12.   "
13. Ibid., p. 210.   "Any explanation can provide an occasion for conversion."   MacIntyre quotes the return of Shatov's wife in Dostoevsky's *The Devils* and Wordsworth's brother's death, and comments that only those over-impressed by metaphysics would want to suggest that any logical process is involved.

3 Some other contributions to the debate 1: Richard Swinburne and Alister Hardy

There has been little continuing debate about innovation in religion among empiricist philosophers. Equipped with the assumptions and vocabulary of empiricism, William James' analysis appears to provide an adequate explanation.

Whether empiricism can adequately account for innovation in religion is a subject that will be dealt with in some detail later; this chapter will examine briefly some pertinent comments by Richard Swinburne and a research project undertaken by Alister Hardy.

Richard Swinburne

In his book *The Existence of God* Richard Swinburne sets out to construct a cumulative, inductive argument for the existence of God. In the course of the argument he enters into debate with Alasdair MacIntyre on the subject of religious experience.

Swinburne argues, "Many have experienced God (or some supernatural things connected with God) and hence know and can tell us of his existence" [1]. If this is so, religious innovators are clearly those who have fresh experiences of God and express them in ways that are relevant to their cultural situation. "God may," Swinburne says, "be known under different names to different cultures" [2].

Like James he believes that all real religious experiences are perceptions of the same thing:

Religious experiences in non-Christian traditions are

experiences apparently of beings who are supposed to have similar properties to those of God, or experiences apparently of lesser beings, or experiences apparently of states of affairs, but hardly experiences apparently of any person or state whose existence is incompatible with that of God. If there were vastly many experiences apparently of an omnipotent Devil, then that sort of evidence would exist; but there are not such experiences [3].

Swinburne assumes the accustomed empiricist definitions and ways of talking. "An experiences is," he says, "a conscious mental going-on" [4]. He notes that descriptions of experiences include words like "seems" or "appears". If these words are used to describe what the subject is inclined to believe on the basis of his present sensory experience, Swinburne calls their use "epistemic". If they are used to compare what an object looks like with the way other objects normally look, he calls their use "comparative". He then defines a religious experience as an experience, "which seems (epistemically) to the subject to be an experience of God (either of his just being there, or doing or bringing about something) or of some other supernatural thing" [5]. Like William James he points out that the crucial feature of this definition is that what makes an experience religious is the way it seems to the subject [6]. He then goes on to ask what it is for the subject to be right.

He launches into talk of perceptions not mediated by the normal senses [7], of private perceptions (which are not private in the sense of my being the only one with a telescope, or the only one with a hand in my pocket, but are like toothache, or dreams in that we only "experience" them in the empiricist sense, when they are our own), and even of private objects, which he defines as objects, "which can cause certain persons to have the experience of it seeming to them that (the object) is there without there having that effect on all other attentive persons who occupy similar positions and have similar sense-organs and concepts" [8]. As an example of a private object he offers, "a person who can choose whom to cause to have the experience of its seeming to them that (he) is there" [9].

Swinburne classifies religious experiences in a way that is similar to James. He has five categories: an apparent perception of a supernatural object in the perception of an ordinary, or of an

14

unusual public object, a private sensation of a normal or of an unusual kind, and an experience which does not involve sensations. He calls it an exclusive and exhaustive list [10], but it is hard to see what it excludes. In fact Swinburne says himself, "Many people view almost all the events of their life not merely under their ordinary description but as God's handiwork" [11].

Armed with these assumptions and this vocabulary Swinburne takes issue with MacIntyre. He suggests a "Principle of Credulity" which states that in the absence of special considerations, when it seems (epistemically) to someone that something is present, then it probably is present [12].

MacIntyre had suggested [13] that there were special conditions that had to be taken into account when looking at religious experiences. Using Swinburne's words he said, "Our supposing that the way things seem is the way things are, is not an ultimate principle of rationality, but itself requires inductive justification." MacIntyre believed this justification was not available in religious experiences in the same way that it was in ordinary experiences; we can infer from seeing smoke to the existence of a fire, or from seeing signals change to the existence of a train, only if we have previously experienced a connection between the two. When we are talking about God, MacIntyre had suggested, even the possibility of making such a connection is absent.

Swinburne appears to overlook MacIntyre's point that a connection can only be made if it is possible to have an undisputed perception of the object in question. An onset of asthma can count as a perception of there being a cat in the room if on previous occasions on which an asthma attack has struck we have incontrovertibly seen the cat in the room. This is possible because it is part of the concept of a cat that we all know what counts as a perception of one. An onset of shivering may not in the same way count as a perception of a devil being in the room, as long as it is part of the concept of a devil that they are usually invisible and can appear to someone "privately" in an infinite number of forms. If we do not know what counts as an incontrovertible perception of a devil we can never establish the connection that shivering is caused by their presence.

It is of course an important theological truth that devils are not the same sorts of things as cats, and theologians, on the whole, realize that we need different procedures for establishing the authenticity of appearances of spiritual beings.

Swinburne bases his argument on the perception of tables. "It is ordinarily supposed," he says, "that people are justified in taking what looks like a table to be one even if they do not at the same time recall their past experiences with tables, and even if they cannot immediately do so" [14]. We can agree that people are justified in taking what looks like a table to be one when they have learnt how to use the word "table", that is, when they know what counts as a perception of a table. Swinburne has not yet established how we learn what counts as a perception of God.

Swinburne goes on to say it is clear that people can recognize things they have never seen before by being given a description of their properties. God, he suggests, can be recognized by his description as, "A "person" without a "body" who is unlimited in his "power", "knowledge" and "freedom"" [15]. I am sure I am not alone in being lost as to what would count as a perception of a person without a body (with or without quote marks around the words); there is no agreed use for this concept.

Swinburne's own assessment of the special conditions under which apparent perception may be seriously questioned includes those, "of a kind with others which proved in the past not to be genuine perceptions" [16]. The crucial question, which Swinburne does not ask, is how one knows whether or not past perceptions of a particular class of object were genuine or not if there is no agreed way of telling what counts as a genuine perception of objects in that class.

MacIntyre's argument raised the difference between apparent perceptions which can under some set of circumstances be proved to be genuine and apparent perceptions which cannot be proved to be genuine under any set of circumstances. Swinburne's description of God as a private object, whatever else it means, clearly puts God into the second category. (This is of course an empiricist philosopher's description of God, not one used by any living religious tradition.)

For people to recognize God in their experiences they must already be in possession of a concept of God which specifies some ways of telling which experiences are of religious value. This is what religious traditions do.

If Swinburne's argument falls here, which I believe MacIntyre to have shown, the empiricist's analysis of religious innovation has been seriously undermined.

Alister Hardy

The practical problems that arise if an attempt is made to apply an empiricist analysis of innovation in religion are interestingly illustrated by the work of another man. Sir Alister Hardy was not a philosopher; he was a natural scientist, but his attempt to set up a research programme on religious experience, based on empiricist assumptions is illuminating.

Hardy held a simplified version of William James' idea that all religions derive from a specific universal feeling:

> Just as science is science in any country of the world, so the fundamental nature of religious experience may be recognized as universal and as the basis of all the world's faiths... What man calls God is a human experience. Any authority in the sacred writings of the various religions of the world is derived from the experience of the holy men of each of these particular faiths. It is the nature of this initial experience that has again and again been distorted by the speculative theories which theologians of the different cultures have built over it [17].

In 1969, having retired from a distinguished career in the natural sciences, Sir Alister founded the Religious Experience Research Unit in Oxford (now known as the Alister Hardy Research Centre) in order to begin a scientific study of religious experience. The plan was to collect and classify accounts of such experiences in order to find out what the experiences were like, who had them, under what conditions, and what effects they had in their lives.

From the start the researchers had a problem that is as far from a solution today as it ever was. It is this: if you believe there is a certain kind of experience that is prior to any kind of theology (any kind of talk), and you want to find out what it is like, what question do you ask in order to get people to tell you about it? They resisted naming the experiences "religious" because they wanted to get behind the formulated language of organized religion, and they could not describe the experience because that would prejudice the responses they got.

They were trying to investigate what they believed to be perceptions of the spiritual world. But, in the language of empiricism, such experiences are private, that is there are no independent or public ways of identifying them. How then are people to know which experiences to tell the researchers about?

After years of work the Alister Hardy Research Centre settled on the following question: "Have you ever been aware, or influenced by, a presence - whether you call it God or not - which is different from your everyday self" [18].

That seems to me like an admission of defeat. The question does not define the category of experiences they want to hear about; we are aware of the presence of thunderstorms, cats, house plants and foreigners, which are all, in very significant ways, different from our everyday selves, but the researchers do not want to hear of our experiences with these mundane objects; while the Research Unit in fact includes in its reports, accounts of experiences openly described as "coming from within the self" [20]. The question, as it stands, does not define the sort of experience considered sacred by any known religion and, lastly, and probably more seriously, it does not avoid prejudicing the answers received because it contains the trigger-word "God", even if it then tries to distance itself from it.

Without the reference to God a large range of mundane experience would fit the question; with it, the question works. People respond, sometimes it is admitted with some extra prompting, by talking about experiences of strange light, feelings of a benevolent presence or of being moved to virtue or courage. But why do they tell of these experiences? They have almost certainly also had experiences of strange darkness, of feeling completely alone and abandoned, or of being moved to immorality and cowardice. These also exactly fit the question as it stands. The crucial point is that they have a concept of God, which they have learnt from their culture, however hazy and however far they have tried to distance themselves from it. They know that God stands for light and love and righteousness.

The project is going confidently ahead, but the philosophical problems that it stands upon illustrate the difficulty of applying empiricist ideas about the priority of experience in religion. If it is not possible to pick out which experiences can tell us about God unless we have a concept that tells us what he is like and what counts as a perception of him, our concept of God cannot, in the way the empiricists describe, derive from our experiences, and innovation in religion cannot be accounted for in the way they describe.

Notes

1. Richard Swinburne, *The Existence of God*, p. 244.
2. Ibid., p. 266.
3. Ibid., p. 267.   This extract is reproduced by permission of Oxford University Press.
4. Ibid., p. 244.
5. Ibid., p. 246.
6. Ibid., p. 247.
7.   "
8. Ibid., p. 248.
9.   "
10. Ibid., p. 252.
11.   "
12. Ibid., p. 254.
13. See e.g. Alasdair MacIntyre, "Visions", pp. 257 ff.
14. Richard Swinburne, *The Existence of God*, pp. 255-6.
15. Ibid., p. 256.
16. Ibid., p. 260.
17. Alister Hardy, *Science, Religion and World Unity*, pp. 1 and 7.
18. For a report of this work see Alister Hardy, *The Spiritual Nature of Man*.
19. For examples see Ibid., pp. 35-39, 150 and 151.   In conversation a researcher told me that they do not discount any reports on any grounds.   In other words they do not take into account the possibility that people can be mistaken about the source of their experiences.

4 Some other contributions to the debate 2: Peter Winch and D.Z. Phillips

Some philosophers influenced by the work of Wittgenstein have attacked empiricism in religion from somewhat different positions to that of MacIntyre, which raise different implications for innovation in religion. The failure of theories based on the priority of language to come up with a satisfactory account of innovation in religion will be considered in more detail later; this chapter will examine briefly some pertinent comments made by Peter Winch and D. Z. Phillips.

Peter Winch

Peter Winch enters into a debate with MacIntyre about the possibility of change in the basic rules of a language system. Without going into the details of Winch's complex ideas about the nature of social institutions, we need only to note that he suggests that all meaningful behaviour is governed by rules and that these rules are to be found embedded in the institutions of societies [1]. The criteria for what counts as real and true, and for what counts as evidence and proof, all belong to the social institutions within which any questions are asked. Our language and our social relations are so closely related they are, "just two different sides of the same coin" [2].

MacIntyre questions this argument on the grounds that, if standards of intelligibility originate in social institutions, the possibility of their developing by criticism is ruled out [3] - a situation that would deny the possibility of one sort of innovation in religion. Winch replies that he emphasized the open character of the rules. "In changing social situations," he says, "reasoned decisions have to be made about what is to count as, "going on in the same way". In my view the point is that what determines this is the further development of rules and principles already implicit in the previous ways of acting and talking" [4]. Winch imagines the situation as one where people are trained to follow norms which involve the phrase, "and so on". They are then open to new possibilities in the interpretation and use of this phrase [5]. Modifications in grammar are possible, but only if they are intelligibly related to existing ways of speaking [6]. MacIntyre has, Winch says, overlooked the fact that criteria and concepts have a history [7].

Winch is open to the possibility of change in religious institutions and language, but he is as closed as MacIntyre to the suggestion that independent rational deliberation on what James would have called, "experiences of the real world" can have a role in such change. He agrees that it is important not to lose sight of the fact that peoples' ideas and beliefs must be checkable by reference to some independent reality. But on the subject of the role of "the independently real" in peoples' thoughts, he mentions two things. Firstly that it is only within a particular system of language that the concept of reality has a use: "God's reality is certainly independent of what any man may care to think," he says, "but what that reality amounts to can only be seen from the religious traditions in which the concept of God is used. It is within the religious use of language that the conception of God's reality has its place" [8].

Secondly he says that reality is not what gives language its sense: "What is real and what is unreal shows itself *in* the sense that language has. Further, both the distinction between the real and the unreal and the concept of agreement with reality themselves belong to our language" [9]. Nature does make herself heard, but this is only, "by way of the factual circumstances in which language is applied" [10].

This emphasis on the arbitrary and self-contained nature of language systems, characteristic of a particular Wittgensteinian tradition, clearly leaves some question marks over the mechanism of innovation in religion. MacIntyre's statement that a man can make one of his own experiences his criterion of authority and Winch's observation that criteria and concepts have a history, only go so far in providing answers.

This emphasis, if pressed strongly in relation to religion, would lead us to expect that innovation in religion can only take the form of gradual internal developments that are not determined by any experiences or reasons that originate from any source external to a particular set of religious institutions.

Winch however is neither committed to the totally arbitrary, nor the totally independent, nature of religious language systems. He makes the suggestion (to which MacIntyre also alludes [11]) that religions are not primarily kinds of language systems at all, but systems of practices or activities and suggests that we think of religious talk, "as growing out of the primitive ritualistic observances" [12]. Of course such talk could have come first, he concedes, but until it is connected with rituals of reverence or worship we, "should have no reason to attach any religious significance to it" [13]. (The difficulties with this view will be discussed later along with an unsatisfactory analogy Winch draws between the relationship between behaviour and language in pain and religion [14].)

Winch does not develop these ideas in relation to innovation in religion but they clearly have a bearing on the subject. Religious practices are, he says, expressions of the feeling for, "a sense of the significance of human life" [15]. They arise as, "a man tries to contemplate the sense of his life as a whole" [16], or as, "a primitive, human response to certain characteristic human situations and predicaments, that is, to use a phrase of Wittgenstein's - part of the natural history of mankind" [17].

Winch also sees the relation between practice and theory in religion as being two-way. Although there are different pressure on each, the traffic between them, "goes in both directions and there is give and take," he says [18].

For Winch therefore, although he does not develop the idea, there seems a possibility that what we might call pre-lingual social institutions, such as religious rituals, could change in response to the changing historical situations of human communities, and that such changes could produce subsequent changes in religious language systems.

D. Z. Phillips

In his early writing D. Z. Phillips takes up the idea of theology being the grammar of religious language and, developing it somewhat further than Winch, raises some different thoughts about innovation in religion. He rehearses similar arguments

22

against empiricism in religion:

> Religion is not the product of an individual. A religion existed before the birth of the individual and will continue to exist after his death. He acquires his religion in the way he acquires his language, namely by being born into a particular society... His hopes and fears, thoughts and plans, are only intelligible in the context of the society in which he lives [19].

He makes similar statements about the criteria of use of such concepts as truth, facts, evidence and reality. It is within religious discourse that we find what is meant by the reality of God, he says. There is, "no question of a general justification of the criteria for distinguishing between the real and the unreal" [20].

Phillips concludes from these two ideas, and from his observations of the role religious beliefs play, that theology has an internal role in religion, and religious language an expressive role in the life of the believer.

Because our language tells us what our experiences mean, there is no possibility of seeing a move from experience to formulated religious beliefs as any sort of conclusion from evidence or any sort of rational inference, and because there is no possibility of a general, independent criteria for distinguishing the real from the unreal, the true from the false, religions cannot be justified or disproved from outside the language systems which comprise them. Finding or losing faith, Phillips concludes, can never be the result of collecting evidence or thinking rationally; when it is said that people must be given reasons for believing in God, he says he simply does not understand what could be involved in this enterprise [21]. The role of theology can not be the justification of religious statements from a supposedly external viewpoint, nor any kind of inference, explanation, or interpretation of our pristine experiences of the world; it can only have an internal role [22].

Phillips' elucidation of the grammar of religious language also leads him to argue that talking about God - an absolute, eternal, necessary being - is nothing like talking about a physical object that we can touch and see and that might or might not exist. (This God is again more of a philosophical construction than a theological one.) Religious beliefs have an unshakeable

23

character that is not like having an opinion; they are not reached by assessing evidence or collecting facts and, since they cannot be falsified by factual evidence, using them is not like using a hypothesis or a theory. In fact as nothing counts either for or against them, they cannot count as assertions about how the world is. Believers and unbelievers do not contradict each other; they just use different language games.

Phillips concludes that religious language is expressive. Although it may sound, on the surface, as though believers are asserting propositions about how things are, their language is in fact just showing something about the way they feel about the meaning of life and death - emphasizing what seems to them to be significant. It does not refer to, describe or mean anything beyond itself [23]. Religious language is used to express what goes deep in people's lives [24], to show the force of what is being said or done. Going on to draw metaphysical conclusions from such language is a mistake, caused by, "confusion about the grammar of our language" [25]. It makes no sense to ask why people use such forms of language. Speaking of a belief in the reality of the dead Phillips says, "No explanation of the beliefs can be given which reduces them to fantasies born of prior conditions. If one asks why people should believe in the reality of the dead, why the dead should be held in awe, reverence or dread, one can only reply that people *do* react to the dead in this way, that is all" [26].

What interests me here is the process by which people might change their reactions to the dead. Phillips' remarks on how religious beliefs can change, are related to his discussion of the Wittgensteinian idea of world pictures - pictures that people use to regulate their lives [27]. He asks if religious beliefs are similar to Wittgenstein's world pictures. His answer is that they are similar in that they seem to form a bedrock beyond which questions seem senseless, and disagreements about them cannot be located within the mode of discourse in which they are expressed. Such disagreements are not disagreements about facts but disagreements about ways of looking at the world. It makes no sense to ask if the pictures people use are correct since notions of correctness only have a meaning within a world picture. In this sense they can be said to be groundless. But religious beliefs are different from world pictures in that someone who cuts himself off from religious beliefs can not be said to have cut himself off from reason, rather there seem to be alternatives that

24

he can reasonably claim. Dissenters do not so much contradict what is being said as decide they have no use for the whole perspective represented by it.

Phillips talks about people losing their faith in God. It is not, he says, a matter of disbelieving, "one thing among many of the same kind, but to see no sense in *anything* of that kind. What has become meaningless is not some feature of a form of life, but a form of life as such" [28].

How this can happen, Phillips discusses in a dialogue with J. R. Jones [29]. If no sort of evidence is involved in assessing the truth of a religious picture how is it that scepticism can undermine religious belief? - Jones asks. Phillips answers that when an individual loses his faith it is a question of his attention being won over by a rival secular picture - a question of his energies being focused in another direction, and the old picture, once powerful in his life, losing its grip. But, he continues, we must distinguish between cases like this and cases where changes in the culture lead to religious pictures losing their hold. Jones asks him why, when this happens, it doesn't make sense to suppose that people could make up new pictures and then try and induce belief in them. Phillips answers that it is because:

> These pictures have a life of their own, a possibility of sustaining those who adhere to them. Part of the answer to the question why it would be nonsensical to imagine theologians... creating pictures... to meet the crisis of the age... is that whatever they created would precisely be their creation, and you would have a curious reversal of the emphasis needed in religion, where the believer does not want to say that he measures these pictures and finds that they are right or finds that they are wanting. On the contrary, the believers wish to claim that it isn't they who measure the pictures, since in a sense, the pictures measure them [30].

J. R. Jones adds that the problem with new pictures is that they would be, "trying to be made to become, operative as beliefs... in the absence of the surroundings of, belief - all that goes with believing in a tradition of belief... in an historical faith." He adds, "I can't see that anything could be a substitute for that" [31].

Phillips' view of religion seems here to restrict the possibility of religious innovation to communities, or individuals within communities, beginning to react to and talk about the deep things in their lives in a different way, so that the traditional world pictures they have been using begin to lose their hold. But it seems that these changes in reaction can not be logically related to anything that happens in their lives - any rational thought about their experiences - and that they happen in spite of the fact that the way the world looks and feels to them is determined by the language system they have inherited. As with MacIntyre there does not seem to be any intelligible mechanism, or even room for any mechanism, by which new religious world pictures are constructed.

And yet, like Winch, Phillips does not want to be so restrictive. In a book written some years after these remarks he denied both that he meant what people had taken him to be saying, and that Wittgenstein's ideas required any such interpretation. "Rightly understood... nothing Wittgenstein says rules out the possibility of dialogue, understanding, criticism, change or decline where religious beliefs are concerned" [32]. "If we cannot give any rational justification for religious beliefs," he asks, "does it not follow that religious beliefs have been made safe, incapable of being affected by personal, social or cultural events?" But his answer is, "No such conclusion does follow, and it is certainly not one that I have ever embraced" [33]. "Certain religious pictures decline... a picture may die in a culture, because believing it is not an isolated activity... other cultural changes can affect people's worship" [34].

He continues to uphold Wittgenstein's remarks that, "Logic is to be found not "outside" language but only within the various language games themselves," but adds that, taken at face value, this claim, "runs counter to what actually happens. Surely people do respond to religious beliefs by saying, "That belief makes no sense"... Religious beliefs and practices are criticized" [35]. He tries to resolve the dilemma by proposing that we see religious rites and practices as a form of language and that we see an interaction - "a two way traffic" - between the different language games. When religions celebrate the harvest, he says, "May not aspects of the rituals and prayers themselves be changed by these various events and activities? There is no reason to think that Wittgenstein cannot allow such an answer" [36].

So again the answer appears to lie in seeing religions not

primarily as language systems but as aspects of culture, whose institutions interact in some way with other institutions and other aspects of culture. "Christianity does not wear culture like a garment," Phillips says, "Christianity is a part of the culture... The religious element is a contribution to the culture and not simply a reflection of it" [37].

MacIntyre's, Winch's and Phillips' accounts of religious belief, although based on sound philosophical theory, seem to leave several questions unanswered. They see a variety of ways in which individuals and communities can be related to religious belief systems; they can inherit them, they can use them to regulate their lives, and they can stop using them, while in communities such systems can develop and they can lose their hold.

But where, if they exist, do James' "makers of religions" and MacIntyre's "founders" fit into this scheme? How, if at all, are new world pictures created by individuals or communities? How far and in what way can factors external to a religious language system affect its development or use? Do individuals and communities make choices and judgements about world pictures and if so on what basis?

It is in search of answers to these questions that I turn now to the story of a religious innovator.

Notes

1. Peter Winch, *The Idea of a Social Science*, pp. 32 ff.
2. Ibid., p. 123.
3. Peter Winch, "Understanding a Primitive Society", p. 27.
4. Ibid., p. 11.
5. Ibid., p. 31.
6. Ibid., p. 27.
7. Ibid., p. 32.
8. Ibid., p. 12.
9. Ibid., p. 13.
10. Peter Winch, "Meaning and Religious Language", p. 209.
11. Alasdair MacIntyre, "The Logical Status of Religious Belief", p. 188.
12. Ibid., p. 198.
13. Ibid., p. 200.
14. This will be discussed in Chapter 9.

15. Peter Winch, "Understanding a Primitive Society", p. 36.
16. Ibid., p. 37.
17. Peter Winch, "Meaning and Religious Language", p. 202.
18.   "
19. D. Z. Phillips, *Religion Without Explanation*, pp. 88-9.
20. D. Z. Phillips, *Faith and Philosophical* Enquiry, p. 70.
21. Ibid., p. 79.
22. Ibid., pp. 5 ff.
23. D. Z. Phillips, *Religion Without Explanation*, pp. 144-150.
24. Ibid., p. 114.
25. Ibid., p. 111.
26. Ibid., pp. 134-5.
27. Ibid., pp. 160 ff. See also Ludwig Wittgenstein, "Lecture on Religious Belief", pp. 55 ff.
28. D. Z. Phillips, *Faith and Philosophical Enquiry*, p. 46.
29. Ibid., pp. 111 ff.
30. Ibid., pp. 117-8.
31. Ibid., p. 118, 119 and 117.
32. D. Z. Phillips, *Belief, Change and Forms of Life*, p. xi.
33. Ibid., p. 15.
34.   "
35. Ibid., p. 20.
36. Ibid., pp. 26-27.
37. Ibid., pp. 94-95.

5 An introduction to the case study

We have seen how some philosophers use historical characters to exemplify the case they are trying to make, and how, when the subject is religious innovation, the character most likely to be mentioned is the founder of the Quaker movement, George Fox.

The following chapter will consider the story of this alarming man, who railed against the religious people of his day and introduced a subversive branch of religious thought based on the belief that people can find God in the quiet of their own minds. It will consider the background to his life and the things he said about himself and his experiences and beliefs in his journals, as well as the records of historians and Quaker commentators.

But first, the use of historical case studies in philosophical enquiry needs to be defended. Some philosophers argue that theories are neither enhanced nor damaged by case histories: their truth and value does not depend upon what happened at any particular point in time, but on internal consistency, elegance and fruitfulness. The theoretical weaknesses of present theories of innovation in religion will be dealt with in some detail in future chapters, so what is the role of an historical case study at this point?

Philosophical theories that take the form of an analysis or explanation of social phenomena need, in order to be of substantial use, to keep some sort of hold on actual instances. It is open to theorists to say that their analysis outlines the essential elements of the phenomenon and that instances that do not fit their theory are unauthentic or idiosyncratic, but there comes a point at which such theories lose credibility because they cannot be made to fit what are generally agreed to be definitive or standard instances. A theory of the nature of religion loses credibility in this way if, for instance, it simply assumes that the nature of religious activity is quite different from what most religious believers take it to be.

Trying to fit the story of a particular instance to a theory that claims to explain a human phenomenon can be helpful in philosophy even when the story is an entirely fictional one; for one theory the exercise may reveal that no plausible story can be told that fits it, for another, the story may so engage our imagination that we are persuaded that it could be correct. Good examples of this procedure can be found in philosophical writing on the subject of self-deception [1]. And if fiction can help philosophers' arguments in this way, how much more can biography, where the story told has its roots in history rather than imagination.

When two incompatibly opposed theorists both choose, from a wide range of possibilities, the same sequence of historical events to exemplify their theories, the situation begs investigation, but we should be wary of claiming too much from the results. The role of this case study is not to provide any kind of proof of the inadequacy of empiricist or priority-of-language theories of innovation in religion, but to raise questions and suggest alternative avenues of thought.

The choice of George Fox rests not only on James' and MacIntyre's use of his story. We have, in his case, the advantage of access to his personal journals, numerous independent primary sources and wide and fairly uncontentious reports of the historical events through which he lived. But of course we only have his accounts of his experiences; we can only surmise the facts of his upbringing and there is ample evidence not only that parts of his journals were written long after the events they describe, but also that they were doctored by Fox's followers [2]. Nor should we forget that Fox, his editors and later commentators, all had their own theories about how religions change and grow.

It is hoped that some justification for the method will be found in its results - that it will become apparent that the recorded events cast serious doubt on the adequacy of the philosophical theories which claim to be supported by them, and point towards a more fruitful approach to explaining innovation in religion.

The main question under review is how well the story of George Fox fits William James' and Alasdair MacIntyre's theories about the process of religious innovation. So what should we expect from the story if either of these theories were correct?

William James

If George Fox is to exemplify William James' ideas about religious innovation we would expect to find that Fox's religious training would be of little importance to the new ideas he developed, since he rejected the religious concepts he was trained in, the religious experiences of his elders and contemporaries and the religious practices to which he had become accustomed; while his intellectual, emotional, social and political training would be irrelevant, except in so far as it led him to attend more closely than his fellows to a special kind of experience. The beliefs he came to hold, and the concepts in which he expressed them, would not be born out of acquaintance with the religious or intellectual ideas of his day, but be inferred from his own experience of an unchanging spiritual world. The difference between Fox and his predecessors would primarily be explained in terms of differences in the extent to which he had, and attended to, a certain kind of experience, rather than any other differences in upbringing.

Fox would be able to describe some of his experiences as religious because of their special quality. He would "recognize" them as, "direct communion with the divine". Due to the unchanging nature of these spiritual experiences we should expect to find that his new ideas had more continuity with the ideas of other religious innovators than with the current religious or secular ideas of his own time.

Fox would find the religious concepts of his day inadequate for making sense of his religious experiences. By attending carefully to his own special experiences he would be able to re-define what God was like and coin new ways of talking about him. These new concepts would be names for the things he became acquainted with in his own experience and they would be discontinuous with the religious concepts of his day.

By teaching others these new concepts Fox would enable them to attend more closely and respond more effectively to their own religious experiences. To some, the advantages of these new concepts would become clear and they would accept and appropriate them. The religious movement started by Fox would be discontinuous with the religion of his day because the Quakers would take more notice of a universally available experience and have a new set of concepts for talking about it.

Alasdair MacIntyre

If George Fox is to exemplify MacIntyre's ideas about religious innovation we would expect to find that Fox's religious training, especially his participation in worship, would teach him what God was like and how to know which experiences tell us about him. His training in language would teach him the publicly observable criteria of use of current religious concepts.

Fox would know which of his experiences had religious significance and value because of this training. Some of these experiences, or some other experience of life, would lead him by a non-logical route to reject the current sources of religious authority and to commit himself to a different one - a different way of deciding which experiences, utterances and practices have religious authenticity.

In rejecting the idea of religious authority which he inherited, Fox would reject the system of ideas and practices that was based upon it. He would set up a new criterion that religious utterances would henceforth be judged in the light of what he had experienced. It is not clear how a new set of concepts and a new belief system would emerge from a criterion of this sort except that it would not be logically inferred from anyone's experiences.

Fox would be seen to have started a new religion by setting up a new criterion of religious authority - one of his own religious experiences - from which would grow a new system of thought and behaviour, used by those who accepted this criterion as their own. The movement he started would be discontinuous with the religion of his day because it would be built upon a new source of authority, which was a particular kind of experience.

Notes

1. See e.g. Soren Kierkegaard, *The Sickness unto Death*, John Douglas Mullen, *Kierkegaard's Philosophy*, and Ilman Dilman and D. Z. Phillips, *Sense and Delusion*.
2. See the prefaces and introduction to *Journal of George Fox*, John Nickalls (ed).

6 George Fox

George Fox was born in 1624 into an era of political, social and religious turmoil and anarchy. It was at the age of nineteen that he left home and set off on a spiritual quest; five years later, in 1647, he resolved his search and began life as a travelling preacher. This period in which he grew up and developed his ideas were arguably one of the most disruptive periods in English history and in the English church. Between 1629 and 1640 England was ruled by Charles 1, with the assistance of Archbishop Laud and his bishops. They set out to increase the power of the priesthood and to impose anti-puritan measures on a largely uncooperative populace. In 1640, when Fox is eleven, public distaste explodes and Archbishop Laud is impeached and imprisoned; in 1641 a censorship that has been in force for years is lifted; in early 1642 the bishops are excluded from the House of Lords and, by that summer, civil war, with all the consequent extra mobility and disruption of traditional standards and hierarchies, has broken out; in 1643 episcopacy is abolished and a mostly Presbyterian Assembly of Divines is set up to reform the Church of England. By 1644 numerous radical religious movements are beginning to emerge - for example it is this year that the Particular Baptists sign their first confession of faith. In 1646 when Fox is seventeen, the Levellers, the first democratic political movement in modern history develops, led by John Lilburne and in 1649 the first communist community is set up by the Diggers, led by Gerrard Winstanley. (Both of these men are later to become Quakers.) By the end of 1648 the King is beheaded, Oliver Cromwell has been made Lord Protector and the whole country has been set on its head.

John Lampen says of these times:

33

The revolution in religious thought which had challenged the monolithic medieval church and produced the Reformation was over 100 years old. The years of Commonwealth in England were a time of extreme and independent views, bitter controversy, and uncertainty about the nature of religious authority. Many groups of people had been abandoned by the established churches or withdrawn from them: generally known as "Seekers", they waited for a revelation of God's truth [1].

In spite of the fact that George Fox makes almost no mention of these events in his journals, it must be impossible to understand or evaluate his life and ideas without setting them against a background of economic, agricultural, industrial, political, social, intellectual and educational revolution, without reference to the fact that he lived through a period when, for a mixture of reasons, long accepted and firmly fixed forms of social authority and government fell apart and men were forced to re-think many of the theories they had depended upon for centuries.

Another factor, the significance of which cannot be over-estimated, was the fairly recent arrival of the printed English Bible and its gradual distribution among an increasingly literate laity. Fox's forebears had grown up under the guidance of an educated priesthood with exclusive access to a Latin Bible. The very idea of lay people having opinions and making judgements in religious matters was a portentous new development.

Fox's religious training

By the time of Fox's childhood, Puritans, and other Separatists, as well as Calvinists within the Church of England, were preaching the importance of the individual's conscience and experience over the institutions of the Church.

They were stressing the importance of studying the Bible and questioning Church traditions and ceremonies. They were crying out against the power of the priests and the injustice of their tithes. New ideas were giving people the courage to stand up to their social superiors and to kick against the authority, traditionally seen to extend from their fathers, through the local gentry, to the King and thence to God himself.

34

An interesting insight into this world can be seen from reports of Archbishop Laud's Metropolitan Visitation of the Province of Canterbury, made in 1634 and five by his Vicar General, Nathaniel Brent [2]. In many instances there are reports of the Vicar General having to charge the clergy of, "divers points of inconformity".

In St. Edmundsbury in April he took away a licence to preach from a Mr. Peartree, "in regard of his great ignorance, being not able to tell me what "ecclesia" did signify," and in Oundle in May he had to admonish a schoolmaster for instructing his scholars out of the wrong catechism. A commentary on these passages [3] explains that Radical Protestants of this time believed that "ecclesia" or "church" meant the congregation, not the ruling hierarchy of bishops, with the implication that church discipline should be controlled democratically, not from above, while the "wrong catechism" was "almost certainly a Geneva Calvinist catechism".

In his journals Fox tells us that his father was known as, "a Righteous Christer" and his mother was, "an upright woman of the stock of the martyrs". Fox says of his childhood that he, "had a gravity and stayedness of mind and spirit not usual in children" and a dislike for seeing adults, "carry themselves lightly and wantonly towards each other... When I came to eleven years of age," he says, "I knew pureness and righteousness, for while I was a child I was taught how to walk to be kept pure. The Lord taught me to be faithful in all things" [4].

It is clear that, looking back on his childhood Fox felt that he had been trained in godly living; he spoke of himself as having been, "brought up into the covenant, as sanctified by the Word which was in the beginning...". He contrasted himself with those who, "being strangers to the covenant of life with God, they eat and drink to make themselves wanton with the creation, devouring them upon their own lusts, and living in all filthiness... without God" [5]. He believed that this training depended upon the fact that from a young age he had been able to recognize the voice of God. Fox does not make it clear what he means by the phrase, "the Lord showed me...", which he uses of his childhood and this means that we cannot satisfactorily answer some of the questions posed, but it is perhaps significant that, unlike the great majority of later Quaker journalists, Fox does not recount any specific religious experiences in his childhood.

Up to age of 18, we can presume that Fox was absorbing

religious practices and concepts from at least three sources - from the ceremonies of the Laudian priests, from his own reading of the Bible and from the preaching of the Arminians and Calvinists

That this is so is supported by some early entries in his journal. When at the age of 19 he sets off on a spiritual search, he recounts how he pursues his target in several different ways and ends in despair. At first he, "went to many a priest to look for comfort but found no comfort from them" [6]. He would also, "get into the orchard or the field with my Bible by myself" [7]. Then:

> After I had received that opening from the Lord that to be bred at Oxford or Cambridge was not sufficient to fit a man to be a minister of Christ, I regarded the priests less and looked more and more after the dissenting people... But as I had forsaken all the priests, so I left the separate preachers also, and those called the most experienced people; for I saw there none among them all that could speak to my condition [8].

Fox's religious experiences

One of the most striking things about George Fox's journals, in the light of the expectations with which one comes to them, is the small amount of space he gives to descriptions of religious experiences. In the nearly 800 pages of his diaries (in the present edition), the word "experience" occurs only six times and only just over 20 dreams and visions are described in any detail. Yet in another sense Fox's day by day life is described as a continuing experience of God's guidance, protection and instruction.

The following passage from the *Journal* will give the flavour. Here Fox describes a vision in characteristically sparse detail and goes on to use two much loved phrases, "I was moved of the Lord," and, "The Lord opened to me":

> And the next day we passed on, warning people as we met them of the day of the Lord that was coming upon them. As we went I spied a great high hill called Pendle Hill, and I went on the top of it with

much ado, it was so steep; but I was moved of the Lord to go atop of it; and when I came atop of it I saw Lancashire sea; and there atop of the hill I was moved to sound the day of the Lord; and the Lord let me see a-top of the hill in what places he had a great people to be gathered. As I went down, on the hill side I found a spring of water and refreshed myself, for I had eaten little and drunk little for several days.

And so at night we came to an alehouse and stayed all night and declared much to the man of the house, and writ a paper to the priests and professors concerning the day of the Lord and how Christ was come to teach people himself by his power and spirit and to bring them off all the world's ways and teachers to his own free teaching, who had brought them and was the Saviour. And the man of the house did spread the paper up and down and was mightily affected with Truth. And the Lord opened to me at that place and led me to see a great people in white raiment by a river's side coming to the Lord, and the place was near John Blaykling's where Richard Robinson lived.

And the next day we passed on among the fell countries and at night we got a little ferns and brackens and lay upon a common and the next morning went to a town where Richard Farnsworth parted with me and I was alone again [9].

It is important to note here that in the period in which Fox wrote his diary, (this early portion was dictated to his stepson-in-law in 1675), the recounting of religious experience was a common, if fairly new, activity. An historian comments of this time:

A particular feature of sectarianism was the extension of the Puritan emphasis on the individual's relationship with God. An important expression of this was the need to have had some sort of conversion, to have experienced God personally. Recounting this experience of God became a condition of membership in some independent and sectarian congregations... The reporting of religious

37

experiences acquired a tremendous importance. Many people kept diaries and many spiritual autobiographies were published [10].

There is an example of such an account, written in 1653, shortly before Fox dictated his journal, by John Rogers. He begins, "We have sufficiently proved... the assertion of the use of experiences declared in the Church, being much for the honour and glory of God..." He then continues to give, "testimony to the truth or further experience of John Rogers, preacher of the Gospel... In every year since I can remember, I have been enriched with so many and such remarkable experiences; as might make some of you rather admire than believe." He recounts some of these, beginning from the age of 10. At one point he speaks of, "inward malady and melancholy," and goes on:

> This sad condition day and night lasted upon me, until I was persuaded that there was a God... and he would hear prayers if I continued but knocking... I threw myself upon the bed, whilst my eyes were glazed with tears! and there I lay, in a sudden sleep which seized upon me... when I awakened I was so much changed that I was amazed at myself, at the suddenness of it; for I dreamt I was comforted, and my heart filled with joy, and when I awaked it was so indeed... And after that I began plainly to see myself... why I despaired and was so long and so lamentably lost, that was because I sought in the wrong place for justification, and therefore a wrong way for salvation [11].

The experience that in 1642, at nearly 19 years of age, set Fox off on his spiritual pilgrimage is recounted in his journals as follows: at a fair two friends, one of whom was Fox's cousin and both of whom he calls professors (meaning that they made a profession of religious faith) propose a drinking game and Fox is shocked and grieved, "that any that made profession of religion should offer to do so." He leaves them, but being unable to sleep that night he recounts that he, "cried to the Lord, who said unto me, "Thou seest how young people go together into vanity and old people into the earth, and thou must forsake all, both young and old, and keep out of all, and be as a stranger to all. Then at the command of God," he recounts, "I left my relations and brake off all familiarity or fellowship with young and old" [12].

For the next few years he wandered in various degrees of temptation and despair, "under great misery and trouble" [13]. Typically he visits a priest at "Mancetter" and, "reasoned with him about the ground of despair and temptation, but he bid me take tobacco and sing psalms" [14].

In 1646 Fox begins to speak about "openings". The first four things he records the Lord "opened" to him were - that Christians must have a personal experience of God, that Oxford and Cambridge-trained gentry should not have a monopoly of the priesthood, that the Church does not consist of buildings but of people and that God could speak directly to people's hearts [15].

Without intending to belittle these insights in any way or pass judgement on their source, it needs to be pointed out that the four ideas they expressed represented fairly common solutions to the common problems being faced by English people in the first half of the seventeenth century, nor would they have been seen exclusively as religious ideas, for in that period the religious and secular worlds were irretrievably intertwined.

We have already seen how lay access to the Bible, the teachings of the Puritans, growing mobility and literacy, and the break up of family traditions were contributing to make the intrusive rules of the established Church under Archbishop Laud repugnant to large numbers of ordinary English folk. These disruptions were also leading the Puritans towards a more personal religion, the ordinary folk towards a suspicion of the gentry and the Calvinists towards a rejection of the hierarchy, censorship and discipline imposed by the priests.

Nor is it hard to speculate on the way these ideas hang together, for if authority in matters of religion is not to be the prerogative of an elite group, there must be another source of authority that is accessible to ordinary folk. What could be more accessible to them than their own experiences?

That these ideas were common property is confirmed by contemporary documents. Thomas Edwards (in 1645, the year that Fox's openings begin), decries the spread of, "the sects and sectaries." He mentions around ten different sects that he knew and points out how they were all intermixed, with the same, "great vein going through the whole; in one word liberty of conscience and liberty of preaching." Listing the practices they have in common he mentions, "the disturbance and overthrow of economical, ecclesiastical and political relations and government - insolences, pride and arrogancy, acts of immodesty and incivility - power and will, carrying all before them and throwing down all that stands in their way" [16]. Such could well describe the path that George Fox had revealed to him in the "openings" of that year.

The second document was written by Thomas Hall in 1651. He lists the tenets held by the Anabaptists of his time. Among them are - that all gifted persons may preach without ordination - that God reveals his will not only by the written word, but also by dreams and visions - that the Saints in this life are pure, without spot and need not use the petition, "Forgive us our sins," - that no Christian ought without a safe conscience take an oath, nor by oath promise fidelity to a magistrate - and that universities, humane arts and learning are needless. He continues: "They deny that preaching, praying, sacrament, singing of psalms and all ordinances are legal. The spirit is all. They give a supreme and independent power, in all ecclesiastical causes and censures, to their single congregations" [17]. One could be forgiven for mistaking that for a description of George Fox and his followers.

Fox's openings are remarkable in that they are not unique for his time, rather they are inspired by the general intellectual problems of his day, answered by Bible truths, expressed in biblical language and defended by reference to Bible passages. Fox himself later refers to them as, "openings of the Scriptures" - "When I had an opening they answered one another," he says, "and answered the Scriptures" [18]. For an example of this we could look at Fox's opening, "That God who made the world does not dwell in temples made with hands." This exact phrase is used by Stephen in his sermon in Acts 7 v.48 and again by Paul in his lecture to the Greeks in Acts 17 v.24. Fox argues for the truth of his opening from this very fact. He says, "The Lord showed me, so that I did clearly see that he did not dwell in these temples ... for both Stephen and the Apostle Paul bore testimony" [19].

As we look at Fox's account of this period of searching for religious truth, written, we should not forget, some 26 years later, it is most obviously interpreted as a period in which, in common with many of his fellows, Fox was struggling to establish a religious authority for himself.

There were three factors jostling in contention. There was the authority of the religious establishment, the authority of the Bible and the authority of his own insights, which he felt came directly

40

from Christ. I would suggest that it is impossible to see this personal crisis of authority separate from the pressing intellectual problem of Fox's day - the crisis of political sovereignty, which we can see coming to fruition some years later, notably in Thomas Hobbes' *Leviathan* written in 1651.

During this period of unrest we can see Fox increasingly rejecting the authority of the priests and preachers, who do not seem to be able to help him find peace, and turning to the authority of his own openings.

The feeling that the priests could not help him, partly because their moral standards were so low, but that God could teach him himself, grows and culminates in 1647 in the experience that brings Fox peace and on which the rest of his life is built. Having forsaken all the priests and the separate preachers for, "there was none among them that could speak to my condition. And when all my hopes in them and in all men were gone, so that I had nothing outwardly to help me, nor could tell what to do, then, Oh then, I heard a voice which said, "There is one, even Christ Jesus that can speak to thy condition", and when I heard it my heart did leap for joy" [20].

Fox resolved his inner conflict in a way that satisfied him for the rest of his life by resolving the question of religious authority. He determined to be guided solely by his own inner light. He says, "My desires after the Lord grew stronger and zeal in the pure knowledge of God and of Christ alone, without the help of any man, book or writing. For though I read the Scriptures that spoke of Christ and of God, yet I knew him not but by revelation, as he who hath the key did open and as the Father of life drew me to his Son by his Spirit" [20].

Although Quaker commentators take this claim of Fox's seriously [21], the influence of the language and thought of the Bible on the content and expression of his openings is so abundantly obvious that they cannot ignore it. Geoffrey Nuttall in his introduction to the *Journals* says, "His principle of loving forbearance, to take a single but telling instance, was clearly influenced as much by the example of Jesus in the Gospels as by any inward voice. No one, in fact, knew his Bible better than Fox did, nor could quote it in argument more devastatingly" [22].

Philip Wragge says that the, "inward teacher" was independent of, "the outward one: rather was the former informed by the Scriptures and guidance checked by them, and Fox usually referred to them in controversy... Yet," says Wragge, "he was not

41

over dependent on the outward letter" for he saw, "in that light and spirit which were before the Scriptures were given forth and which led the holy men of God to give them forth" [23].

This "unity in the truth" was something that later Quakers came to expect. John Lampen says, "Early Friends found that their experiences bore out the Scripture: "He will guide you into all truth". That is, they expected to find that the insight given by the Spirit to one man could not contradict that given to another; nor could it disagree with the teaching of Jesus" [24]. In practice of course this "unity" was not so much a discovery as a criterion of authenticity.

Quaker commentators seem more easily able to ignore the equally obvious connection between Fox's ideas and both the pressing intellectual problems of his day and the range of answers being proposed by his fellows. Geoffrey Nuttall, in his introduction to the *Journals* says, "Like Paul, (Fox) was anxious to claim independence of others in the discovery of his message; and in fact no substantial dependence has been established." He then concedes:

> For centuries weavers had bourne a name for independence and radicalism in religion. In Leicestershire Lollard traditions had lingered since Wycliffe was Rector of Lutterworth, not so far from Fenny Drayton were Fox was born. To the atmosphere of his own time he owed more than he knew or would allow. To all intents and purposes, nevertheless, Fox was, what Penn calls him, "an original, being no man's copy" [25].

Apart from Fox's openings which continue for the rest of his life, he recounts in his journals dreams, visions and voices, rapture, prophesy, discernments and healings, answered prayer, and natural and unnatural events that he sees as God's preservation, guidance and vengeance on his enemies. It cannot be disputed that Fox's journals present him as an extraordinarily charismatic, probably psychic and powerful character with a highly developed conscience. But one of the things which stands out in the journals is the lack of description of anything that you could call a religious experience, in the sense in which someone like William James uses the expression. A few dreams are described in some detail, but mostly it is the information he concludes from the vision that is recorded, and much of that is in very mundane language.

The impression given is not that some experiences in Fox's life stand out for Fox as being from God because of their special quality, but that everything that happens to him, everything he feels and thinks and does, is seen in terms of his relationship with God.

A rare example of a vision described in some detail and in rich dream language is recounted in the *Journals*:

> And I had a vision about the time that I was in this travail and sufferings, that I was walking in the fields and many Friends were with me, and I bid them dig in the earth, and they did and I went down. And there was a mighty vault top-full of people kept under the earth, rocks, and stones. So I bid them break open the earth and let all the people out, and they did, and all the people came forth to liberty; and it was a mighty place... And I went on again and bid them dig again, and Friends said unto me, "George, thou finds out all things," and so there they digged, and I went down, and went along the vault; and there sat a woman in white looking at time how it passed away. And there followed me a woman down in the vault, in which vault was the treasure; and so she laid her hand on the treasure on my left hand and then time whisked on apace; but I clapped my hand upon her and said, "Touch not the treasure". And then time passed not so swift [26].

A more characteristic account can be found on page 14:

> And one day when I had been walking solitarily abroad and was come home, I was taken up into the love of God, so that I could not but admire the greatness of his love. And while I was in that condition it was opened unto me by the eternal Light and power, and I therein saw clearly that all was done and to be done in and by Christ, and how he conquers and destroys this tempter, the Devil and all his works, and is atop of him, and that all these troubles were good for me, and temptations for the

43

trial of my faith which Christ had given me.

Fox recounts occasions when he was able to prophesy events that occurred later. On page 147 he tells how, in 1653 he was with a judge and a colonel and, "was moved to tell them before that day fortnight the Long Parliament should be broken up and the Speaker plucked out of his chair. And that day fortnight Colonel Benson came again and was speaking to Judge Fell and said that now he saw that George Fox was a true prophet; for Oliver had broken up the parliament by that time."

It also appears that Fox had a gift of healing. Page 631 of his journals has an incredible story of a man in Barbados who fell from a horse and was found dead from a broken neck. Fox manipulated his neck and brought him back to life so that he was able to continue his journey the next day.

As an example of answered prayer, guidance and protection, the following section is from one of Fox's journeys by ship, in 1673:

> And when we came near Cape Henry, about the 8th hour, in the morning, we espied a ship on the coast where pirates used to be, which occasioned some fear and trouble to fall upon the seamen. But the Lord God, whose I am and we are, let me see in a vision two ships to the westward that should make towards us but should do us no hurt. So when about three or four days after we espied another ship westward, which occasioned some fear to the seamen, the Lord opened it unto me that was the other ship he showed me in the vision, which was no enemy. And then I desired of the Lord God that if it was his will we might see no more ships until we came to England, to keep the fear out of the people, and the Lord answered me, so that we saw none until we came into King's Road, the Bristol harbour [27].

Another example of how Fox interprets events as acts of God can be found on page 505. Fox has been mentioning some who stood against him. "When I came into the country again," he recounts, "all these aforesaid were dead and ruined in their estates and several others of our persecutors whom the Lord blasted and ruined; and though I did not seek to execute the law upon them for their acting contrary to their own laws against me, yet the

44

Lord had executed his vengeance upon them. "

John Lampen tells a story about Fox from a source other than his journals and draws out from it his view of the distinctiveness of Fox's religious experiences:

> A girl in Dorset on her way for the first time to hear George Fox preach, found herself thinking, "What is it that condemns me when I do evil and justifies me when I do well?"... After a while in the meeting George Fox stood up and said: "Who are thou that queriest in thy mind, "What is it I feel...?" I will tell thee. Lo... the Lord of Hosts is his name. It is He, by his Spirit, that condemns thee for evil and justifieth thee when thou dost well. Keep under its dictates, and He will be thy preserver to the end" [28].

This story, John Lampen comments:

> brings beautifully together a number of the strands which confirmed for the early Friends their experience of God within themselves. Not conscience itself, which is a human faculty, but the Light which illuminates it; the awareness of truth and love and beauty in the deep parts of our minds; the sense of the power of nature..; the impetus... to action which sometimes comes most inconveniently..; the almost miraculous sympathy with the feelings and thoughts of another, which most of us know rarely, but Fox had to a high degree: all these are familiar to agnostic and "irreligious" people. But Fox calls us to recognize them as the traces of "that of God" in us, and to identify them with the God revealed in the Bible working through his Spirit [28].

This quote brings out what the journals themselves suggest; Fox did not have a different range of experiences from other people; others feel the pull of conscience, have dreams, psychic visions and sudden insights, but they do not see them as having any *religious* significance. In fact some modern Quakers pursue similar experiences today within an almost completely secular framework of thought. Fox differed from his contemporaries by

45

attending to a different set of experiences as being those with religious authenticity and value - he saw in the mundane events of his life the hand and the voice of God.

Fox's religious concepts

Fox's disputes with the priests were not about creeds and doctrines, but about authority and practice - about the nature of the church, and about how Christians should behave. Early in his career (1647) Fox was, "moved to go to the steeplehouse to tell the people and the priest, and to bid them to cease from man whose breath was in their nostrils, and to tell them where their teacher was, within them, the spirit and the light of Jesus" [29].

On page 35 Fox describes the mission which to which he felt God had called him:

> I was glad that I was commanded to turn people to that inward light, spirit and grace by which all might know their salvation, and their way to God... I was to bring people off from all the world's religions which are vain, that they might know the pure religion and might visit the fatherless, the widows and the strangers and keep themselves from the spots of the world... And I was to bring them off from all the world's fellowships and prayings and singings which stood in forms without power. And from Jewish ceremonies, and from heathenish fables, and from men's inventions and windy doctrines... and from all their images and crosses and sprinkling of infants with all their holy days (so called) and all their vain traditions... Moreover when the Lord sent me forth into the world, he forbad me to put off my hat to any, high or low, and I was required to "thee" and "thou" all men and women without any respect of rich or poor, great or small [30].

Two points emerge - firstly the relative unimportance of conceptual formulations to Fox, and secondly his constant use of the concepts of the Bible. The first of these is still central for Quakers. George Gorman says, "In this attempt to present a picture of Quakers in the 1980s no reference had been made to

Quaker priests or ministers, nor to a Quaker creed or the use of outward sacraments. The simple fact is that Quakers do not have them" [31].

The second point now seems irrelevant; speaking of the spirit that binds Quakers together, Gorman says, "Friends speak of this in a number of ways. Some simply say, "the spirit" or "love". For others the name "Holy Spirit", "Inward Light" or "the living Christ" is the most appropriate name" [32]. Lampen says:

> Although he (Fox) protested against the formal and dogmatic elements in the religious teaching and practice of his day, he used the traditional language of theology, which may now seen outdated or unfamiliar to some readers. The religious debates of his time had the advantage of this agreed vocabulary, the language of the Bible... For many of us this language has now been so debased that it no longer gives us the words in which to talk about experiences which are intensely meaningful to us [33].

And yet Fox did introduce some unfamiliar concepts. One of these is "the inward light". John Lampen tells us that this light is identified with the "Word" of John's Gospel [34]. In fact it is lifted directly from John 1 v.9 and is detailed by John's other New Testament writings. (The difference between the Quakers and the mainstream of Christianity has been explained in terms of their over-dependence upon the writing of John, and relative neglect of the writings of St. Paul. This can be demonstrated by Fox's and the later Quakers' unorthodox view of salvation, described by Nutall as, being transported, "even in this life into paradise, into such a paradise as Adam and Eve knew before they fell, thus giving men triumph over their sinful propensities" [35].)

We should not forget however that Fox claimed that all his theology was revealed to him directly from God. On page 34, having propounded various fairly orthodox Christian doctrines in the words of the Bible, Fox says, "These things I did not see by the help of man, nor by the letter, though they are written in the letter, but I saw them in the light of the Lord Jesus Christ and by his immediate Spirit and power, as did the holy men of God, by whom the Holy Scriptures were written... and what the Lord opened in me I afterwards found was agreeable to them."

However this strange claim is to be interpreted the records are not consistent with the idea that Fox made up concepts in order to name and respond more effectively to things he became acquainted with in his religious experiences; the concepts were already in existence.

Fox's religious legacy

If Fox did not introduce his followers to a new set of concepts. What was it then he left, that inspired a religious movement that is still vigorous today? Was it a belief system, creeds or doctrines? Was it a new criterion for religious authority? Was it access to a certain sort of experience? Historical records and Quaker commentators seem unanimous. To a minor extent it included all of these but only in so far as they were all wrapped up in his unique legacy.

George Gorman puts it this way: "The unique Quaker contribution in the eighties as in all previous decades, is in the manner of their silent corporate worship, for the Quaker meeting for worship is the core of the Religious Society of Friends" [36]. Earlier he had said, "While most modern Friends would not naturally use Fox's language to describe their experience, they would be absolutely at one with him in his strong conviction that in being quiet and still, it is possible to discover a life giving, creative power in the depths of human personality" [37]. Philip Wragge says:

> Fox also had a great organizing ability... it was soon
> apparent that some form of Church organization was
> needed, especially in an age when some Protestants
> tended to confuse liberty with licence. Fox aimed at
> a Christ-governed Society of Friends; guidance was
> given as the gathered group waited upon God and
> the individual leading must be checked by the
> judgement of the group. He saw that discipline was
> necessary to maximize freedom and on his release
> from Scarborough in 1666, he spent four years
> setting up Monthly and Quarterly meetings... His
> organization gave shape, stability and permanency to
> Quakerism without cramping individual liberty and

48

it remains almost unaltered down to the present day
[38].

Howard Brinton says of the meeting for worship, "In the form here described, this is the only practice of the Society of Friends which has existed from the start without going through a process of development. Its discovery was the discovery of Quakerism" [39].

What Fox left his followers was, in the opinion of all these commentators a practice, an activity with a meaning, an institution. As far as concepts, ideas and beliefs are concerned those that Fox left and have endured are those that relate to the Meeting. Brinton says:

> The Quaker bases his method on belief in a God-centred spiritual universe, the inner truth and meaning of which is in some degree accessible to man... As scientists agree on a certain well established body of scientific facts inherited from the research and discovery of the past and subject to continual revision so the Quakers have accepted a certain body of religious and social doctrines inherited from the past and subject always to new interpretations as more Truth is apprehended [40].

As far as criteria of orthodoxy are concerned Brinton says, "The basis of the test is not facts arrived at but the method used... The Society of Friends accepts into membership a person who is willing to follow the Quaker method regardless of where it may lead."

The process by which the Meeting came to have this authority is instructive. The idea of each person following their own inner light was bound to lead to crisis in a developing organization, and it did. In 1656 George Fox clashed violently and with devastating results with another emerging Quaker leader, James Naylor [41].

Although Fox does not tell the whole story in his journals we do have the letters he wrote for general distribution at this time [42]. It was clear to all that some sort of discipline was necessary in the new sect but these letters reveal Fox rejecting the most obvious solution and making no attempt to set up his experiences or his teaching as any sort of authority. (William Penn says of Fox that, "He exercised no authority except over evil" [43].)

49

Fox reminds the Quakers about, "the witness of God in everyone, in which they come into peace... and fellowship with one another." And his direct exhortation is, "Keep your meetings in the power of the Lord." In response to the need for control in the church, Fox repeats his belief in the authority of, "the inner light of every man" and, "the unity of truth", and refuses to set up any other criterion of judgement on what God might reveal to those who wait upon him. In his third letter he makes this even more clear, "Let it be your joy to hear or see the springs break forth in any, through which you have all unity in the same feeling, life and power. And above all take heed of judging, ever, any one openly in your meeting." He continues with a few suggestions about how to keep order but the principle remains, "So in all this you have order, you have edification, you have wisdom... which takes away the occasion of stumbling the weak and occasioning the spirits of the world to get up. You will hear and feel and see the power of God."

To this day Fox's method of reaching truth and maintaining order remains. In his *Guide to Quaker Practice*, Howard Brinton explains that the principle set up by Fox is not one of the anarchy of individual insight but, "The principle of corporate guidance, according to which the Spirit can inspire the group as a whole, is central. Since there is but one Truth, its Spirit, if followed, will produce unity. To achieve this unity is always possible and the Society of Friends has practised the method of achieving it with considerable success for three centuries" [44].

Certainly Fox left access to a certain sort of experience the experience of waiting in silence in a community for a unified revelation from the spirit of truth. Fox's legacy to the world was an institution, justified and explained by a set of beliefs, acting in itself as a criterion of authority and creating a range of experiences, beliefs and behaviour patterns for those who practise it. Fox's new institution was explained in terms of a very old set of concepts that to many Quakers today are obsolete, although the institution still has its power.

There is in fact little doubt that it was Fox's action in instigating an institutional structure upon his sect that ensured its survival; for other sects which spoke in very similar, if not identical, terms about very similar, if not identical, experiences melted away when their leaders died [45].

But from where did Fox get the idea behind this particular institution - that authority and power could safely and usefully be invested in the agreement of ordinary men and women? He would undoubtedly have said that God revealed it to him. Let no judgement be made about the source but note that England was, in this half of this century, struggling through the birth of modern democracy.

As an example of the view from which people were moving we could look at *The Canons* of June 1640. The parish clergy were to read the following, "explanation of the regal power" at Morning Prayer once in every quarter:

> The most high and sacred Order of Kings is of Divine Right, being the ordinance of God himself, founded in the prime laws of nature, and clearly established by express texts both of the Old and New Testaments. A supreme power is given to this most excellent Order by God himself in the Scriptures, which is, that kings should rule and command in their several dominions all persons of what rank or estate soever whether ecclesiastical or civil... For any person or persons to set up, maintain or avow in any their said realms or territories respectively, under any pretence whatsoever, any independent coactive power... is to undermine their great royal office, and cunningly to overthrow that most sacred ordinance which God himself hath established, and so is treasonable against God as well as against the King [46].

But that view was under attack. A very contrary one was being expressed for example by the Levellers - "the first democratic political movement in modern history" [47], which developed under the leadership of John Lilburne; also by the Diggers, who took steps towards setting up a communist society in 1649 under the leadership of Gerrard Winstanley.

Richard Overton wrote a paper addressed to Cromwell's parliament on behalf of the Levellers in 1649:

> Ye were chosen to work our deliverance and to establish us in natural and just liberty agreeable to Reason, and common equity, for whatever our forefathers were, or whatever they did or suffered, or were enforced to yield unto, we are the men of the

51

present age and ought to be absolutely free from all kinds of exorbitancies, molestations or arbitrary power, and you we chose to free us from all without exception or limitation, either in respect of persons, officers, degrees or things: and we were full of confidence, that ye would have dealt impartially on our behalf, and made us the most absolute free people in the world. Ye should, in the first place, declare, and set forth King Charles his wickedness openly before the world, and withal, to show the intolerable inconvenience of having a kingly government... Ye only are chosen by us the people, and therefore in you only is the power of binding the whole nation, by making, altering or abolishing the laws [48].

Thomas Edwards, outraged by the stand taken by Overton and Lilburne describes them in 1646 as, "against religion and civil government tending to nothing else but the overthrow of the fundamental constitution of this Kingdom in Kings, Lords and Commons and setting up the body of the common people, as sovereign lord and king" [49].

Gerrard Winstanley, like John Lilburne later to become a Quaker, argues for democracy in secular government in words and ideas remarkably similar to those Fox used to argue for democracy in church government:

Not one word was spoken in the beginning, that one branch of mankind should rule over another. And the reason is this, every single man, male or female, is a perfect creature of himself; and the same spirit that made the globe dwells in man to govern the globe; so that the flesh of man being subject to reason, his maker, hath him to be his teacher and ruler within himself, therefore needs not to run abroad after any teacher and ruler without him; for he needs not that any man should teach him, for the same anointing that ruled in the Son of Man teacheth him all things [50].

Notes

The extracts from Fox's *Journals* in this chapter are reproduced with permission from the Library Committee of London Yearly Meeting of the Religious Society of Friends, and those from J. Philip Wragge and John Lampen, with permission from Quaker Home Service.

1. John Lampen, *Wait in the Light,* p.l.
2. "Archbishop Laud's Metropolitan Visitation of the Province of Canterbury in 1934-5", Christopher Hill et. al. (ed), *Seventeenth Century England; a Changing Culture 1618-1689,* pp. 12-13.
4. John Nickalls (ed.), *Journal of George Fox,* pp. 1-2.
5. Ibid., p. 2.
6. Ibid., p. 4.
7. Ibid., p. 7.
8. Ibid., p. 11.
9. Ibid., pp. 103-104.
10. Christopher Hill et. al. (ed.), *Seventeenth Century England; a Changing Culture 1618-1689,* p. 42.
11. John Rogers (1653), "Beth-Shemesh: A Tabernacle for the Sun", Anne Hughes (ed.), *Seventeenth Century England: a Changing Culture Vol 1: Primary Sources,* pp. 151-152.
12. John Nickalls (ed.), *Journal of George Fox,* p. 3.
13. Ibid., p. 4.
14. Ibid., p. 5.
15. Ibid., pp. 7-8.
16. Thomas Edwards (1646), "Gangraena", Anne Hughes(ed.), *Primary Sources,* pp. 131-132.
17. Thomas Hall (1651), "The Pulpit Guarded: The Epistle to the lay Preacher", Anne Hughes (ed.), *Primary Sources,* pp. 144-145.
18. John Nickalls (ed.), *Journal of George Fox,* p. 8.
20. Ibid., p. 11.
21. See e.g. William Penn's preface to *Journal of George Fox,* p. xliii.
22. John Nickalls (ed.), *Journal of George Fox,* p. xxvii.
23. J. Philip Wragge, *George Fox,* p. 22.
24. John Lampen, *Wait in the Light,* p. 20.

25. John Nickalls (ed.), *Journal of George Fox*, p. xxv.
26. Ibid., p. 578.
27. Ibid., pp. 662-663. Interestingly compared with Acts 27.
28. John Lampen, *Wait in the Light*, p. 13.
29. John Nickalls (ed.), *Journal of George Fox*, p. 20.
30. Ibid., pp. 35-36. It is interesting to note how many phrases in this long dissertation come directly from the New Testament.
31. Anne Hoskins and Alison Sharman (eds.), *Quakers in the Eighties*, p. 6.
32. Ibid., p. 7.
33. John Lampen, *Wait in the Light*, p. 6.
34. Ibid., p. 35.
35. John Nickalls (ed.), *Journal of George Fox*, p. xxvii.
36. Anne Hoskins (ed.), *Quakers in the Eighties*, p. 5.
37. Ibid., p. 2.
38. J. Philip Wragge, *George Fox*, pp. 16-17.
39. Howard Brinton, *Guide to Quaker Practice*, p. 9.
40. Ibid., p. 8.
41. See, John Nickalls (ed.), *Journal of George Fox*, p. 268, although one must look elsewhere for the whole story.
42. John Nickalls (ed.), *Journal of George Fox*, pp. 280-283.
43. Preface to John Nickalls (ed.), *Journal of George Fox*, p. xliv.
44. Howard Brinton, *Guide to Quaker Practice*, p. 31.
45. Another exception is of course the Anabaptists, whose novel institution of Believers' Baptism has also survived.
46. J. P. Kenyon (1966), "The Stuart Constitution 1603-1688 Documents and Commentary", Anne Hughes (ed.), *Primary Sources*, pp. 58-59.
47. G. E. Aylmer, *The Levellers in the English Revolution*.
48. Richard Overton (1646), "A Remonstrance of many thousands Citizens and other Freeborn People of England to their own House of Commons", Anne Hughes (ed.), *Primary Sources*, pp. 169 ff.
49. Thomas Edwards (1646), "Gangraena", Anne Hughes (ed.), *Primary Sources*, p. 175.
50. Gerrard Winstanley (1649), "True Levellers' Standard Advanced", Anne Hughes (ed.), *Primary Sources*, p. 188.

7 An assessment of the case study

We can now look back at the expectations aroused by William James and Alasdair MacIntyre in the light of the story of George Fox, to see if it does, as they claim, support what each sees to be the mechanism of religious innovation.

William James

William James' theory seems to have fared badly. Not only does what we have learned about Fox's life fail to exemplify it, it is hard to imagine any possible set of facts that could. Fox's three-pronged training from the established church, the Sectarians and his own reading of the Bible, instructed him in various views about what God is like and how to tell which experiences have religious significance and value. If he had not been thus instructed in the concept of divinity, it is hard to see how he could have recognized any experience as being "communion with the divine".

The experiences that Fox saw as having religious significance do not appear to be substantially different from the experiences of his contemporaries, nor did he recognize them by their special spiritual quality. Certainly Fox's conscience and his sense of calling were highly developed, his psychic visions were clear and frequent and the quiet voice within was strong and consistent, but his decision that these amounted to communion with God is most plausibly seen as an interpretation, only possible because of his training.

It is contrary to the facts of the case both that Fox rejected the religious concepts of his day, in isolation and as a result of his private religious experiences, and that he coined new concepts to name the things he had experienced. He rejected the practices of the priests and the institutional structures that authenticated them, in common with a great many of his contemporaries, in an intelligible response to a particular historical situation. He embraced what he saw to be the concepts and practices of the writers of the New Testament as they appeared to him to apply to the intellectual and practical necessities of his life.

His ideas show a marked similarity to, and the definite influence of, many of the secular and religious ideas of his time. Fox did not teach his followers a new set of concepts for talking about an old experience; he introduced them to a new institution.

Alasdair MacIntyre

MacIntyre's theory has fared better. It seems consistent with what we know of Fox's life that his training in religious language - by sharing in the liturgy of the established church, listening to the Sectarian preachers and studying the Bible - were formative of his religious ideas and his assessment and interpretation of his experiences. But something led him to reject all the established religious authorities. We can agree with MacIntyre that non-rational factors may have had a part to play in this decision. (His emotional reaction to his cousin's drinking habits, perhaps.) But I think we must also acknowledge, in disagreement with MacIntyre, that he found the religious institutions of his day inappropriate for reasons that we can appreciate and understand even looking back from several hundred years later. The new institution that he introduced also clearly fitted the demands of the situation.

Fox introduced a new source of religious authority, but MacIntyre must again be wrong when he says that the criterion of authority for this new religion was one of Fox's own experiences. In the place of the established criteria, Fox took as his authority in religion his own inner voice. It is unlikely that this idea was original, and what Fox accepted as genuine communication from God was in fact rigorously judged by what he read in the Bible. The quality or content of any of his experiences did not, however, become an authority for anyone else. Fox himself never suggested that they be used in this way, nor in fact did he teach that each listen uncritically to his own inner voice; the source of religious authority that he set up was the authority of the Meeting, to which all had to submit.

Quite apart from the record of history it is surely not possible for a memory of an experience to become the basis for a comparative test, even for subsequent experiences of the same person, let alone those of others [1]. The only thing that could become the basis for such a test would be what someone said about their experiences, but Fox did not leave detailed descriptions of his experiences by which others could judge theirs. What he left was a method of recreating a certain kind of experience and a method for testing its genuineness. Within MacIntyre's theory it is hard to see the role that experience has, both in the decision of an individual to reject the current religious criteria of authenticity and in the setting up of a new system of worship and belief based upon new criteria. But it is not hard to see why Fox rejected the religious institutions of his day. It was a move that in some ways seems inevitable in view of the historical situation. It is also not only easy to imagine how new religious experiences and beliefs and new ways of talking about them, can arise from the practice of a new institution; it is possible to follow it happening in the growth of the early Quaker movement [2].

So while many of the other new religious and political movements spawned at this time faded away, Fox's one inspired and original religious idea secured the survival of the Quaker movement. And to this day Quakers seek religious truth by sitting in silence waiting for a unified revelation from the Spirit of Truth.

Notes

1. See e.g. Ludwig Wittgenstein, *Philosophical Investigations*, para. 258.
2. See e.g. the growth of the Quaker commitment to pacifism and reason under the leadership of William Penn.

8 A critique of empiricist theories

The phenomenon of radical innovation in religions raises problems within theories that are based on the priority of experience. The story of George Fox has also been shown to fail quite notably to exemplify them [1]. The theoretical failure of empiricism in relation to religion has been attacked by a wide range of arguments from modern philosophers and theologians. This chapter will briefly comment on these and the specific problems they raise in accounting for innovation in religion from an empiricist base.

An empiricist theory of innovation in religion would, put simply, be something like this; some of our experiences are a direct perception of "the spiritual world", or of supernatural beings. These experiences are private by nature and are the source of our religious concepts and beliefs, activities and institutions. Innovation in religion occurs when individuals have these experiences in a specially intense or fresh way, have a sense of recognizing them for what they are, see them as evidence for the existence of a supernatural world and use them to criticize and change the religious concepts and institutions of their day.

There are three main difficulties with this model:

Some of the empiricists' concepts are indefensibly anomalous

Nicholas Lash expresses the view that the empiricists' concept of experiences as "conscious mental goings on" is a strange one. He asks: "Why on earth should this exceedingly queer account of experience in general, and of religious experiences in particular,

58

prove so persuasive that many highly intelligent people simply take it for granted?" [2]. A painful experience at the dentist or a distressing experience after over-indulgence in food and drink, or an irritating experience in a committee meeting, are not "conscious mental goings on" but, "aspects of my interaction in the public world of flesh and facts and language, with dentist's drills, indigestion, good company and tedious discussion." Lash accuses William James of underestimating, "the public institutional, structured character of all our experience" [3], and concludes that finding God is not like coming across a particular fact or thing. God is rather to be found, "in all the kinds of things which we do and suffer, achieve and undergo" [4].

T. R. Miles says, "Those who have equated "experiences" with "mental events" have introduced an innovation without being aware that they were doing so, and that the result is gratuitous confusion" [5]. His conclusion is:

> A person can describe his *religious* experiences -
> that is, his experiences when he tries to come to
> terms with cosmic issues - in the same way logically
> as he can describe, for instance, the experiences
> which he had last summer in Norway; in neither case
> does it make sense to ask if his experiences were
> mental events or if they made him aware of
> something non-material [6].

When we examine the experiences which people, not over-influenced by empiricist philosophy, call religious [7], we see that they include descriptions of shared events and activities, of encounters with a range of ordinary objects and people, as well as descriptions of feelings, emotions, moments of insight, and more unusual, inner sensations. They do not appear always to see "the experience" as an inner sensation that accompanied their participation in an event or encounter; they speak as though the happening or the meeting *is* the experience and it is often one that is shared.

Empiricists see religious experiences as perceptions of spiritual reality. These perceptions differ from what we might call "perceptions of material reality" in that they are private, but this idea of a private perception is an odd one. If I am standing in a crowd and, putting my hand in my pocket, discover I have some keys there that I should have left at home, I have, in one sense, had a private perception; no-one around has shared the discovery with me.   But this is not the sort of experience that the empiricists are describing.   Swinburne explains that a religious experience, if it is a perception, is normally a perception that someone else in the same physical relation to the object, with the same instruments, sense organs and concepts and the same amount of attention, does not perceive [8].   Gods, according to Swinburne, can chose to whom (and to how many) they reveal themselves.   This leads him to talk about God as a private object.   But this is an anomalous use of the word "object".   The nearest example seems to be found in talk about dreams or pains, but we do not normally refer to objects in relation to either of these subjects without some clear qualification or much confusion.

The problem with purely private experiences is, as Wittgenstein has pointed out [9], that it is impossible to see how words referring to them can be formulated and used.   In order for a concept to become part of a language it must have some publicly observable criteria of use, so that people can agree what are correct and what are incorrect instances of its use.

Not all empiricists are committed to all of Swinburne's arguments.   It is possible to be an empiricist and find room for the idea of a shared religious experience, but any idea of a special kind of perception of a non-material world raises similar problems with criteria of use.

Experiences cannot be recognized as religious prior to the possession of religious concepts and therefore cannot be the source of concepts and beliefs.

The empiricist model of religious innovation depends upon the supposition that people can recognize experiences as having religious authenticity and value prior to, and independently of, the religious beliefs and concepts they have inherited from their culture.   It depends, that is, upon religious experiences being distinguishable from non-religious experiences by their quality. "The essence of religious experiences," says James, "the thing by which we finally must judge them, must be that element or quality in them which we can meet nowhere else" [10].   William James' immense catalogue of the varieties of religious experience, covering almost every imaginable human emotion and sensation, would seen to contradict this; can they all have a common quality?

More plausible is James' alternative and in some ways incompatible suggestion that peoples' experiences are religious in so far as they are recognized by them as being related in some way to what they consider to be divine [11], a suggestion that implies the priority of concepts over percepts.

Similar, but no less explicit, accounts of religious experience are to be found in more recent writers. Sir Alister Hardy claimed in 1979 that he had collected, "over 4,000 first-hand accounts, which show that a large number of people even today possess a deep awareness of a benevolent non-physical power which appears to be partly or wholly beyond, and far greater than, the individual self". He continues:

> The experience when it comes has always been quite different from any other type of experience they have ever had. They do not necessarily call it a religious feeling, nor does it occur only to those who belong to an institutional religion or who indulge in corporate acts of worship... it usually induces in the person concerned a conviction that the everyday world is not the whole of reality: that there is another dimension to life [12].

Like James he discovers that people experience, "the abstract power" in a wide variety of ways - he suggests 92 categories in which to put them - and adds: "Spiritual awareness appears to be universal to human kind" [13].

Sir Alister's evidence and the conclusions he draws from it are flimsy. I do not want to argue that it is false that people all over the world experience some sort of help, comfort, strength or peace from a not obviously physical or merely internal source, at certain times in their lives. I want to point out that they, at other times, experience dereliction, overwhelming temptation, despair and anxiety. The question that needs to be asked is how people decide which of their varied experiences to tell Sir Alister's researchers about?

Sir Alister argues that he is not interested in the experiences people call "religious" or "spiritual", but with experiences of a certain kind, whatever people want to call them. This puts him in an insoluble linguistic dilemma, for, in order not to prejudice the results, he neither wants to name the experiences he wants to hear about, nor to say what they are like. The problems with the question he asks have been discussed in Chapter 3. The accounts that it evokes [14] reveal that it is peoples' personal theology, which may differ from, but is always continuous with, the theology of their culture, which determines which, if any, of their experiences they choose to put in Sir Alister's nameless category. This is the common thread that holds the 4,000 accounts together. There is no common quality running through them by which they could be recognized.

The practical problems of this research programme, based on empiricist assumptions about religious experience, support quite vividly the argument that it is not possible to recognize experiences as religious - as coming from God, or as being experiences of a spiritual world - without some training in religious concepts. The experiences cannot therefore be the source of the concepts.

As an additional argument there is an alternative way in which we can be said to perceive something different from the people immediately around us - that is if we see the same object, but see it *as* something different [15]. A group of people see a dark shape cross the lawn: the hunter sees it *as* a leopard. An audience listen to a piece of music; the expert hears it *as* a sonata. A family watch a show of temper; the mother sees it *as* an expression of jealousy. The notable thing about "seeing as" is that in order to recognize a perception as a perception of something in particular, it is necessary to be in possession of the appropriate concept - to know, that is, what counts as a perception of that class of thing. The hunter knows what features of a dark shadow make it correct to describe it as a leopard. Experts know what features of a piece of music make it correct to describe it as a sonata. The mother knows how to recognize jealousy when she sees it.

Applying this idea to religious experiences seems to assume that in every religious experience there is some *thing* being perceived, which is not the case; when, for example, people say they hear God speaking through meditating on a Bible story, there is no thing that they experience as the voice of God, in the way a primitive tribe might interpret a roll of thunder.

John Hick in fact develops this idea to cover the believer's experience of, "living within the ambience of the unseen God" [16], of the prophets', "consciousness of God as actively present in their contemporary history" [17], the disciples, "seeing Jesus as the Christ" [18], or bread and wine being, "experienced as channels of divine grace" [19]. But, however it is interpreted, this ability to apply a particular concept to a particular experience comes not from having fresh and clear perceptions but from having been trained in the use of words. Private experiences, in the empiricist sense, cannot be the source of religious concepts.

Experiences cannot be used as evidence for the existence of a supernatural world

T. R. Miles asks the question: in what sense can religious experience be compelling? His answer is: "Certain experiences can *invite* a particular answer to cosmic questions; they cannot logically demonstrate that such an answer is correct" [20]. Alasdair McIntyre says:

> An experience of a distinctively "mental" kind, a feeling state or an image cannot of itself yield any information about anything other than the experience. We could never know from such experiences that they had the character of messages from the divine, unless we already possessed a prior knowledge of the divine and of the way in which messages from it were to be identified. The decisive evidence for the claim would then be anterior to the experience and not derived from it, whereas what we are concerned with here is how far the experience itself can provide such evidence [21].

He goes on to point out that, in order to establish that experiences of a certain kind count as evidence for the existence of something else, one must have an agreed rule of inference [22].

It is just these sorts of publicly agreed rules that are precluded by the private nature of the empiricist's concept of religious experience. As was argued in Chapter 3 we could in certain circumstances count the onset of an asthma attack as evidence that there is a cat in the room, because we are agreed on the normal way of telling if a cat is present (we know what cats look like) and we could have established that this person's asthma has in the past invariably connected with the presence of a cat. If devils are private objects in the empiricist sense there are no agreed criteria by which we can decide what counts as an incontrovertible instance of there appearing. There is as a consequence no way of establishing that an onset of shivering is invariably connected with their presence. Shivering is not evidence that a devil is present.

In fact, if devils are private objects, nothing can be counted as such.

Notes

The extracts from T. R. Miles are reproduced by permission of Macmillan Ltd. and from Alister Hardy by permission of Oxford University Press.

1.   See Chapters 1, 3 and 7
2.   Nicholas Lash, *Theology on the Way to Emmaus*, p. 144.
3.   Ibid., p. 146.
4.   Ibid., p. 154.
5.   T. R. Miles, *Religious Experience*, p. 13.
6.   Ibid., p. 23.
7.   This will be done in Chapter 17.
8.   See Richard Swinburne, *The Existence of God*, pp. 248-249.
9.   Ludwig Wittgenstein, *Philosophical Investigations*, See e.g. I paras. 258 and 293.
10.   William James, *The Varieties of Religious Experience*, p. 62.
11.   Ibid., p. 50.
12.   Alister Hardy, *The Spiritual Nature of Man*, p. 1.
13.   Ibid., p. 2.
14.   For a selection of these accounts see Sir Alister Hardy's book, *The Spiritual Nature of Man*.
15.   See John Hick, "Religious Faith as Experiencing-as", pp. 20 ff.
16.   Ibid., p. 27.
17.   Ibid., p. 31.
18.   Ibid., p. 32.
19.   Ibid., p. 35.

20.   T. R. Miles, *Religious Experience*, p. 56.
21.   Alasdair McIntyre, "Visions", p. 256.
22.   Ibid., p. 257.

9 A critique of priority-of-language theories

The phenomenon of radical innovation in religions raises some problems within theories that are based on the priority of language [1].

As the discussion of the case study suggested, the problem with these theories is not, as it was for empiricist theories, a matter of there being major difficulties with the philosophical assumptions on which they are based. It is rather that the particular ways in which these assumptions have been applied to religion, has produced problems for explaining the role of innovators.

Put simply, a model of innovation in religions based on the priority of language would look like this: religions are not the product of individuals; they belong in the first place to communities. Religions as language systems are rule-following activities. Individuals learn about them by being trained in the use of the language of a particular religious tradition. They learn how the concepts of truth, reality, evidence and proof are to be used in a religious context, and they learn to recognize which experiences, actions and utterances are authentic and have religious value.

Innovators are those who at some stage in their lives reject this training and suggest a change in the rules; they introduce new ways of talking - different rules for using the relevant concepts, different criteria for assessing religious experiences, actions and utterances. Their success depends upon the reception of these new rules by what then becomes a new religious community.

A major problem area for these sorts of models is that if our concepts of reality, the meaning of our experiences and our ways of reasoning, are determined by the rule-following language systems we learn through cultural training, neither independent rational deliberation nor experiences of an independently perceived world, can have a role in the criticism and change of such systems.

As a basic position this seems to be right but the further one presses it in relation to religions the more intractable the problems seem to become in accounting for radical innovation. The more religions are seen solely in terms of language systems and the more arbitrary and isolated language systems are seen to be, both in relation to one another and in relation to the world of our experience, the more difficult it becomes to give a coherent and plausible analysis of the phenomenon of religious innovation. For, as the case-study suggested, innovators do criticize and change religions, and they appear to be responding to their experience of changing historical situations, and to produce solutions that are intelligibly related to the problems those situations have set.

If religions are primarily language systems and if language systems are isolated and arbitrary, it follows that religious beliefs cannot be justified or disproved from outside, nor can the criteria on which they are based be questioned from inside the system. They are, in this sense, groundless, and this would appear to have three implications that are relevant to innovation.

Changes in allegiance from one set of beliefs to another cannot be seen as conclusions from evidence or any sort of rational inference from experience

As MacIntyre puts it, when he hears the Christian story, "either a man will find himself brought to say, "My Lord and my God," or he will not" [2].

But biographies confirm that for many individuals the "leap of faith" that is involved in commitment to sources of religious authority is felt to be precipitated or even forced by reasons that are not divorced from rationality and experience. Many ordinary Christians are ready to tell the story of how they came to faith. Rational arguments from relevant experiences figure too frequently for us to accept MacIntyre's remarks without question [3].

Theology has an exclusively internal role within the language system that constitutes the religion

As Phillips puts it theology's function in religions is not to justify religious statements from a supposedly external viewpoint, nor to try to draw conclusions from, or impose an order on, the facts we independently encounter in the world. "Theology is," he says, "the grammar of religious language" [4].

But, if this is right, it is hard to account for 2000 years of Christian argument, apologetics and preaching. Theology does have an internal, or grammatical role, that starts with the authority of Scripture, Church and Spirit, but it has also been producing arguments for faith since the apostles and the Greek Fathers [5]. It is concerned with answering the apparent human need for cognitive order, for explanations of what our lives mean, the significance of particular events and the construction of coherent and consistent answers to questions about the meaning and destiny of human life. Theology, rather than being exclusively concerned with internal consistency, is vitally concerned with its own relationship to secular thought, language and behaviour, and with a rational assessment of their competing claims. The history of religions suggests that religions survive and fall on their ability to adapt to changing intellectual climates and social experiences. Perhaps a religion with an exclusively internal theology (Christianity without apologetics, social ethics, feminist, urban or liberation theology) could survive, but it would not bear much relation to any of the religions with which we are most familiar.

The construction of new religious belief systems is arbitrary [6]

How do new, or radically changed, conceptual belief systems come into being if they are not, in any sense, intelligible moves from experience? How are world views - the pictures that people use to make sense of their lives - constructed if they are not the result of rational deliberation on, or appropriate responses to, or provoked by, peoples' life histories and changing social experiences? What does St. Paul's theology amount to if it is not an attempt to make coherent sense out of the apostles' encounter with Jesus? Here there are only questions, because if religious

68

beliefs are groundless in the sense we have been considering, there are no satisfactory answers.

There are however three unsatisfactory answers. The fact is that none of the philosophers we have been considering is committed to the idea that religions are solely ways of talking nor that language systems are completely isolated or completely arbitrary. They each make an attempt to explain how religions are constructed and develop and how individuals make decisions about adopting or abandoning them.

Alasdair MacIntyre

Alasdair MacIntyre believes that religions are justified by reference to the acceptance of an ultimate authority. That they are ultimate, he says, precludes going beyond them to look for any sort of external justification. He believes, that is, that the credibility of a religion is established internally. But when Winch declares that standards of intelligibility originate in social institutions - that their intelligibility is also established internally - MacIntyre argues that this cannot be so, because it would rule out the development through criticism of the standards of intelligibility current in a society [7]. He does not attempt to say what the crucial difference is between credibility and intelligibility, that the one can be based on standards independent of particular language systems and the other not. Nor do I think that such an argument is possible. We learn both what it is true to believe and what it makes sense to say from our language training and yet radical criticism of both does arise. This is the nub of the problem and MacIntyre has done nothing to solve it.

As we have already seen, MacIntyre attempts to solve the problem of innovation in religion by suggesting that people can start new religions by setting up new criteria for deciding what is authentically religious, and that this is done by proposing that a pre-eminent experience of their own, will be what future experiences are judged by [8].

There are considerable theoretical difficulties with this suggestion which Wittgenstein has made clear [9]. The memory of an experience cannot be used to test further experiences because we have no external criteria by which to judge whether we have remembered it correctly. An innovative interpretation or description of an experience could take something like this role in a new religion, but this leaves us with a, still unexplained, decision on the part of innovators to change the rules about how to interpret and describe their experiences.

Another problem with MacIntyre's proposal is that while insisting that religious beliefs cannot be inferred from experiences, he asserts that a new religion can grow from its founder's pre-eminent experience. This experience becomes, he says, the criterion by which others' experiences are judged to be authentic. But he makes no attempt to explain how the beliefs and activities of this new religious community can develop from their commitment to this new criterion, nor does such an explanation seem possible within the confines of this theory.

Peter Winch

Peter Winch responds to MacIntyre's criticism of him by explaining how he believes language systems develop. Institutions are, he says, based on rules, but these rules have an open character. "In changing social situations, reasoned decisions have to be made about what is to count as, "going on in the same way"". It is a case of, "the further development of rules and principles already implicit in the previous ways of acting and talking" [10].

To Winch language systems change by means of gradual, internal developments of the rules that govern institutions. He appears as closed as MacIntyre and Phillips to the suggestion that such developments can be a rational response to anything outside the system. This description of how religions change is consistent with the assumptions of a priority of language theory and is an accurate description of one kind of change. Religions do seem to develop gradually in response to the need for internal consistency; and all new religious movements seem to be logically related to what went before.

And yet it is inadequate as an explanation of the sort of radical innovation that is the subject of this book - of changes that appear to be appropriate responses to changes in the secular intellectual climate or people's social experience, or changes that seem to involve a wholesale rejection of the current ways of going on and the proposal of a radically new set of rules and criteria.

There are two areas of Winch's characterization of religions that are theoretically unsatisfactory and that are relevant to the problem of innovation in religion. He draws an analogy between religious language and pain language that doesn't work in some crucial areas and he attempts, unsuccessfully, to identify a set of practices that can be called "religious" independently of associated beliefs.

Winch's analogy [11] is helpful in many ways. It is helpful to see how religious practices have their roots in primitive natural activities like moments of silent contemplation, joy or prostration. It is helpful to remember that the "natural cry" of pain becomes moulded by culture and replaced by established institutions such as talking about pain and that, in the same way, the "natural" expression of wonder or reverence can become moulded into and replaced by worship rituals. It is helpful to remember that we learn how to talk about pain by observing natural pain behaviour and to see that we can also learn to talk about God by observing worship.

At this point however the analogy breaks down. For pain is a sensation and talk about pain is talk about the sensation. But neither God nor religion are sensations. Not only is a feeling of awful reverence a complicated emotion, rather than a simple sensation, but also when we talk about religion or about God we are not talking about this emotion. We do not learn about God by observing natural expressions of reverence; we learn about God by participating in a variety of established activities, and when we talk about religions we talk about these symbolic, rule following, social practices (and the beliefs associated with them) that, among other social functions, express a range of sophisticated emotions of which reverence is only one.

Being distinctly different from talking about pain, talking about God does not develop in the same way. Pain is pain, however it is expressed, but when radical innovation occurs in religions, which emotions and experiences are to be seen as authentically religious is among the things that are open to criticism and change. It is hard to imagine a revolutionary innovator criticizing the pain behaviour of his community and proposing radically new ways of feeling and behaving that would be received by them as an appropriate development of the concept [12].

As well as making this unsatisfactory analogy Winch attempts, also unsatisfactorily, to identify practices as religious independently of any associated beliefs. We can recognize creatures who are in pain even though they have no concept of pain, in the sense that they have no pain language and no beliefs about pain. Possibly, although I find this difficult to imagine, we can recognize creatures that are in a state of awe even though they have no concept of awe. Winch's proposal that we can recognize creatures as being engaged in religious activities without any reference to religious beliefs is, however, open to substantial criticism.

Wonder and reverence, fear, submission, devotion, and every other "primitive" emotion evoked by religions can also be expressed in an entirely mundane or secular context. (Pain cannot be expressed in a "non-pain" context.) In order to call a practice religious we have to have some understanding, not only of what the participants are doing, but of what they think they are doing. We need to know what the practice means to them - what function it has in their lives - even if they themselves have never formulated these thoughts or meanings as specific beliefs.

When we say the activities some creatures are engaged in must be religious, it is because we speculate about what they believe, not what they feel. When naturalists say that elephants must be engaging in religious activity when they appear to mourn or fete their dead, it is not because they think they see, implied in the elephant's behaviour, a religious emotion; the emotion they would see would be grief, or possibly hope, but neither grief nor hope are necessarily religious emotions. They think they see implied a religious belief - a belief in the continuing significance of the dead.

The case of tribesmen looking to the mountains in order to show reverence to their gods is, Winch maintains, different from the case of their looking towards the mountains to seek animals to hunt because the latter is an explanation of why they look, the former only expresses a conceptual connection. This is because, he says, the term "animal" can be given a sense independently of this habit of the tribesmen looking towards the mountains while the term "god" derives its sense only from its connection with the rituals. But does the sense of religious concepts derive only from their connection with religious activities? On the contrary, religious traditions supply their followers with public criteria which give a sense to their talk of what they see as spiritual realities [14]. In Exodus Chapter 19 Moses explains that God meets his people on the mountain in fire and smoke and talks to them in thunder. His presence can be confirmed by the fact that if they touch the mountain when he is there they will die. God's presence on the mountain is, within this tradition, given a sense independent of the habits of his worshippers, in much the same way that seeing brown shapes darting among the bushes gives sense to their activity of looking for animals on the mountain.

While in some Christian traditions the Eucharist does seem to have become the central focus of the participant's understanding of God, in others it still gets its sense from an historical event, of which it is a memorial. Both the activities and the beliefs of a religious tradition are necessary for it to be recognized as a religion.

These criticisms of Winch suggest that religions are not most helpfully seen primarily as a sort of sensation or emotion, nor as a sort of activity, nor as a sort of language, but as a sort of institution, which implies the combination of an established practice with an established meaning.

D. Z. Phillips

D. Z. Phillips' characterization of religious language as expressive, rather than referential and truth affirming [15] is crucial to his failure to account adequately for innovation in religions.

Phillips claims that when he looks at the way religious believers speak - the role that religious language has in their lives - he finds that talking about God is nothing like talking about physical objects, and that religious beliefs have an unshakeable, unconditional character that is not like having an opinion or using a testable hypothesis. Rather than being supported by evidence or reasons, they are stated in a way that makes them unfalsifiable. They are held in position by their role in undergirding a whole way of talking and living. Disagreements between people using different world views are not disagreements about facts, but disagreements about ways of looking at the world. It makes no sense to ask if the pictures they are using are correct since notions of correctness only have a meaning within a world picture. In this sense religious beliefs can be said to be groundless rather than justified.

Phillips' argument draws on Wittgenstein's ideas about bedrock propositions and world pictures [16]. Bedrock propositions enjoy a special status because of the place they occupy in a language system. Within the system they are rarely stated and never questioned. They are held to be certain, not because they are conclusions from experience, or can be justified by reasons, but because, if they were not true, the whole way of life that is built upon them would collapse. Phillips argues that religious beliefs are like Wittgenstein's bedrock propositions. They are held without grounds; their necessity is grammatical.

It is this view of religious language that leads him to say that he simply does not understand what could be involved in having reasons for believing in God [17] (or the reality of the dead [18], or the forgiveness of sins [19]). And it is this puzzlement that makes his explanation of innovation in religion so problematic. But is Phillips' characterization of religious language a fair one - and is it a fair interpretation of Wittgenstein's remarks? Can one suppose that orthodox monotheistic beliefs involve no truth claims about a self-subsistent entity who is independent of anyone's beliefs? Are the beliefs of ordinary religious believers not falsifiable assertions, or not supported by any kind of evidence? Do they have a grammatical necessity and are they always held unconditionally?

Phillips makes three identifiable mistakes that are all, to some extent, caused firstly by a hardening-up of Wittgenstein's remarks, that in my opinion moves them beyond what he intended, and secondly by taking as his observed model an unorthodox, philosophical form of religious belief rather than that of ordinary believers.

Whether any religious belief is meaningful, susceptible to evidence, has a grammatical necessity and is held unconditionally are separate questions which depend upon the particular belief in question and the way it is used by the particular believer.

The observation that talk of God is not like talk of physical objects does not imply that God can have no sort of ontological status and that claims about his existence are therefore not meaningful assertions

That the grammar of talk about God is not like the grammar of talk about physical objects, has been accepted and discussed in several sections of this thesis. Saying we believe there is a hat stand in the hall next door is not at all the same as saying we believe there is a God in heaven. We can mean on the one hand that we are not certain whether there is a hat stand there or not, we do not care very much, but know without hesitation how to go

74

about finding out. We can mean, on the other hand, that we are prepared to live and die by our belief that it is so, but cannot see how to prove it to someone who is not, as nothing that happens seems to count either way.

Answering the criticism that religious people think they are addressing a being when they address God, Phillips says:

> I have no doubt, however that *the same* believers who say that the existence of God is a fact would, if pressed, admit... that there is no question of God ceasing to exist, of having existed for a certain length of time, or having come into existence... I should have thought it followed from this that the reality of God cannot be what Hume called a matter of fact and existence [20].

But, as Norman Malcolm argues, it is a mistake to think that there is only one kind of meaning for assertions of existence. He maintains, "There are as many kinds of existential propositions as there are kinds of subjects of discourse" [21].

Phillips is impressed by the Christian's talk of the eternal - the absolutely necessary and unlimited - nature of God's existence, especially as expressed by Kierkegaard [22]. He sees this talk as quite different from talk about the existence of material things, which are finite, contingent and may or may not exist at any particular time [23].

Theologians who tend towards this view of God have argued that beliefs about the existence and nature of God must be held unconditionally and his properties must be inalienable, on the grounds that belief in a God who might exist, is probably faithful and may be able to save, is not religiously adequate. It is not adequate, they say, because it can not do what religious beliefs are supposed to do, that is, overcome the disturbing contingency of human life [24].

But all through history people have believed in gods who have contingent, limited, properties and involve themselves with their creation. If, as at the time of Joshua, you believe your neighbour's gods are unfaithful and vicious, if, as in Tibet, your god is your king, if, as with many Hindus, you have a hierarchy of gods with different functions and characteristics, the properties of your god are clearly contingent. We can only presume that if these people's faith is adequate for them it has some other purpose than overcoming the disturbing contingency of human life.

The grammar of religious language is quite different from that of material objects, but we believe in the reality of, and make meaningful assertions about, things other than material objects. We talk of diseases, dreams, universities, emotions and ideas. The ontology of material objects is not the only ontology we understand.

As with other kinds of talk, the ways of life in which religious language is embedded give their followers public criteria for talking about religious concepts. Religious believers talk of images and oracles, of theophany and incarnation, they tell stories and perform rituals, they describe what are claimed to be contemporary manifestations of the divine spirit.

It may be impossible to make meaningful assertions about the timeless, impassive, necessary God of the philosophers. It is not impossible to make them about the gods people worship in living traditions. Joseph Runzo is right to talk of Phillips, "lean ontology" which is, he says, "neither the only theological orthodoxy nor the only logical orthodoxy" [25].

The observation that religious beliefs can be used in a way that gives them grammatical necessity does not mean that they can not also have a "matter of fact" use that makes them susceptible to evidence

As Wittgenstein suggested, religious beliefs can be used as bedrock propositions, held in place not by evidence, but by their role in supporting a superstructure of beliefs and activities. But it is not the case that religious beliefs, as a class, have the grammatical necessity of bedrock propositions.

Whether a belief is constitutive of the conceptual foundation of someone's life, depends upon the particular instance of its use. Many religious beliefs can be shown to have a "matter of fact" use in the lives of believers - to be part of the conceptual superstructure built on a secure foundation. They still may not, in that case, be susceptible to evidence from outside the system, but they are susceptible to evidence from within it.

If we consider a typical religious belief - the belief that God has spoken [26] - we find that within the criteria of everyday, secular language the belief that God has spoken is nonsense; God does not have a mouth and noises that we recognize as language do not

76

emerge from it. (Yet within the criteria of a particular religious tradition it has an imperative nature; when God speaks we must obey.) But religious traditions supply public criteria which give the statement a sense - thunder is God speaking (perhaps only the priests understand what he is saying), or an oracle, or dreams, or the words of a prophet, or a sacred book are believed to be the voice of God. The belief that God has spoken is, in this context, a meaningful, falsifiable assertion. It can be equated with the fact that the prophet has spoken, the oracle has declared, the thunder has sounded.

The belief that God has spoken may be used as a bedrock proposition. For a believing Jew, for instance, it may be a foundation for the whole of his way of thinking and behaving, the picture by which he regulates his life. However as a claim related to a specific occasion it denies, for example, that the utterance being considered has been made by a false prophet (or that the oracle has not been used correctly). Religious traditions supply criteria for making decisions about the credibility of prophets and oracular messages. Believers know what counts as evidence for and against the claim that God has, on this particular occasion, spoken or not. The Old Testament is, for example, clear and consistent about the conditions which count against the claim that God has, on a particular occasion, spoken through one of his prophets [27]. In this context the belief that God has spoken has a "matter of fact", not a grammatical, role in the language of believers.

Phillips claims that the belief that sins are forgiven is held in a grammatical way - that, devoid of justification or evidence of any kind, it is the position from which some people choose to view the world - an expression of what they feel to be deeply significant about their lives and relationships. I find this use of this particular belief plausible but idiosyncratic. Within every Christian tradition there are reasons for believing in forgiveness and judgement that can be rehearsed and questioned. From the belief that Jesus is Lord can be derived beliefs about channels of authority, ways of arguing and criteria for what counts as evidence and justification - all that is needed to firmly ground the belief that sins are forgiven [28]. (This does not imply that the belief that Jesus is Lord is not susceptible to evidence, nor that it is necessarily held groundlessly. It can, for example, be derived from the Gospel stories or from beliefs about ethical values.)

This is not to deny Wittgenstein's assertion that at the bottom of all our beliefs are some beliefs that are held groundlessly - beliefs that we do not allow to rise and fall with evidence, but are held in place by the way we live. (The beliefs that take these positions are different for different people and at different times in their lives.) Nor is it to deny that the way of life that rests upon these foundations supplies boundaries within which we can ask questions, construct reasons and make decisions - the criteria by which we decide what our experiences mean, what is real and valuable and true.

What has been demonstrated is that most religious beliefs do not, most of the time, have a grammatical role in the lives of believers. These religious beliefs, like most other sorts of beliefs, are part of the building rather than the foundation of a thought system.

This leaves the question of whether there are any religious beliefs that are held groundlessly in the sense that Wittgenstein implied in his discussion in, *On Certainty* [29]. If there are, perhaps the place to look for them would be somewhere like Frazer's, *Golden Bough* [30] where the apparent belief that the dead must be revered, or that sacrifice must be made, is reported to be widely shared.

The observation that religious beliefs can be held unconditionally does not mean that they can not also be held tentatively

Phillips found, from his observation of religious beliefs that they *can* be held unconditionally, but whether a belief *is* held unconditionally or not is a separate question from whether it is susceptible to evidence. People take a different amount of interest in evidence. How easily one accepts the authenticity of a divine message is powerfully influenced by how much one wants or needs it to be true, or untrue. People can hold unconditionally, beliefs that are susceptible to evidence and hold tentatively, beliefs that are not [31]. The propositions held at one time in our lives as bedrock propositions can, in the context of others being held firm, be questioned and thoughtfully considered. If religious faith is as Phillips appears to claim, people can either participate in it, or be uncomprehending observers. They cannot understand and not believe, nor believe and be temporary observers. The experience of meaningful

78

dialogue between believers and non-believers makes this claim implausible.

For Jewish believers to claim that God has spoken can be, for them, a foundational proposition. To reject the claim would be for them to reject the history, religion and culture of their race. It would involve the collapse of a whole way of talking and living, a whole way of interpreting their experience of the world. For such believers nothing will count as evidence against it; in the sense that it is part of the foundation of their world view, we can say that is not susceptible to evidence; within the tradition it cannot be questioned because the tradition rests upon it, but without the criteria of use supplied by the tradition it does not make sense.

This does not mean however that such a belief can never be questioned or held tentatively - meaningfully observed from within or without [32]. Jews do reject their heritage and cease to believe. To the hesitant proselyte it is a matter for careful calculation whether the eternally faithful God of the Jews is or is not a reality. Even an Anglican bishop can claim that his faith is a, "risky commitment to a glimpsed possibility in the face of reasonable human hesitation about whether it is really possible" [33].

A believing Jew may go to college and discover Marxism. An alternative world view opens up before her. The serpent whispers, as he did to Adam, "Has God spoken?" [34] How is she to chose between the two pictures? What now counts as evidence or reasons? Phillips answer is - nothing, but the fact is that something does count, for Jews do become Marxists (as Phillips will concede) and some are happy to discuss plausible reasons for their choice (which he will not).

Phillips' asserts that if we discard our bedrock propositions we do not discover that our views are false; we experience the collapse of those conditions which make the having of any views - true or false - possible [35]. But this is not what happens.

The society in which we live does not consist of one or two discrete, monolithic language systems, but a conglomerate of overlapping and competing ways of interpreting our experiences and living in the world. The beliefs that, at any time, for any individual, form the bedrock, can shift and change [36]. Any belief can at some time be brought to the surface and questioned in the context of others being held secure. We can slip into an apologetic mode and come back to worship, imagine to ourselves what it would be like to look at the world through the eyes of a Christian, try it and then stop to ask, as John Betjeman does in his poem *Christmas* [37], whether it is all "really true".

Phillips concedes something like this when he observes that rejecting a religious view of life is not like cutting oneself off from reason [38]. The fact is that we possess several ways of using the word "reality", and have at our disposal a variety of ways of classifying and giving meaning to our experiences and constructing arguments. If presented with new possibilities we can hold some of these beliefs secure while asking questions of others: would taking this on board enrich our lives or disturb our quest for cognitive consistency?; how much of what we presently use and value would fall if this belief was relinquished, and is it worth it? These sorts of questions may not be direct responses to experiences, especially not experiences in the empiricist sense, but they do constitute intelligible reasons for accepting, rejecting or reforming our religious beliefs.

MacIntyre's, Winch's and Phillips' attempts to reconcile Wittgensteinian insights about language with the observed phenomena of radical innovation in religion have been shown to be, in some respects, unsatisfactory. The next chapter will consider if there is another way forward.

Notes

1. See Chapters 2, 4 and 7
2. Alasdair MacIntyre, "The Logical Status of Religious Belief", p. 205.
3. MacIntyre chooses to consider Wordsworth and Shatov, but he could have chosen C. S. Lewis (see his autobiography, *Surprised by Joy*) or Michael Goulder and John Hick, (See their dialogue, *Why believe in God?*)
4. D. Z. Phillips, *Faith and Philosophical Enquiry*, p. 6.
5. A significant factor in this development of Christianity is the fact that the early church spread among the Greeks, who were in a sense outsiders in relation to the Hebrew world from which it emerged and felt compelled to find ways to fit it into their ways of thinking.
6. Phillips' discussion with J. R. Jones about loss of belief, *Faith and Philosophical Enquiry*, pp. 111 ff.) is referred to in chapter 4.

7. MacIntyre's discussion with Winch is referred to in chapter 2.

8. Alasdair MacIntyre, "The Logical status of Religious Belief", p. 200 fn.

9. Ludwig Wittgenstein see for eg: *Philosophical Investigations*, I paras. 258 and 293.

10. Peter Winch, "Understanding a Primitive Society", p. 27.

11. See Peter Winch, "Meaning and Religious Language", p. 197. My criticism of this analogy is largely inspired by Stuart Brown's paper in the same volume pp. 233 ff.

12. It might be thought that the rise of Christian Science fitted this description but it involves an altogether wider set of proposals than envisaged here and its development in fact illustrates the complexity and variety of emotions and experiences that can be considered religious.

13. See Peter Winch, "Meaning and Religious Language", pp. 196 ff.

14. (As quoted by Winch later in his paper) Simone Weil, *First and Last Notebooks*, p. 147, "Earthly things are the criterion of spiritual things ... Only spiritual things are of value, but only physical things have a verifiable existence."

15. See chapter 4 where Phillip's later denial that he meant what people have taken him to be saying here is also discussed.

16. D. Z. Phillips, *Religion without Explanation*, pp. 160 ff.

17. D. Z. Phillips, *Faith and Philosophical Enquiry*, p. 79.

18. D. Z. Phillips, *Religion without Explanation*, pp. 133.

19. Ibid., p. 164.

20. D. Z. Phillips, *Faith and Philosophical Enquiry*, p. 71.

21. Norman Malcolm, "A Contemporary Discussion", p. 59.

22. Phillips demonstrates the influence of Kierkegaard e.g. Ibid., pp. 33 and 204 ff. and *Religion without Explanation*, p. 131.

23. D. Z. Phillips, *Religion without Explanation*, pp 174 ff.

24. Phillips discusses this view in *Faith and Philosophical Enquiry*, p. 60.

25. Joseph Runzo, *Reason, Relativism and God*, p. 180.

26. These arguments were suggested by Stuart Brown's book, *Do Religious Claims make Sense?*

27. See Deuteronomy 13 and 18 vs.15-19, Jeremiah 23 and Ezekiel 12 v.21-14 v.11. If what is said is not consistent with the nature of God as revealed to Moses or encourages behaviour contrary to the law, the prophet is a false one

28. See e.g. Matthew 9 vs.1-7 and Acts 2 v.38 and 10 vs.39-43

29. Ludwig Wittgenstein, *On Certainty*, paras. 110, 204, 307, 499, 559 etc.

30. James Frazer, *The Golden Bough*.

31. Roger Trigg's, *Reason and Commitment*, is helpful on how beliefs to which one is committed can, at the same time, be doubted.

32. Colin Lyas in, "The Groundlessness of Religious Belief", p. 189, argues that he holds the belief that his name is not Herman Munsterberg unconditionally, although it is technically susceptible to evidence.

33. David Jenkins, in an interview with Walter Schwarz, *Guardian Weekly*, November 15 1987.

34. Genesis 3 v.1.

35. D. Z. Phillips, *Religion without Explanation*, p. 165.

36. See Ludwig Wittgenstein, *On Certainty*, para. 97.

37. John Betjeman, *John Betjeman's Collected Poems*, p. 188. And is it true?/And is it true?/This most tremendous tale of all ...That God was man in Palestine/And lives today in bread and wine?"

38. D. Z. Phillips, *Religion without Explanation*, p. 167.

Part 2
INSTITUTIONAL THEORIES

10 The search for a different sort of theory

What is required of a good philosophical theory of innovation in religion? It should be philosophically sound - soundly argued from sound assumptions, economical, and consistent with a sound general theory of religion. It should also be possible to tell a plausible story of an instance of innovation in religion that fits the theory in a satisfying way. If this turns out to be difficult the temptation is to describe a form of religious innovation that fits the theory being proposed and then claim this is "real" religion and other forms we may come across are gratuitous annexations. This is an unsatisfactory procedure, especially if the instances generally considered to be standard or definitive end up in the second category.

It has been suggested in this book that present theories based on an empiricist view of religion fail in both of the two requirements, while present theories based on the priority of language in religion fail most notably in the second. It seems in general that empiricism makes the role of tradition unnecessary while priority-of-language theories make the role of innovators impossible.

The task now is to see if it is possible to start from what seem to be the sound assumptions of the priority-of-language theories and move towards a theory of innovation that adequately accommodates standard stories of religious innovation.

I begin by accepting that, as adequately argued by MacIntyre, Winch and Phillips, the use of the concepts of reality and truth (and the cluster of concepts that surround them) are learnt and substantially determined by, cultural training; and by accepting the implication of this, namely that there is no source of criteria for giving intelligibility or credibility to talk or experiences that is independent of culture.

Religious traditions are systems of practices and beliefs that provide such criteria. They depend on the idea of following rules and therefore have the internal authority that we associate with tradition - the authority of established and handed-down practices and beliefs.

The features of standard forms of religion that our theory should accommodate can be summarized as follows: most of the major world religions are essentially committed to the idea of truth. When believers say their beliefs are true they do not mean that they are true within the criteria of their own culture, but that they correspond in some way to how things stand. They also believe that people who have incompatible beliefs are wrong, in a way that will one day become evident. They hold that their faith is not explicable solely in anthropomorphic terms - as the product of people and their ideas, but involves, in some way, the intervention in human history of something that is beyond it.

Religions can act as a base for the criticism and change of other aspects of culture. This has been demonstrated by the role of the Christian Church in communist states. The same can be said of other aspects of culture, such as art. Other aspects of a culture can, on the other hand, act as a base for the criticism of a religious tradition or its loss of authority. Literary and historical criticism is, for example, seen by some to have eroded the authority of the Bible.

While it is true that religions, with their determining rules, are inherited by individuals and buttressed by tradition, religious innovators do criticize and propose changes in religious traditions in a way that can be seen as an intelligible response to changing historical situations. In the process, systems of belief and action, including criteria of authority, "bedrock propositions", and "world pictures" are discarded and new ones created, that can be seen to be intelligibly related both to what preceded them and to the historical changes that precipitated them.

Whether these new traditions take root depends on their reception by a group of people, who then form a new religious community. The reception of new ideas and the abandonment of old ones, is a process that is not detached from an individual's experiences, or from reasons. During the process systems of thought are questioned and compared and intelligible decisions are taken.

One of the roles of theology is to work towards cognitive consistency within a particular tradition, but it is also concerned with intelligibly relating the tradition to other aspects of the intellectual climate and people's social experiences.

What Wittgenstein intended to convey by his remarks about religious beliefs being a form of life, theology being grammar, and rule-following activities being autonomous and isolated has been a long-standing matter of debate. The writers considered in the previous section, have in their interpretations, I believe, taken each of these remarks too far.

In one of Wittgenstein's senses you can not give up a form of life and you can not relate to people (or lions [1]) with a different form of life from your own. In this sense there can not be several independent forms of life in one culture. W. D. Hudson asks if one form of life can isolate itself and claim a logical ultimacy of its own. He comments, "Surely not, if the language used to constitute it is common to other forms of life as well, as most, if not all of the language used to express religious beliefs is" [2].

Religious traditions cannot be totally autonomous, nor totally isolated from one another, or from other aspects of the culture in which they operate; they just have different histories. Theology has to be done continually as religious traditions relate their institutions to changes in the surrounding aspects of culture.

There are several remarks in Wittgenstein's work to suggest that forms of life (consisting of both practices and talk) are, in some senses, constrained by the world and by our psychology [3]. Important here is his insistence on the fact that, in some senses, rules are followed blindly [4] - that it is, "not a kind of *seeing* ... It is our *acting* which lies at the bottom of the language game" [5]. And this acting is, for Wittgenstein, essentially communal [6]. A proper appreciation of these ideas must raise the importance of institutions, in the sense of communally established activities that express aspects of the human psyche, in any consideration of innovation in religion.

Wittgenstein's remarks about rule-following activities do not make them immune from intelligible criticism and radical change. Anthony O'Hear, for example, argues that there is something deeply anti-relativistic about Wittgenstein's analysis of rule-following [7]. For Wittgenstein the whole idea of following a rule depends on the ability to distinguish between being right and thinking one is right. Once people have learnt this distinction through membership of an epistemic community they can, O'Hear argues, see the possibility that some of the beliefs widely held in their community may also be wrong. Wittgenstein is careful to point out what does not amount to an effective challenge to our life and belief but he does not say there are no effective challenges, nor that such challenges may not, in principle, be amenable to some sort of reasoned assessment. Wittgenstein's discussion of the shifting river-bed is relevant here. He says, "The same propositions may get treated at one time as something to test experience, at another as a rule of testing" [8]. In fact Wittgenstein, as O'Hear points out, is himself not averse to criticizing practices well-embedded in his own culture.

The remaining chapters of this book will explore the possibility of reconciling these philosophical assumptions with these features of standard forms of religion by considering religion, not primarily as a kind of experience, nor primarily as a kind of language, but as an aspect of culture - a kind of social institution - by constructing, that is, an institutional theory of religion.

Some clues as to how this way of considering religion might help have already emerged. Seeing religions as more than language systems will help explain more clearly: the conflicting pressures for continuity and for change within an institution (tradition v. innovation); the way in which religions are not isolated; the way in which religions are not arbitrary and; the way in which religions are assessed and chosen.

Tradition and innovation

Social institutions involve rules (conventions) about ways of talking, reasoning and interpreting experience, ways of behaving, both practically and symbolically and ways of relating; they involve channels of authority, social roles and institutional structures. Although intimately related, these various factors can in some sense have lives of their own - developing independently and attracting an independent authority. This clarifies the dynamic tensions that can arise within a religion. It is interesting to consider here, as an example, the tensions that arise between liturgy and theology in a changing social climate such as that represented by the feminist movement.

A symbolic activity that has a social function has within it both pressure for continuity and, if the social situation changes, the possibility of pressure for change. There can be tension between practice (This is how it has always been done), and theory (Our lives have changed and it no longer feels the same to us). These tensions do not necessarily have to be conscious or verbalized. A previous feeling of authority just fades (towards the Bible) or people just stop using a particular institution (private confession). Alternatively the conflict can become intense (the ordination of women) and can become focused on an individual (George Fox).

Interacting aspects of culture

Modern cultures are not made up of a diversity of discrete world views and isolated language systems. A common language spans a profusion of almost individually tailored combinations of attitudes, values, beliefs and behaviour. The different spheres of life in which the same people move are not isolated from each other. A week in a city office, a university common room or a tower block flat affects what is looked for in the Eucharist on Sunday; concepts learnt in the factory and the lecture room find their way into liturgy; new ethical problems posed in the laboratory demand a new look at Scripture, a rethinking of old doctrines; the ideas of writers, artists, economists and artisans interact with priests and theologians (some of them are in their congregations and classrooms). There is no neutral independent source of reasons or experiences from which to view the world but, if religion is one aspect of culture among many, it can be viewed from others and compared, combined, reformed or rejected.

Culture and life

If, as Wittgenstein maintained, nature makes herself audible [9], one way that we hear her is in the rules that govern social institutions (in the sense of established, symbolic, rule-following, activities). They are, in the end, what people just do. These rituals have functions for human societies and for individuals that relate to their life histories. They express, focus and give a meaning to, and a way of sharing and controlling, the exaltation and anxiety that surrounds a birth, the grief and hope that surrounds a death, the pride of adulthood, the wonder of harvest,

89

the value of comradeship, the fear of battle. Ritual activities attract an intrinsic authority (tradition) but the power of rituals changes with changing social circumstances (innovation). The threat of the enemy recedes; the harvest loses its wonder; other fears and wonders unimagined by our ancestors arrive to take their place. Life feels different and some adaptation of the institutional system is demanded if it is to survive. Practices can be adapted or die out, or the same actions can be given different meanings, perhaps different words are said to accompany or explain them.

There is no neutral independent source of experiences from which to view the world, but changing historical situations produce changes in how people feel about their lives and therefore produce pressure for changes in the social institutions whose meaning and power derive from those feelings.

Choosing a world-view

If religions are complex institutional systems interwoven with other such systems in the lives of modern people, they can, like any part of any system, at some time in a person's life, be taken out and questioned in the context of other parts of the total system being held firm. Doubters can calculate the net effect to their cognitive, social and emotional lives of retaining or rejecting a belief or an attitude and make reasoned decisions about it. These decisions can be rationally pondered responses to the experience of changing historical or personal circumstances without depending in any way upon general criteria of rationality, or experiences of an independently real world.

How then are we to suppose changes occur in rule-following activities? Soccer is a rule-following activity that serves a social function. How do changes occur in the rules of the game? The rules of how to play football (and the rules relating to other roles associated with the game such as referee, manager, spectator etc.) are part of our inherited tradition. As such they have an intrinsic authority which is augmented by various local, national and international regulating bodies. But pressures for change emerge that are related to factors outside the world of football, and succeed in forcing changes that relate intelligibly to the source of these pressures.

Changes in the social function of the game (and of its

90

economics) related to the increasing importance of the spectator, can be seen to have led to changes in the off-side rule. An increased level of violence in society and on the pitch has led to the introduction of new rules about warnings and sending-off, and new concepts - the "yellow card" and the "red card". Changes in the physical conditions in which the game is played (in a small hall or yard for instance) can lead to changes in the rules about the number of players required. The story of the rise of Rugby Football and its subsequent split into rival leagues would make an interesting comparison with the rise of a new religion or sect.

These considerations all seem to point towards the possibility that some kind of institutional theory of religion might be a fruitful base for an adequate explanation of radical innovation in religion.

Institutional theories in the fields of art have, however, not been entirely successful. The next chapters will consider what can be learnt from them.

Notes

1. Ludwig Wittgenstein, *Philosophical Investigations*, I para. 223.
2. W. D. Hudson, *Wittgenstein and Religious Belief*.
3. E.g. Ludwig Wittgenstein, *Zettel*, para. 364 and *On Certainty*, paras. 616-7.
4. Ludwig Wittgenstein, *Philosophical Investigations*, I para. 219.
5. Ludwig Wittgenstein, *On Certainty*, para. 204.
6. Ludwig Wittgenstein, *Philosophical Investigations*, I paras. 198-201.
7. Anthony O'Hear, "Wittgenstein and the Transmission of Tradition", From the script of a lecture delivered at the Royal Institute of Philosophy in November 1989.
8. Ludwig Wittgenstein, *On Certainty*, paras. 96-98.
9. Ludwig Wittgenstein, *Zettel*, para 364.

11 Institutional theories in aesthetics

What is Art? The question is an old one. Socrates wanted to know what all the things we call art have in common [1], and the question was asked without any very satisfactory answer for centuries. It was Wittgenstein who arrested the inquiry by the suggestion: "Don't say: There *must* be something common... look and see whether there is" [2], and by the indication of an answer: "The application of a word is not everywhere bounded by rules" [3].

The question became, in some quarters, no longer acceptable. But by the end of the 1960s, with new ways of looking at art seeming to indicate the possibility of a new sort of answer, some philosophers [4] began to argue that perhaps it was after all worth asking. Maybe there was a path somewhere between the Platonic conclusion that "Art" was the name of an inaccessible mystery, and the Wittgensteinian conclusion that it was not the name of anything. Maybe you could say something valid and interesting about art by looking, not at the natural properties of objects, or the natural attitudes of individuals, but at the relationship between art and culture - not at brute facts but at institutional ones [5]. Ideas proliferated but actual theories were scarce and their critics vociferous.

This question about art can be asked in many different ways. Asked in a rigorous way it becomes a search for an essentialist definition of art, but it can, at the other end of the scale, become a quest for a more helpful analysis of the way the concept of art is used.

An institutional theory of art is an attempt to answer this question, at either end of the scale, by referring to institutional facts. It does not, that is to say, seek to define or analyze the concept of art in terms of natural properties or relationships, but in terms of properties and relationships that depend upon the agreement of human communities [6].

To explore the field of institutional theories of art this section will briefly review the ideas of J. Margolis and Richard Wollheim, neither of which terminates in an institutional theory, some works of T. J. Diffey and Arthur C. Danto, which could be said to point towards an institutional theory, Jerrold Levinson, who presents just such a theory, although he denies that that is what he is doing and finally, the work of George Dickie.

J. Margolis

In a paper entitled, "Works of Art as Physically Embodied and Culturally Emergent Entities", J. Margolis points to a similarity between works of art and persons in that they both appear to possess two sets of properties. One set they have as physical objects and these they possess, "independently of any cultural consideration and even independently of the existence of any culture". The other set of properties are, "culturally significant properties," that, "cannot be ascribed to the merely physical objects in which they are embodied" [7].

These latter constitute the work of art and are characterized by having an "interior purposiveness". He draws an analogy with a signal;

> A man raises his arm to signal; the action has that intentional property. Apart from human society there is no such action, no more than a movement of the arm; within the conventions of a culture the action may be seen as such, embodied in the arm's movement... To identify an act of signalling one must identify a suitable physical movement that by reference to an appropriate tradition or rule or custom or the like may fairly be taken as embodying the act. So the very existence of the action depends on a cultural context [8].

Applying the analogy to art he suggests that it is only relative to some cultural tradition that anything can be identified as a work of art" [9].

Richard Wollheim

In a book entitled *Art and its Objects*, Richard Wollheim explores the implications of seeing art as "a form of life", a phrase taken from Wittgenstein's later philosophy [10], a phrase which Wollheim says, "appears as descriptive or invocatory of the total context within which alone language can exist: the complex of habits, experiences, skills, with which language interlocks in that it could not be operated without them and equally, they cannot be identified without reference to it" [11].

One of these implications is that we should not think there is something which we call the artistic impulse or intention, and which can be identified independently of, and prior to, the institutions of art [12]:

> There is no way in which we can ascribe manifestations to this artistic instinct until there are already established in society certain practices recognized as artistic; the sexual instinct, on the other hand, manifests itself in certain activities, whether or not society recognizes them as sexual...
> In the case of sexuality, the connection between the instinct and its satisfaction in the world is immediate, in the case of art it is mediated by a practice or institution (...the parallel in the sexual sphere to talking of an artistic instinct would be to postulate a "matrimonial" instinct) [13].

It does not follow, according to Wollheim, that there is no such thing as an artistic impulse; there is still the impulse to produce something as a work of art, but what gives art its unity, "is that the objects that centrally belong to it have been produced under the concept of art" [14].

Later in his essay Wollheim talks about seeking, "not a definition, but a general method for identifying works of art" [15]. He says the method might take the form of picking out certain objects as original or primary works of art, and then setting up some rules which successively applied to the original works of art will give us... all subsequent or derivative works of art.

94

Wollheim discusses the way in which it could be true to say that art is dependent upon life:

> It is clear that, when we look at a painting or listen to a piece of music, our perception rests upon projection and responsiveness to form, processes which we may believe to be in operation from the beginnings of consciousness. It has been said, with reason, that the crux or core of art may be recognized in some effect as simple as the completely satisfying progression from a cobbled street to the smooth base of a building that grows upward from it. Here, then, we have the dependence of art on life [16].

He points out that, in art, these original processes are constrained, but what is peculiar to art is not a new kind of feeling, or perception or awareness, but a new conjunction of elements already in existence.

These observations of Wollheim's suggest that it might be possible to define art in terms of its relationship to institutional facts. But this is a temptation which Wollheim, as we shall see later, vigorously resists [17].

T. J. Diffey

In a paper called, "The Republic of Art", T. J. Diffey suggests it is the institutionalized presentation of an object that is crucial when we claim it is a work of art. We are not, he says, expressing a brute fact about the object, but an institutional fact. Being a work of art is, Diffey says, a status conferred upon an object by the judgement of the public [18].

He argues that if, as some claim, there are no necessary and sufficient conditions for the application of the term "work of art", the term has no connotation. However, if we demand something less vigorous we can exhibit the logic of the phrase. As far as it is denotative, one can proceed by listing well known works: "That is," he says, "to enumerate institutional facts" [19].

But how do you accommodate innovators who seek to re-create the concept of art? It is the case in art, Diffey maintains, that it is possible to re-create the concept of art, but at the same time, it is not true that anything anyone chooses to call art is art.

To steer between these extremes it is necessary to consider how the status "work of art" is conferred on something. He suggests this might be done, "by reviving the metaphor of the Republic or Commonwealth of Letters, extending it to include all the arts, and then taking it literally" [20].

First stage membership of the republic is by self election, and effective, or second-stage, membership is by recognition, and it is the republic which confers the status of "work of art" on things that are already identifiable as, for instance, a novel, or a play. One can not intend to produce a work of art, only wish or hope that it will be one and, although it seems impossible for the republic to make a mistake, in fact, as in the award of degrees, value judgements are involved and mistakes can be made [21]. Merely personal users of the term may be ignored, scorned or fail to carry the support of the republic.

But Diffey poses several other questions that he does not answer: how does the republic make up its mind?; must there be reasons for conferring or withholding status?; is there one republic or many?; is this really a single concept? These ideas point towards an institutional theory of art, but, with the author's connivance, fail to arrive at one.

In a later paper Diffey develops some of these ideas in a different direction. Most of the paper deals with objections to institutional theories that suppose that, "when we know how things are accredited as art we shall know what art is" [22]. This idea is, he says, subject to a number of philosophical objections (which we shall consider later). He adds, "Wittgensteinians are right that a formula defining art would be useless; for example we do not need a definition of art to spot works of art since works of art are identified not by philosophical definition but by history" [23]. He pleads for a compromise between rejecting the question: what is art? altogether and answering it by reference to the way works of art are accredited. He wants to urge that the question of what art is, is something, "which is settled historically, but which yet can legitimately be a matter of dispute" [24].

Arthur C. Danto

Arthur C. Danto wrote a paper about New York painting. In it he imagines four identical neck ties - one Picasso has painted all over blue, the others have been painted blue by a child, a forger and Cezanne. According to Danto only the first tie is a work of art:

> One way to see the matter is this: Picasso used the necktie to *make a statement*, the forger employed the tie to copy what Picasso made a statement with but made no statement by means of his... The child and Cezanne are simply making a noise. Their objects have no location in the history of art... art had not developed appropriately by the time of Cezanne for such a statement to have been intelligible, nor can the child in question have sufficiently internalized the history and theory of art to make a statement, much less *this* statement [25].

Later in this paper Danto introduces the concept of ascriptivity, which is a property of predicates when they attach to objects by reference to conventions and which apply less on the basis of certain necessary and sufficient conditions than of defeating conditions not holding [26]. He suggests "artwork", perhaps like "person", is an ascriptive term rather than an exclusively descriptive one [27]. Danto proposes two defeating conditions for objects not to be art works - that they are copies and that they are not created by artists [28].

In a later paper Danto elaborates his thoughts and introduces two important new ideas. Although he does not press them into serving an institutional theory they are consistent with and can be incorporated into, an institutional account.

The two new ideas are the concept of "the artworld" and the role of theories in constituting it. Danto begins by saying that we know which objects are works of art because we know how to use the word "art", and to apply the phrase "work of art", correctly, but he goes on to warn, this is not as simple as it might seem, for these days one needs to know about artistic theories in order to know that one is on artistic terrain [29]. Danto looks back at the history of art and, drawing an analogy with science, speaks of changes which are not so much revolutions in taste as theoretical revisions of considerable proportions, "involving not only the artistic enfranchisement of these objects, but an emphasis upon newly significant features of accepted artworks, so that quite different accounts of their status as artworks would now have to

97

be given [30].

Turning to some 20th century American artists such as Robert Rauschenberg and Andy Warhol, Danto explains how acquaintance with a particular theory is necessary if one is to see how it is that their contributions count as art [31]. He refers to one particular example of Andy Warhol's work;

> What in the end makes the difference between a Brillo box and a work of art consisting of a Brillo box is a certain theory of art. It is the theory that takes it up into the world of art, and keeps it from collapsing into the real object which it is... Of course without the theory, one is unlikely to see it as art, and in order to see it as part of the artworld, one must have mastered a good deal of artistic theory as well as a considerable amount of the history of recent New York painting [32].

Danto proceeds to describe the relationship between new art theories and existing ones in terms of the addition of new artistically relevant predicates. Which predicates end up being seen as artistically relevant is, he says, of almost purely sociological interest, nor would the things they confirm as artworks be artworks, without the theories and histories of the Artworld [33].

Jerrold Levinson

In a paper called "Defining Art Historically" Jerrold Levinson develops what he calls an alternative to the institutional theory of art. In fact he specifically denies that, "an analysis of arthood" must involve institutions and that the institutions of art in a society are essential to art. He says, "The making of art is primary; the social frameworks and conventions that grow up around it are not" [34]. But he retains, "the crucial idea that artworkhood is not an intrinsic exhibited property of a thing, but rather a matter of being related in the right way to human activity and thought" [35]. He is, I suggest, using the word "institution" in an unusual way here. The activities of human communities are, in a normal use of the word, institutions, and if his theory depends upon the relationship between art and these activities it is, in that sense, an institutional theory.

Levinson sets out to construct this relationship in terms of the intentions of single, independent, individuals, rather than in terms of acts performed in an institutional setting.   This intention makes reference to the history of art - what art has been - as opposed to, "that murky and somewhat exclusive institution, the artworld" [36].   The core of his proposal is, he says, to give an essential historicity to an account of what it is to regard something as a work of art.

X is a work of art, he suggests, if it is a thing intended for regard as a work of art - that is, regarded in any of the ways in which prior art works are or were correctly regarded [37].   In order to expand this definition he goes on to suggest that the person concerned must have appropriate proprietary rights over the object, that he must intend in the sense of, "making, appropriating or conceiving for the purposes of," and he must do it in a manner Levinson characterizes as "non-passingly".   By "correctly regarded", he means to include "standardly regarded". He summarizes this position by saying: "To be art at (time) t is to be intentionally related in the required way to something which is art prior to t" [38].   The definition is not circular because what counts as art prior to the present time is a fact (it is what I call an institutional fact).   "To eliminate this reflexiveness would," Levinson says, "be to eviscerate the term "art" of the only universal content which it now retains" [39].

To accommodate what he calls revolutionary art, or art that calls for a totally unprecedented sort of regard, Levinson argues that if they are to be art, the artists's primary intention must be to make his objects art.   He must, "initially direct his audience to take them (or try to take them) in some way that art *has* been taken", or to take them, "in some other way in contrast to and against the background of those ways".   He must as least "consciously nod in the direction of past artistic activity" [40].

George Dickie

George Dickie took the ideas of Arthur Danto and transformed them into a full blown institutional theory of art.   He did not pursue the idea that the continuity of art theories were of primary importance in defining art;   he turned instead to the concept of the artworld, amalgamated it with Diffey's idea of conferring status and proposed that it was possible to define an art object as, "an artifact... a set of the aspects of which has had conferred upon it the status of candidate for appreciation by some person or persons acting on behalf of a certain institution (the artworld)" [41].

If this theory is to work as a definition it obviously needs careful descriptions of what is meant by an artworld and an artifact, by acting on behalf of an institution, by conferring status and by being a candidate for appreciation. These descriptions Dickie outlines.

He uses Danto's idea of "the artworld" - the broad social institutions in which works of art have their place; but refines it: "When I call the artworld an institution I am saying that it is an established practice, not that it is an established society or corporation" [42]. He takes theatre as an example of one of the systems within the artworld: "The roles of actors and audience are defined by the traditions of the theatre. What the author, management, and players present is art, and it is art because it is presented within the theatreworld framework" [43]. Each system within the artworld has its own origins and history and each has its own procedures and lines of authority even if they are on the level of customary practices rather than being explicitly codified [44]. But the different systems have in common the fact that they are the framework for the presenting of particular works of art. And who belongs to the artworld? Dickie seems to answer this question ambiguously. The essential core he sees as consisting of artists who create, presenters and "goers" who appreciate. "All the roles are institutionalized and must be learned in one way or another by the participants," but he adds: "In addition, every person who sees himself as a member of the artworld, is thereby a member" [45].

To explain what he means by an artifact Dickie says that a natural object such as a piece of driftwood or a painting done by a gorilla, can be made into art by such an action as hanging it on the wall, or entering it in an art exhibition. It is thereby, "artifactualized without the use of tools - artifactuality is conferred on the object rather than worked on it" [46]. A great deal apparently depends upon the institutional setting; exhibited at the Field Museum of Natural History in Chicago by her keeper, Betsy the Gorilla's paintings are not works of art; exhibited a few miles away at the Chicago Art Institute by its director, they have undergone a dramatic change. They remain Betsy's paintings,

100

Dickie explains but, "they would be the art of the person responsible for their being exhibited". (Betsy not being able to conceive of herself in such a way as to be a member of the artworld, and hence to confer the relevant status [47].) However any member of the artworld is capable of acting on behalf of the institution, even if they act alone [48].

Dickie describes the conferring of status on works of art as analogous to the way in which a person is certified as qualified for office, or two persons acquire the status of common-law marriage within a legal system, or a person is elected president of the Rotary, or a person acquires the status of wise man within a community. The status of "work of art" is acquired, "by a single person acting on behalf of the artworld and *treating an artifact as a candidate for appreciation*" [49].

But, being a candidate for appreciation does not require that the object actually be appreciated even by one person. Neither does the theory rely on any special sense of the word "appreciation". All that is meant by it, says Dickie, "is something like "in experiencing the qualities of a thing one finds them worthy or valuable"". It is the kind of, "institutional structure in which the art object is embedded, not the different kind of appreciation that makes the difference between the appreciation of art and the appreciation of nonart" [50].

The institutional theory of art may sound like saying a work of art is an object of which someone has said, "I christen this object a work of art". Dickie concludes that it is rather like that, "although this does not mean that the conferring of the status of art is a simple matter. Just as the christening of a child has as its background the history and structure of the church, conferring the status of art has as its background the Byzantine complexity of the artworld" [51]. Yet there is a difference - in the case of art there do not seem to be ways in which the conferring can go wrong, because the artworld, "admits and even encourages frivolity and caprice without losing its serious purpose" [52]. Mistakes can only be made in the sense that you can lose face if no one appreciates an object you have proposed, or if it turns out to be a fake.

Dickie gives a fuller account of his theory in a later book. Here he argues that the concept of a work of art can be used in three different senses - a primary or classificatory sense, a secondary or derivative sense and an evaluative sense [53]. His definition of art, he claims, applies only to the primary sense. Use of this

101

sense, which indicates simply that a thing belongs to a certain category of artifacts, occurs infrequently because it is usually perfectly clear whether or not something is a work of art in this sense. It is, however, Dickie claims, a basic concept that structures and guides our thinking about our world and its contents [54]. We say driftwood is art, he explains, because it resembles some paradigm work of art or because it shares properties with paradigm works of art [55].

Some years later, in book called *The Art Circle* George Dickie replied in detail to the criticisms that had accumulated against his institutional theory of art, and gave the most plausible institutional account of art so far.

What needs to be borne in mind in this later account is that, as Dickie explains, its scope, context, aims and method, as well as its conclusions, are substantially different from traditional theories of art and previous attempts at institutional theories [56]. He admits that the version of the institutional theory of art which he previously worked out was, "mistaken in a great many of its details". His new account is, he says, a contextual theory; what he now means by an institutional approach is all in the modest, but not trivial, idea that, "works of art are art as the result of the position they occupy within an institutional framework or context" [57]. This framework he later describes as, "a cultural practice" [58].

He now believes no institution, in the sense of a group of persons of whatever size or formality, is essential for artmaking. As a result he rejects his ideas about conferred status and conferred artifactuality, the status of candidate for appreciation and the idea of acting on behalf of the artworld [59]. Instead he states simply that if artists create works of art, at least in part because they have thoughts about art (thoughts that involve some degree of understanding about the concept of art, about art itself), "derived from their language and acculturation", a possibility is opened up that a condition for their works being works of art might be the existence of some thing we could call the institution of art [60].

He goes on to demonstrate the difficulty of accounting for the production of art outside a framework of this kind, and suggests how art could have begun by describing how artifacts, originally associated with such things as religious or magical activities, could come to have characteristics of some interest in themselves, "over and above the interest they had as elements in the religious or whatever kind of other activity in which they were embedded. At about this point," he comments, "it becomes meaningful to say that primitive art had begun to exist, although the people who had the art might not yet have a word for its art" [61].

Such an institutional theory of art places virtually no restriction on what art may do - there is no specific aesthetic function. It requires no specific sort of aesthetic experience, perception, appreciation, attitude or set of properties, that function as an aspect of the essential nature of art [62]. All an institutional theory does, he claims, is describe the conditions necessary for a particular activity or practice that has emerged as an historical development [63].

Notes

1. See Plato's *The Republic*.
2. See, for example, Ludwig Wittgenstein, *Philosophical Investigations*, I para. 66. These ideas of Wittgenstein's were worked out in relation to art notably by Paul Ziff, "The Task of Defining a Work of Art" and Morris Weitz, "The Role of Theory in Aesthetics".
3. Ludwig Wittgenstein, *Philosophical Investigations*, I para. 84.
4. A selection of this work will be reviewed later in this chapter.
5. Elizabeth Anscombe discusses what brute facts are in, "On Brute Facts", p,6. What institutional facts are will be discussed in more detail in Chapter 14.
6. Not agreement in opinions but in form of life, see Ludwig Wittgenstein, *Philosophical Investigations*, I para. 241.
7. J Margolis, "Works of Art as Physically Embodied and Culturally Emergent Entities", pp. 189-90.
8. Ibid., pp. 192-3.
9. Ibid., p. 191.
10. See for example, *Philosophical Investigations*, I paras. 19, 23 and 241.
11. Richard Wollheim, *Art and its Objects*, p. 120.
12. Ibid., p. 121.
13. Ibid., p..122.
14. Ibid., pp. 123-4.
15. Ibid., p. 159.

16. Ibid., pp. 117-8.
17. See Chapter 12.
18. T. J. Diffey, "The Republic of Art", p. 147.
19. Ibid., p. 148.
20. Ibid., p. 150.
21. Ibid., p. 152.
22. T. J. Diffey, "On Defining Art", p. 19.
23. Ibid., p. 18.
24. Ibid., p. 20.
25. Arthur C. Danto, "Artworks and Real Things", p. 10.
26. Ibid., pp. 11-12.
27. Ibid., p. 11.
28. Ibid., p. 14.
29. Arthur C. Danto, "The Artworld". p. 10.
30. Ibid., p. 11.
31. Ibid., p. 16.
32. Ibid., p. 18.
33. Ibid., p. 20.
34. Jerrold Levinson, "Defining Art Historically", p. 47.
35. Ibid., p. 232.
36. "
37. Ibid., p. 234.
38. Ibid., p. 239.
39. Ibid., p. 240.
40. Ibid., pp. 241-2.
41. George Dickie, "What is Art?". p. 23.
42. Ibid., p. 22.
43. "
44. Ibid., p. 24.
45. "
46. Ibid., p. 29.
47. Ibid., p. 30.
48. Ibid., p. 25, "A number of persons are required to make up the social institution of the artworld," says Dickie, "but only one person is required to act on behalf of the artworld and to confer the status of candidate for appreciation."
49. Ibid., p. 25.
50. Ibid., p. 27.
51. Ibid., p. 31.
52. Ibid., p. 32.
53. George Dickie, *Art and the Aesthetic: An Institutional Analysis*, p. 25.

54. Ibid., pp. 26-27.
55. Ibid., p. 25.
56. George Dickie, *The Art Circle*, p. 111.
57. Ibid., p. 7.
58. Ibid., p. 52.
59.   "
60. Ibid., p. 53.
61. Ibid., p. 56.
62. Ibid., pp. 85 ff.
63. Ibid., p. 111.

12 A critique of institutional theories in aesthetics

Institutional theories of art attempt in some manner to answer the question: what is art?, by referring not to brute facts but to institutional ones, that is, not to natural properties or relationships but to properties or relationships that depend upon the agreement of human communities.

As we have seen such theories vary in the context, vigour and content of their claims. All have been subjected to substantial criticism. These criticisms fall into two classes, those which criticize the entire programme and those which criticize the particular theories proposed.

Critics of the entire programme

Some of those who criticize the whole idea of institutional theories are, as I have already suggested, using the word "institution" in an unusual way. Jerrold Levinson, for example, wants to deny that the institutions of art in a society are of prime importance to its art. He does not want art to be defined in terms of, "its institutional networks" but in terms of, "its concrete history." He does not want art to be art by reference to the, "murky... institutions of the artworld", but to the intentions of individuals that are, for him, crucially related to the history of art, that is, to which objects have been counted as art in the past [1]. This is of course indisputably a matter of institutional facts by the normal use of the word [2]. Using the word normally it would be hard to sustain an argument that institutions are not important to the concept of art, nor to the concept of religion.

106

At very least it cannot be denied that most adults in most communities have an understanding of what religion is, directly derived from their encounters with cultural practices. This fact alone must make institutions an important factor in the use of the concept, and the extent of their importance an issue worth pursuing. Other critics seem to be expressing a general dislike for rigorous essentialist theories. They want to hold on to Morris Weitz's claim that the conditions for a thing to be art are indefinitely corrigible [3]. Richard Wollheim, who is committed to demonstrating the institutional character of art, denounces institutional theories because they claim to pick out works of art by describing properties which are essential to them. He says that this is an enterprise that, "more sceptically inclined philosophers, often expressing an indebtedness to Wittgensteinian ideas, have declared not possible" [4].

Kendall L. Walton says in a review of Dickie's earlier book that he welcomes its emphasis on the role of the world of art in social institutions, but adds, "My own view is that the search for a definition (of art) is a philosophical dead end. We do not need one." It is not, he explains, that he thinks the concept can not be defined but, "simply that a definition would serve no good purpose, that it is not likely to provide any significant philosophical insight or illumination... Concepts are not mountains," he says, "Their mere existence in a language does not make them worthy objects of analysis," and since the things we regard as art are, "hardly a "natural class", the distinction between what belongs to it and what does not is, I believe, a useless and uninteresting one" [5].

Monroe C. Beardsley [6] sets out the requirements of an essentialist institutional theory of art. Firstly it must be possible to distinguish which actions and objects are essentially institutional and which are not; secondly it must be possible to demonstrate that the existence of some institution is included among the truth conditions of, "A is an artwork".

A brief look at the sort of things institutions are, and the way they begin, and the way in which actions and objects become institutional, will reveal that the first of these requirements can never be met in any rigorous way; and a brief consideration of the way language works will show that the second requirement is similarly, if not an impossible aim, an undesirable one. For institutions grow out of natural ways of doing things [7] and what is essential in the rules of use of a word today may not be

107

essential tomorrow [8]. Descriptions of how words are used are not binding upon the users; metaphor, ellipsis and hyperbole are common and too often slip into standard speech [9]. Many words do not have a literal and a metaphorical use that are helpfully kept distinct. The essentialist's problem lies with the fact that both institutions and language are living things.

And yet there is still a point in asking what art, or what religion, is, not in an attempt to discover a rigorous essentialist definition but in an attempt to analyze the use of the concept and thus to reach a more satisfactory understanding of it and phenomena such as radical innovation in rule-following activities.

Another area of general criticism is the extent to which institutional theories have been preoccupied with a certain style of modern painting and sculpture which, their critics say, should have been precipitated from, rather than accommodated to, the concept of art.

There is clearly a sense in which the Dada movement (characterized by Duchamp's entry of a urinal into an art exhibition with the title *Fountain*), was a deliberate attempt, not to change the concept of art, but to destroy it. Ted Cohen thinks no definition of art should fit (Duchamp's *Fountain*) comfortably. He believes that in the face of objects like this we should not re-define art so that they can be made to fit into the category, but give up the compulsion to decide whether to rule it in or out, while holding on to the conviction that we know what art is [10].

T. J. Diffey says whether readymades are works of art is no longer a live issue; it has been settled, but he still believes there is a point in resisting the incorporation of readymades into art: "To think of anti-art as merely some more recent form of art is to nullify its significance" [11].

Anita Silver points out that since Duchamp's aim was to create a conceptual crisis, a definition of art on which his readymades, "were clear-cut and comfortable instances of the application of the term "art" would be a definition on which the works would lose their point" [12].

Wollheim believes that Duchamp's readymades are highly provocative and altogether ironical in relation to art. To think that they require aesthetic theory to be reformulated in such a way as to represent an object like *Fountain* as a central case, would be, he says, a total misunderstanding of Duchamp's intentions [13].

Religion has problems with borderline cases too; Buddhism and Marxism are often seen as such, or Masonry, or, as seen in the recent disputes over Stone Henge, modern Druidism. But there is nothing like the same passion in the philosophical community for the discussion of whether they are, or are not, religions. Most people are happy to believe they know what religion is without having to make definite decisions about borderline cases. The need to accommodate borderline cases in a unitary concept of religion has had no part in the motivation behind this project.

This is mostly because no attempt is being made to provide a rigorous essentialist definition. We could hope however that it may shed some light on the ways in which people attempt to resolve such disputes.

Institutional theories of art all to some extent depend upon the idea of ascription - the idea that to call an object a work of art is to give it a status, rather than to recognize that it has some natural quality. The theories' critics have variously attacked this idea. Melvin Rader [14] follows Plato's *Euthyphro*, by saying definition must tell us more than what people do with an object. Because their treatment is baseless unless it is a response to the object's intrinsic nature, what is done must presuppose rather than produce definitions of the object. Diffey also rejects the idea that art can be understood wholly in terms of the properties of works of art - the idea that, "when we know how things are accredited as art we shall know what art is". He lists his objections:

1. Common sense says that something is in a gallery if it is a work of art not the other way around.
2. To treat x as y does not entail that x is y.
3. To say that something gets its status as art through certain sorts of accreditation leaves the term "art" unanalyzed.
4. It does not seem to be a real task or anybody's job to predicate "art" of any individual (object).
5. The republic seems, on this argument, to operate at the level of particulars, rather than genres.
6. It cannot be assumed that questions of status and evaluation are not distinct issues [15].

The concept of ascription is however dramatically illuminated by transferring it to the context of religion. Firstly there is far less danger of conflating the question: how does something become a sacred object? with the question: what is religion? This may be because, although the idea of sacred objects is central to some forms of religion. In others it is of negligible importance [16]. An act of consecration can be identified as a discernible (although not necessary) process by which ordinary objects become sacred. An investigation into the reasons for consecrating objects, and the relationship of the act to the value of the objects before and after it has taken place, promises to evaporate many of the difficult questions posed by critics of institutional theories of art.

Transferred to the world of religion, Diffie's list of philosophical objections loses much of its credibility; in the context of a table becoming an altar or a wafer becoming "the Body of Christ", does common sense say something is used in a consecration ceremony if it is a sacred object and not *vice versa*? Does treating something as a sacred object not entail that it is one? Does it seem to be anyone's real task to predicate "sacred" of any individual object? Does it seem right that it operates at the level of particulars? Can it be assumed that questions of status and evaluation are not distinct issues?

Even Wollheim's insistence that there must be reasons for doing it, and since these are prior to the act, the consecration ceremony can not be an essential feature of the making of sacred objects, seems puzzling.

An institutional theory of religion can be expected to help clarify the concepts of ascription, consecration and sacredness, and questions about how far the properties and value of sacred object are culturally emergent.

Diffey raised another substantial criticism of institutional theories of art - the problem of the relationship between classification and evaluation, between status and value. Institutional theories may seem to wrench the two apart and to assert, perhaps arbitrarily, that the classificatory sense is primary to the concept of art and the evaluative sense is secondary.

Richard J. Sclafani criticizes Dickie for saying that when we take a piece of driftwood to be art, we are using the evaluative sense of the concept; we are saying that it resembles or shares some properties with paradigm works of art, not that we really think it is art in the sense that the paradigms are. When we say of a cake, "It's a work of art", he explains, we do not mean that it is art in the same way as the *Mona Lisa*, while with the driftwood example we may well believe just this [17].

110

This criticism, while disagreeing with Dickie's use of the category distinction, suggests that there is an important distinction to be made. But the question remains whether the classificatory sense is primary. Walton says he does not think Dickie's classificatory concept of art is very important in our conceptual scheme. He confesses to be unconvinced by Dickie's argument: "What we feel is important about paintings," he says, "can be expressed and understood, not only without stating whether they are art (in Dickie's sense), but without assuming even any implicit understanding about this" [18]. While Anita Silvers claims that the evaluative and classificatory senses are, "inextricably bound together in usage" [19], and Bruce Morton denies that there is any use in common parlance corresponding to Dickie's classificatory sense [20].

Questions about authenticity and value hang together rather differently in religion. You can have a ritual that is undeniably religious but of little worth, but can you have a vision that is authentic and worthless? There is in religion an important distinction to be made here and it is no less complex or difficult to entangle.

A further criticism of institutional theories of art in general is that they cover only some areas of art - that they are insufficiently comprehensive. It is Levinson who puts this most strongly. Institutional theory, "comes close to conflating art and *self-conscious* art, art and *socially* situated art, art and declared art", he says [21]. While Wollheim says that such theories distort the fact that, "Art in a society is a far more comprehensive phenomenon than the corpus of works of art produced in that society, and its boundaries are extremely difficult to draw" [22]. Care must be taken that this criticism does not apply to an institutional theory of religion.

The final criticism in this section is the claim that institutional theories might lead to a vicious sort of relativism. Frances Berenson says: "If the institutional theory of art is intended to mean that we are all of us trapped in our aesthetic response acquired exclusively from our own societies, as if in tightly closed boxes of the societies to which we belong, then the theory can be shown to be false because contrary to fact" [23].

In religion too, we may not be able to enter fully into the feelings and experiences of those of other faiths or none, but we can to a considerable extent understand some of them. No problem need arise about fitting this fact into an institutional theory of religion. On the subject of whether mutual understanding between societies must in principle be possible or impossible, I agree with W. W. Sharrock and R. J. Anderson, who say, "Wittgenstein's work should not provide us with arguments to favour either side in this controversy but should fortify us against the risk of being tempted to take one... The difficulties of understanding that do arise will not result from their being different ways of life but from their being the particular ways of life that they are" [24].

Relativism in the arts most usually raises its head in this context while the connection between art theories and truth does not on the whole arouse much passion. Although people may want to say the art theory they subscribe to is true, it will often be argued more in terms of pragmatism and fruitfulness than correspondence to the way things stand. In religions, however, truth is often a more important issue. Is the concern that an institutional theory of religion will lead us into an unacceptable form of relativism, a serious indictment? It need not be so. An institutional theory does not imply that either absolute truth claims or cognitive faith commitments are necessarily either meaningless or unjustified [25]. Such a theory might also be expected to shed some light on the religious concept of revelation.

Specific criticisms of Danto's ideas

Critics see Danto as having proposed that for an object to be a work of art it must be treated relevantly in terms of a certain sort of theory. But, Anita Silver says, if there is no way of distinguishing acceptable art theories from non-acceptable ones then, since all objects are candidates, and anyone can call anything an art theory, "it makes it too easy for objects to qualify as art" [26]. Why, she asks, if a theory can make one can opener into a work of art, is it not the case that all can openers are works of art [27]?

George Dickie also criticizes Danto's epistemological claim that artistic theories help us to tell artworks from non-artworks, and his ontological claim that artistic theories make art possible. How, he asks, would the Real Theory of Art help us to distinguish art objects? And exactly how do art theories make art possible? If he means they must be consciously held then he is clearly wrong for, historically, art precedes theories. But he must mean more than simply having ideas about what counts as art, as, "In this weak sense everyone would have a theory about almost everything he did" [28].

Sclafani asks if any art theories of the sort that Danto's theory seems to require exist, and concludes that Danto, "has forced an interpretation which does not fit the facts" [29].

The question of whether art theories are essential to the concept of art, or the status of art works, again seems rather different when transferred to the world of religion; the questions they raise somehow do not seem so difficult to answer: do beliefs have the role of making religions possible? If there are no ways of deciding which beliefs are acceptable, is making objects sacred too easy? Is seeing something as a religious experience, or as a sacred object, a theory-laden activity? Is there anything more to it than learning how to use our language?

An institutional theory of religion promises to help us see more clearly the two-way relationship between beliefs (both in the sense of philosophical theories, and the hopes and expectations of ordinary believers) and the religious experiences and behaviour, of individuals and communities.

Sclafani raises another problem by referring to William Kennick's question, "Which comes first, the first artwork or the first theory?" [30]. But he resolves this by saying, "The notion of a first poem, first painting, first work of art is as unintelligible as the notion of the first sentence, first belief, first language" [31]. He then refers to some of Wittgenstein's remarks in *On Certainty* [32] and asks if getting someone to see something as art is a theory dependent activity. Is getting him to see it as art any more than bringing it about, "that he learn how "art" and its correlates are used in English? And we do this by ordinary example". Does a child not play Irish folk music merely because she has been brought up in an Irish village [33]?

Transferred to religion this is a question which has been a long-standing topic of philosophical interest - is experience or language primary in religion? It is just here that an institutional theory can be expected to illuminate and clarify such questions as: what role does experience have in religion? Can it give us information about a "spiritual world"? What is the relationship between experience and culture here? What factors influence religious innovation? How might we suppose religions begin?

Other critics of Danto see him as having proposed that for

objects to be works of art they have to be relevantly related to a certain group of people - the artworld. They find this concept too vague and broad. Sclafani says that the concept, "may turn out to be so general and so vague that it is rendered vacuous... or, it may require sharpening up to the extent that we will no longer be able to recognize it as a picture of the world of art we are commonly familiar with" [34]. By virtue of what can a person claim membership in the artworld, how can people avoid it, and exactly how do objects become enfranchised in it?, he asks [35]. These and similar questions about the nature and function of the artworld are asked with similar force in relation to Dickie's theory.

Criticisms of Dickie's theory

Every concept Dickie introduces is, his critics claim, vaguely defined and spawn a handful of what seem to be unanswerable questions.

Is Dickie's concept of the artworld a bundle of practices, as he originally claimed, or a group of people, as he goes on to imply by his discussion of membership. (How can you act on behalf of a practice? Monroe C. Beardsley asks, "They seem to lack the requisite source of authority" [36].) It is Dickie's failure to give a clear answer to this question that results in a large extent to the failure of his original theory.

The nub of the problem is expressed in the question: who is a member of the art world? Dickie answers this question ambiguously, which leads William Blizek to say, if it is true that everyone who sees himself as a member of the artworld is thereby an officer of it, "the customary practice is likely to be diffuse and the institution it defines ambiguous," but if membership is limited by the tastes and interests of a select group, the official artworld, this is, "just what Dickie doesn't want". He wants both, "a clearly defined institution (in which case art is recognizable and public) and an open door for creativity". As Blizek points out, a compromise is difficult [37].

Morton suggests that the only answer to this problem is both obvious and fatal, "Our artist acquired status within the artworld by creating a work of art. That is all. But this requires antecedent grounds for identifying works of art." In his view, works of art are logically, and indeed temporarily, prior to the

114

institution of the artworld. "The first work of art (logically) could never have been created, given Dickie's analysis, since there would have been no art world to do the conferring of status" [38].

Anita Silvers claims that Dickie's artworld has no rules, while institutions are always at least partially constituted by rules. She goes on to draw the conclusion, "Most of us could be made to admit that there are some artifacts which simply are not art, no matter who might say they are" [39]. Wollheim also claims the theory, "must point to positive practices, conventions, or rules, which are all explicit in the society (the artworld), even if they are merely implicit in the mind of the actual agent" [40].

The concept of acting on behalf of the artworld also comes under the critic's scrutiny. We have already seen some of the problems here, for if there are no restrictions on who may act on its behalf, or what they may do on its behalf, the concept loses a great deal of content and credibility. One area of disagreement is whether an individual can act alone in this way. Levinson is anxious that they can't and Blizek is anxious that they can. Levinson urges that, "There can be private, isolated art which is constituted as art in the mind of the artist - and on no one's behalf but his own and that of *potential* experiencers of it," and he assumes that, "*just that*, is not enough to make the artwork or else the notion becomes trivial and otiose" [41]. While Blizek wants art, "to remain in the public domain," which conflicts with Dickie's idea that many works of art are never seen by anyone but the person who creates them, but they are still works of art. "The price to be paid for that degree of flexibility is," he says, "excessive" [42].

The question of authority, what sort of rules apply and who applies them, seems to have been one of the most intractable problems for institutional theories of art, and at first sight the move to religion does not seem to help. The Hindu religion, if it makes any sense to use a unitary name, is, for instance, as anarchistic as the modern art world, and there is as little observable structure to say what goes and what does not. But in religion one can perhaps see more clearly the force of tradition - not the power of people, but the authority of practices - of the established ways of doing things.

Wittgenstein thinks the word "agreement" (and we think of it here as agreement *in* forms of life) is related to the word "rule"; "They are cousins," he says, "If I teach anyone the use of the one word, he learns the use of the other with it" [43]. Peter Winch explains this idea more fully: "There is an intimate conceptual connection between the notion of authority on the one hand and, on the other hand, the notion of there being a right and a wrong way of doing things." He goes on to explain that all characteristically human activities involve reference to an established way of doing things. This idea, in its turn, "presupposes that the practices and pronouncements of a certain group of people shall be authoritative in connection with the activity in question". But, as he points out, he has made here no explicit reference to the idea of one person's will influencing another's. Authority, as opposed to power, involves an indirect relation between people, and the intermediary is the established way of performing the activity on which they are engaged [44].

A satisfactory institutional theory of religion will not be based on the idea of the authority of groups of people, or of people acting on behalf of institutions, but promises to clarify the idea of the authority of tradition - of institutional practices - and the way they interact with the experiences and behaviour of individuals and communities.

Most criticism falls on Dickie's concept of conferring status. Morton says that it is not a necessary condition for an object to be a work of art because, "Works of art are logically (and indeed temporarily) prior to the institutions of the artworld." And it is not a sufficient condition because a christening can fail [45]. Beardsley says it is too broad if it can be done by almost anyone, and yet it may be too narrow, because it implies that if a non-poet writes a poem it can't be an artwork until a poet treats it as such [46]. Cohen points out that in the conferring of status in other fields there are always rules and defeating conditions. He proposes changing the analogy with, "ceremonial acts like christening and political licensing, to less canonical ones like promising" [47]. He points out that even with promising, it is possible to try to make a promise and fail (because, for example, what is promised has already happened or is out of the question). While there may be a point in making an impossible promise, it can not give the statement the status of a promise. The attention is drawn in such a case, he says, not to the content but to the act. "If making a thing art is like an ordinary illocution," he says, "then there are prior constraints. There must be a boundary... between making art, and trying but failing to make art. Dickie cannot account for this" [48].

116

Wollheim is also puzzled by the idea of conferring status because he cannot see any act that it can be describing. "Some independent evidence is required for what the representatives of the artworld allegedly do," he says [49]. It has already been pointed out in the discussion of general criticisms how transferring the field of enquiry from art to religion changes the nature of the problems concerning ascription and the conferring of status.

Dickie insists that no special sort of appreciation is required to understand art. Wollheim says: "How can we possibly believe that, in drawing our attention to a certain artifact, (the artist) is putting it forward for appreciation, unless we can also attribute to him some idea of what it is about the artifact that we should appreciate, and further believe that it is because of this that he is drawing our attention to it?" [50].

Materially, Ted Cohen feels that what Dickie says about appreciation is, "too strong even though very general; formally, it lacks a dimension without which it is not acute enough to discriminate art from other things." The very point of Dada, he says, is that the objects were not worthy or valuable, therefore, "being a candidate for appreciation in any but the emptiest sense of "appreciation"... is not part of what it is to be an artwork" [51], while it also lacks any idea of constraint or rules.

These objections do not threaten an institutional theory of religion. Wittgenstein warns about looking for what is common in aesthetic judgements; what we are left with, he says, is, "an immensely complicated family of cases... with the highlight - the expression of admiration, a smile or a gesture etc." [52].

To say that the objects of Dada were appreciated for the irony that flowed from their very plainness, does not empty the notion of appreciation, only of a special *aesthetic* sort of appreciation. Similarly to call, or make, an object or an experience religious *is* to propose that it is *in some way* worthy of appreciation. The specific way in which it can be appreciated is, in some senses open, but for any individual, placed in a specific social context, it is constrained by history - by the way religious objects and experiences have been regarded in the past - constrained not by formulated rules or structures, nor the wills or power of authoritative groups of people, but by tradition - the authority of established practices.

Notes

1. Jerrold Levinson, "Defining Art Historically", pp. 245-247.
2. Precisely how the word "institution" is used in this project is described in Chapter 14.
3. Morris Weitz, "The Role of Theory in Aesthetics", p. 27.
4. Richard Wollheim, "The Institutional Theory of Art", p. 157.
5. Kendall L. Walton. A review of Dickie's, "Art and the Aesthetic: an Institutional Analysis", pp. 99-100.
6. Monroe C. Beardsley, "Is Art Essentially Institutional", pp. 197 ff.
7. Chapter 14 examines institutions in some detail and argues for this proposition.
8. Wittgenstein warns, "There is not always a sharp distinction between essential and unessential." Ludwig Wittgenstein, *Philosophical Investigations*, I para. 62.
9. "Most ordinary language is composed of "dead metaphors"". Sallie MacFague, *Metaphorical Theology*, p. 15.
10. Ted Cohen quotes from: Michael Fried's Catalogue Essay for *Three American Painters*, p. 47: "Dada stands opposed to the notion of value or quality in art," and goes on to say that Duchamp's urinal, "is virtually accompanied by an announcement that traditional appreciation (if there is such a thing) cannot occur." Ted Cohen, "The Possibility of Art: Remarks on a Proposal by Dickie", pp. 72-82.
11. T. J. Diffey, "On Defining Art", pp. 21-22.
12. Anita Silvers, "The Artworld Discarded", p. 452.
13. Richard Wollheim, "The Institutional Theory of Art" pp. 165-6.
14. Melvin Rader, "Dickie and Socrates on Definition", p. 423.
15. T. J. Diffey, "On Defining Art", pp. 19-20.
16. There are some interesting similarities and differences between the questions: how does something become a work of art? and: how does something become a religious object or experience? It needs to be remembered that there are arts where the idea of an aesthetic object is of negligible importance, and where the idea of an aesthetic experience is highly significant, such as dance.
17. Richard J. Sclafani, "Art as a Social Institution: Dickie's New Definition", p. 112.

18. Kendall L. Walton, "A Review of George Dickie's Art and the Aesthetic: an Institutional Analysis", p. 99.

19. Anita Silvers, "The Artworld Discarded", p. 444.

20. Bruce N. Morton, "A Review of George Dickie's Aesthetics: an Introduction", p. 117.

21. Jerrold Levinson, "Defining Art Historically", p. 233.

22. Richard Wollheim, "The Institutional Theory of Art", p. 166.

23. Frances Berenson, "Understanding Art and Understanding Persons", pp. 49-50. On p. 43 she points out that we can to a remarkable extent understand and join in the arts of other cultures.

24. W. W. Sharrock and R. J. Anderson, "Criticizing Forms of Life", pp. 397-398.

25. This question will be dealt with in detail in Chapter 20

26. Anita Silvers, "The Artworld Discarded", p. 443.

27. Ibid., p. 446.

28. George Dickie, *The Art Circle*, pp. 18-20.

29. Richard J. Sclafani, "Artworks, Art Theory and the Artworld", p. 30.

30. William Kennick, "Comments on the Artworld", p. 585.

31. Richard J. Sclafani, "Artworks, Art Theory and the Artworld", p. 26.

32. Ludwig Wittgenstein, *On Certainty*, paras. 475, 141 and 144.

33. Richard J. Sclafani, "Artworks, Art Theory and the Artworld", p. 34.

34. Ibid., fn. to p. 21.

35. Ibid., p. 22.

36. Monroe C. Beardsley, "Is Art Essentially Institutional", p. 202.

37. William Blizek, "An Institutional Theory of Art", pp. 143-144.

38. Bruce N. Morton, "A Review of George Dickie's Aesthetics: an Introduction", p. 117.

39. Anita Silvers, "The Artworld Discarded", pp. 443-444.

40. Richard Wollheim, "The Institutional Theory of Art", p. 162.

41. Jerrold Levinson, "Defining Art Historically", p. 233.

42. William Blizek, "An Institutional Theory of Art", p. 149.

43. Ludwig Wittgenstein, *Philosophical Investigations*, I para. 224.

44. Peter Winch, "Authority", pp. 100-101.
45. Bruce C. Morton, "A Review of George Dickie's Aesthetics: an Introduction", p. 117.
46. Monroe C. Beardsley, "Is Art Essentially Institutional?", p. 202.
47. Ted Cohen, "The Possibility of Art: Remarks on a Proposal by Dickie", p. 76.
48. Ibid., pp. 80-81.
49. Richard Wollheim, "The Institutional Theory of Art", p. 162.
50. Ibid., p. 165.
51. Ted Cohen, "The Possibility of Art", pp. 70-72.
52. Ludwig Wittgenstein, *Lectures and Conversations*, I para. 32.

13 Institutions as forms of human behaviour

Crucial to any institutional theory is the use of the word "institution". The word is however a confusing one for it is commonly used in at least two distinct ways; firstly to refer to forms of behaviour that have become established in particular human communities - such as marriage, theatre or baptism: secondly to refer to groups of people who are joined by their use, understanding or control of such forms of behaviour - such as the Law Society, the Royal Academy or the Church of Scotland.

It is clear that, in religion, institutions in both these senses have a kind of authority. But, as has been suggested by the survey of institutional theories of art, institutional theories constructed around the second of these two senses tend to get bogged down in problems of one sort or another. For if we say religious authenticity or value is defined by the beliefs, actions or pronouncements of a group of people, we end up with insoluble difficulties in defining such a group and saying how the beliefs, experiences and actions of individuals are related to it. (Who counts as a Hindu? How big is a church? What does it mean to be authorized to act on behalf of a faith or a tradition?) This attempt to set up an institutional theory of religion will therefore concentrate on the former use - institutions as forms of behaviour.

Before we begin to ask what forms of behaviour we can call institutional we need to consider the way certain words are used to talk about human behaviour. Behaviour can be called "natural" or "cultural", "direct" or "symbolic", "individual" or "social". These distinctions will be important in our characterization of institutional behaviour, but they are all difficult - being used in special and sometimes confusing ways by biologists, sociobiologists, anthropologists and sociologists.

Natural, cultural and established forms of behaviour

The word "natural" is often, and most usefully for our purposes, used in opposition to the idea of being caused, made or controlled by people. In biological terms it is used to refer to something that is genetically determined or transmitted rather than something that is learned or culturally transmitted. Ted Benton uses it in this way when he distinguishes between "natural" capacities and "historical" capacities. He says natural capacities are those whose possession is, "independent of membership in, or acquisition of, any *specific culture*." He gives as, "obvious examples... the capacities underlying feeding, locomotion and mating". They are, he says, explicable in terms of natural selection and in terms of human anatomy and physiology [1].

Benton is here using the word "natural" to talk about capacities and tendencies rather than behaviour. Using the distinction for human behaviour is fraught with difficulties, for in some senses all examples of human behaviour are determined by "natural" inheritance (genes) and yet no human behaviour is completely determined by them. This fact is widely recognized by scientists of human behaviour. The psychologist, Piaget recognizes it in his work on intellectual development [2]; the sociologist, Raymond Williams recognizes it in his work on culture [3]; the sociobiologist Edward O. Wilson recognizes it in his work on aggression. He says, "The question of interest is no longer whether human social behaviour is genetically determined; it is to what extent. The accumulated evidence for a large hereditary component is more detailed and compelling than most persons, including even geneticists, realize... It is already decisive" [4]; even philosophers have recognized it; Michael Rose in a recent paper in *Philosophy* with Edward Wilson says,

> There is solid factual evidence for the existence of epigenetic rules - constraints rooted in our evolutionary biology that affect the way we think. The incest example shows that these rules, directly related to adaptive advantage, extend into the moral sphere; and the hypothesis of morality as a product

of pure culture is refuted by the growing evidence of
the co-evolution of genes and culture [5].

The use of the word "culture" is, if anything, more entangled than
the use of the word "nature", for as Raymond Williams points out,
it has, historically, been used to refer to a process, a
configuration, the spirit of a community or to whole and
distinctive ways of life [6]. Scientists of behaviour have tended
to use it specifically for something that is transmitted by learning
rather than by genetic endowment. In this sense chimpanzees
are credited with cultural behaviour when, for example, they learn
the use of tools from their parents or peers [7]. Ted Benton tries
to avoid the difficulties of the word by naming his non-natural
category of human capacities "historical" rather than "cultural"
[8]. His examples are the capacity to cook food and the
capacities for aesthetic creation and appreciation. He says that
the possession of any specific historical capacity, "presupposes the
prior possession and exercise of some set of natural capacities"
[9].

An enormous amount has been written about the autonomy of
culture, about the power of biology and about the way they
influence each other. Professional axes have been ground,
political prejudices have been buttressed and moral arguments
corroborated. There is no space and, in a way no need, to pursue
these discussions here. As Ted Benton observes, a sensible
consensus seems to have emerged that culture has a relative
autonomy, which needs to be understood in relation to biological
constraints [10].

Since in some senses then all human behaviour has a natural
and a cultural aspect, while no human behaviour is completely
determined by either nature or culture, it would be both
inappropriate and unhelpful to label any specific piece of human
behaviour with either term.

Scientists of human nature have continued to look for the
elusive species-wide capacities that underlie human behaviour
and to try to follow through individual genetic differences to
determine their effect on behaviour. They have tried to
apportion the relative importance of nature and culture in various
fields, but on the whole stopped using the words "natural" and
"cultural" to label distinct categories of human behaviour. Is
there, therefore, any useful way left for us to make a distinction
of this kind? An attempt will be made in the following chapter

to draw a distinction between *descriptions* of human activities. To signify that the distinction is not the usual one between nature and culture we shall call them "natural" and "established" activities. The following example will preview that distinction: the same activity may be described as "grasping hands" and as "making a contract". "Grasping hands" is a description of a natural activity, because it can be identified prior to and defined independently of, any particular human community. "Making a contract" is a description of an established activity because it is a practice that has become established in a particular community and can only be identified and defined in relation to its use in that community.

Direct, symbolic and ritual behaviour

Symbolic behaviour is behaviour that contains a message or a meaning, behaviour that needs to be understood on at least two levels. It can be described in physical terms and in terms of what it means. The category covers a vast array of behaviour: a rabbit stamps its feet; a bird dances; a chimpanzee grimaces; a mad-man kills a woman who looks like his mother; a girl tears up the photograph of her lover, or draws a map; a clergyman sprinkles water on the head of a baby.

Used in this wide sense it can again be argued that it is not a helpful distinction for talking about human behaviour. Since the time of Durkheim [11] sociologists have argued that all but the most basic aspects of human behaviour can only be understood in terms of the meaning they have for their participants. But again there is a useful distinction that can be made.

Symbolic behaviour can be seen to have its roots in an unconscious expression of mood or readiness to act. As social life develops, anticipating the actions of others has survival value. Such expressive behaviour can therefore develop into a signal system which arouses an innate response. These primitive signalling systems can become complex and detailed as in the courtship dances of some birds or the communication system of the honey bee.

Wilson talks about "anticipatory action" and "intentional movements" being, "in the course of evolution... ritualized into communication signals. The waggle dance of the honey bee is actually a miniaturized rehearsal of the flight from the hive to the food," he says [12]. Eibl-Eibesfeldt puts some human behaviour into just this category. He includes flirting and bowing and greeting with an open hand. "When angry," he says, "we may stomp with a foot, an intention of attack which among Europeans is especially found in small, uncontrolled children; adults usually suppress it," He adds, "I saw the same gesture in an angry Bantu boy" [13]. Later he says, "Darwin points out that the first act of saying "no" (disapproving) in children is the rejection of food, by turning the head to the side from the breast or a spoon." A blind and deaf girl shook her head when she did not want to eat, and also when she refused something, for example, an invitation to play [14].

Peter Winch says, "Action with a sense is symbolic." "The analysis of meaningful behaviour must allot a central role to the notion of a rule; ...all behaviour which is meaningful (therefore all specifically human behaviour) is *ipso facto* rule governed" [15]. "All meaningful behaviour must be social," he says later, "since it can be meaningful only if governed by rules, and rules presuppose a social setting" [16].

How do these remarks relate to this sort of typically non-human behaviour? It seems to me that innate animal communication is meaningful, rule following and social. The signal, such as the rabbit's stamping foot, or the nodding of the courting duck, needs an interpretative rule. The stamp *means* the rabbit has perceived danger, the nodding *means* the duck is ready to mate. The rule could only develop and would only make sense in a social setting. But the rule is not "understood" in the sense we usually mean nor does it have to be learned. The animal is programmed to respond to the signal. It is, to use Wittgenstein's phrase, at "bedrock, and my spade is turned. Then I am inclined to say: "This is simply what I do"" [17]. The meaning of the behaviour can best be explained either in terms of the mood it expresses, the action it anticipates or the response it generates. We shall refer to this kind of behaviour as expressive symbolic behaviour.

In human beings symbolic behaviour is not seen in this basic form except perhaps in early infancy. In even the most primitive societies it is developed and manipulated in a variety of ways:

Expressive symbolic behaviour is moulded by culture

In human societies innate responses to expressive signalling behaviour are either reinforced, allowed to atrophy or actively suppressed, but they are always adapted into specific cultural forms. Eibl-Eibesfeldt says, "Man is extremely inclined to culturally mould and change behaviour in a relatively short time" [18]. Showing anger by stamping is considered childish in our culture; a strongly worded letter is more acceptable. Even behaviour as deeply rooted as smiling has to be reinforced by feedback. In blind children, it atrophies.

Expressive symbolic behaviour can be manipulated so that it not only unconsciously expresses an emotional mood but also controls one

Symbolic actions can be performed to arouse, to relieve, or to redirect, a feeling. When rabbits stamp their feet there is no question of their doing it because it makes them feel better. But people can stamp their feet to express their frustration, as it were to themselves, and so to relieve it. Or a battle party can perform a stamping dance to summon up aggressive feelings before they join the fight. In these kinds of situations the meaning of the behaviour is best understood in terms of what it is used for, or what it achieves. (To say the ground represents the enemy really adds nothing in understanding or clarity.)

Ceremonies that are largely of this type are frustrating to the anthropologist who is looking for representative meanings. Dan Sperber, for instance, argues that the search for the meaning of symbolic behaviour is vain, because it does not always have any [19].

Evans Pritchard, more perceptively, describes ceremonies of the Nuer tribe where:

> A study of the symbols tells us nothing of the nature of what is symbolized... Words and gestures transport us to a realm of experience when what the eye sees and the ear hears is not the same as what the mind perceives. Hands are raised in supplication to the sky, but the sky is not being supplicated... We seem indeed to be watching a play or to be listening to someone's account of what he has dreamt. Perhaps when we have this illusion we are beginning to understand, for the significance of the objects, actions and events lies not in

themselves but in what they mean to those who experience them as participants or assistant... When we reflect on their meaning we perceive they are a dramatic representation of a spiritual experience [20].

D. Z. Phillips confirms this non-representative use of symbols, which are moulded to express or control an emotional mood. He describes a ritual of the Seminoles of Florida. If a mother is dying in childbirth they hold her infant over her face to receive her parting breath. The anthropologist Tylor explains this ritual in terms of the notion of a soul, "A thin unsubstantial human image... independently possessing the personal consciousness and volition of its corporeal owner, past or present." Phillips remarks:

> A mother has given her life for her child and this is expressed in the ritual by the child receiving her parting breath. What more needs to be said?... these acts are not based on hypotheses or opinions concerning strange invisible substances which, by mysterious means, are transferred from one person to another. On the contrary, the gestures are expressions of something [21].

I am not suggesting that such symbolic actions are usually consciously constructed and performed by a society for what they achieve. They are just done; the effects follow.

Human beings have developed representative symbolism

There may be a sense in which animal communication behaviour can be said to be representational. Perhaps the bee's dance represents the route to the food. But I think it is clearer if we call animal communication "expressive" behaviour and keep the term "representative" for a more specifically human type of behaviour.

It takes generations for an innate expressive symbolic rule to become established. Human beings can create a representative rule in an instant. (The salt-cellar is my Volvo and the ashtray is the Rolls.) Such rules can be almost entirely arbitrary or based on some natural connection or innate response, and they can quickly become established in a human community.

To understand such behaviour you need to ask questions which are not appropriate to ask about expressive behaviour: what do the actions, objects and participants stand for?, rather than, what mood does the behaviour express or what is achieved by its performance?

Mary Douglas describes a ritual that uses representative rules:

> The ancestors' antique spear is really a new spear recently bought from an Arab trader. Or the ancestral spear is non-existent, a man making gestures with it by moving his empty hands as if the spear were there. The sacrificial ox stands for the sacrifice, but the sacrificer may not be present at all, even the ox may be represented by a cucumber [22].

Alasdair MacIntyre quotes a more straightforward example: "According to Spencer and Gillen some aborigines carry about a stick or stone which is treated as if it is or embodies the soul of the individual who carries it. If the stick or stone is lost, the individual anoints himself as the dead are anointed" [23].

Ernest Gellner professes to find this behaviour, "simply incoherent". He cites it as a case where, one cannot take the sense from the use because the use affords no sense. He then says it is easy to give the rules for the use of the concept, but adds, "We confront a blank wall here, so far as meaning is concerned" [24].

It appears he can understand the representative component of the behaviour but not the expressive component - a feat that Peter Winch has no problems with at all. Winch explains it as a simple analogy with the practice of carrying a photograph or lock of hair from a lover [25].

Wittgenstein points to both the representative and the expressive components of symbolic behaviour in the same example when he says, "Burning an effigy - kissing the picture of a loved one. This is obviously not based on a belief that it will have a definite effect on the object which the picture represents. It aims at some satisfaction and achieves it. Or rather, it does not aim at anything; we act in this way and then feel satisfied" [26].

It appears that, in some senses, representative symbolism grows out of expressive symbolism but, as it develops, symbolic behaviour can lose its expressive component; drawing a map we could call *merely* representational behaviour.

Human beings tend to be reflective about their symbolic behaviour and to develop theoretical explanations for it, which can take a representative, an expressive or a technical form

Wittgenstein, talking about art, says, "We don't start from certain words, but from certain occasions or activities" [27]. Although it cannot be stated as a fact in respect of institutions as a whole class, it seems, for a number of reasons, more plausible to suggest that institutional activities in general precede, rather than proceed from, their theoretical justifications.

Peter Winch argues for this view [28]. He says that although Wittgenstein does not say directly that practices precede their explanations, his writing suggests it. This argument of Winch's has already been discussed [29]. Although the analogy he draws between the relationship of natural expression in talk of religion and in talk of pain is unsatisfactory, it does not prejudice the point we are interested in here. The analogy is unsatisfactory because talk of religion is not talk of natural sensations and their natural expression, but this does not mean that such talk can not grow, in a more complicated way, from primitive practices.

Reasons for what communities do are, according to this analysis, constructed, discovered or invented to accompany the rituals used by a community. Once this has happened an interesting interactive relationship develops between activities and beliefs, for both appear to have what we might call, "a life of their own" (at least in relation to the individual), while both also profoundly affect the "life" of the other.

The relationship is complex and too much has been written on the subject to cover comprehensively here. MacIntyre summarizes the history of the debate in terms of a, "slide from the striking and controversial falsehood to the non-controversial apparent platitude". Pareto and Marx he accuses of starting from the falsehood, "that beliefs are essentially secondary, a by-product of a social life which drives forward independently". The early Weber he accuses of starting from the contrary falsehood, "that ideas have an autonomous and effective role in social life". Both falsehoods are then modified by the admission of counter examples, "until all the protagonists come together in adherence to a facile interactionism" [30]. He is himself concerned to point out that the relation between belief and action, "is not external and contingent, but internal and conceptual" [31]. It is, he says like the relationship between words and meaning... actions may be said to express beliefs.

We should note firstly that there is a sense in which the activities themselves "make sense of" the chaos of self conscious social life - they can without any attempt at theoretical explanation, give a sense of order and control, or relief from negative feelings. We can see this to some extent not only in primitive communities but in our private neurotic rituals.

Peter Winch suggests that we should not see the rites of unfamiliar communities as misguided techniques for producing consumer goods, (as he accuses MacIntyre of doing). On the contrary we should consider, "The possible importance that the carrying out of certain activities may take on for a man trying to contemplate the sense of his life as a whole" [32].

The rationalizing of symbolic behaviour takes many forms. As we have seen it may or may not develop into conscious beliefs. J. H. M. Beattie talks about beliefs having, "degrees of explicitness from vague and unspoken assumption to formal and exact assertion... Confusion may arise," he says, "from the failure to distinguish between beliefs that are actually held by people and those that are not consciously held by anyone."

The things believed in, in order to make sense of certain forms of behaviour, may or may not then be assumed to have an Existential status. "What is believed in is not, or need not be, taken absolutely literally," says Beattie, "... but rather as essentially metaphorical... as a kind of poetry in fact" [33]. To illustrate this point Beattie takes a story from an article by Bernard Levin in the *Times*. Sir Mortimer Wheeler, so the story goes, was fond of sherry. A woman, ever since she heard this, "had put a glass of it on the television set whenever he was appearing, so that he might take a sip whenever he felt like it" [34]. Beattie comments, "I'm sure that Sir Mortimer's admirer was really (more or less) aware when she "entered into the act" so to speak, that she was carrying out a ritual, valid as such, and not engaging in a "real" relationship. Otherwise she (and the hundreds of others like her) would *really* be crazy" [35].

On the other hand some communities do move quickly from raising hands to the sky in supplication, to believing that there is a helpful deity in the sky, from leaving a gift to alleviate the terror of the storm, to believing that there is a malevolent storm spirit. We cannot, as some empiricists would have us do [36], rule out the clearly ontological component of some of the beliefs associated with symbolic behaviour. Mary Douglas says of the Zande witchcraft system,

> To make the institution work new ideas are produced to fit the pieces coherently together or to sustain the credibility of the whole... The pressure to organize thought introduces new entities into the universe, such as hereditary witchcraft substance in the intestine... One kind of social reality (the Zande), built on one kind of accountability, invested fellow humans with sinister psychic powers, the other (the Nuer) subjected a world filled with spirits and ghosts to the will of a righteous god [37].

The consideration of witchcraft leads to another difference in the way communities rationalize their ritual practices. Communities can differ in the extent and manner in which they credit their symbolic behaviour with a technical efficiency.

It would be a mistake to characterize symbolic behaviour as behaviour that has no technical efficiency. Evans Pritchard has been accused, by Peter Winch, of making this mistake when he characterizes mystical notions as, "patterns of thought that attribute to phenomena supra-sensible qualities which... are not derived from observation or cannot be logically inferred from it and which they do not possess." Ritual behaviour he describes as, "Any behaviour that is accounted for by mystical notions. *There is no objective nexus* between the behaviour and the event it is intended to cause" [38].

The problem with this sort of judgement, as Peter Winch points out, is that it implies that it is possible to have a view of reality and of causal influence that transcends its actual use in a language. Winch mentions the fact that we ourselves have varying views about cause and effect, demonstrated in the difference between the sorts of reasons we give for someone getting married and for apples falling off trees. He continues, "It should not then be difficult to accept that in a society with quite different institutions and ways of life from ours, there may be concepts of "causal influence" which behave even more differently" [39].

Quite apart from all the various problems of understanding

unfamiliar cultures, even from our own conceptions of causal influence it is not implausible to suggest that doing a war dance might make the participants fight more aggressively and that contemplating the grace of God in the symbols of the Eucharist might significantly improve a believer's emotional environment and thus his moral behaviour.

It is also the case that different communities and even different individuals within communities may not agree about the rationalization of their symbolic behaviour. The historic battles about the efficacy of the Christian Eucharist or the more modern battles about the objective reality of the Christian's God could be taken as examples here [40].

Ritual forms of behaviour, settled with their theoretical justifications, seem to undergo a gradual process of differentiation

This differentiation can be seen in various ways - most obviously it follows the way societies tend to fragment into functional categories. What in primitive societies seem all of a piece, in more developed societies divide into disparate aspects of communal life concerned with such functions as education, economics, politics, morals, defence, aesthetics and religion.

Whether these categories of ours are appropriate or helpful in understanding unfamiliar cultures is debatable. As Beattie says, "We have, to begin with, no alternative to labelling, provisionally at least, the institutions of other cultures in terms of the categories of our own". But he warns that, "Social anthropologists should indeed be constantly aware of the difficulties and dangers of extrapolating the terms and concepts of their "own" cultures into their representations of other cultures" [41].

It seems to me - in contrast to what Winch has said about recognizing forms of behaviour as religious before there is any religious talk - that it is only when aspects of the ritual behaviour of a community are given theoretical justifications by that community that we can begin to categorize them into differentiated functional categories. If we see an unfamiliar community dancing, acting, singing, dressing up, how do we know if the activity is religious, political, social, military or aesthetic unless they talk about why they are doing it - unless they describe the human action they think they are performing?

132

It is when we discover that a ritual is justified or explained in terms of a belief in spirits, or a supreme spirit being, or in terms of finding answers to ultimate questions about the meaning and purpose of life, that we categorize it as religious. Trying to categorize the rituals of unfamiliar communities by guessing at the sort of justification that we think might explain them can easily lead to mistakes, for our categories may be quite irrelevant to their behaviour [42]. Even in our own quite recent history we can see the differentiation of symbolic behaviour taking place - for moral, religious and aesthetic behaviour has, in living memory, been far more closely intertwined than it is today.

It is also important to remember Beattie's warning that one form of behaviour can have several kinds of significance at once. The service for thanksgiving after the British victory in the Falkland Islands is just one example of a modern form of symbolic behaviour with multiple, and to some extent conflicting, significance to the people participating in it.

As institutions are seen to fall into a distinct category they then tend to be used and controlled by the same group of people and come to exhibit similarities to other activities in that category. This can be illustrated by following the development of aesthetic behaviour as it emerged from the categories of the religious, the economic and the social in the quite recent history of our own culture.

This section has not been able to do more than touch on the very complex area of human symbolic behaviour, but it is important to do so because an understanding of symbolic behaviour is crucial to an understanding of institutions. While taking the sociologist's point that all human behaviour is layered with meanings for its participants I shall, in line with more normal use, keep the term "symbolic" for behaviour that has a significant representational or expressive component. Thus burning a photograph in with a bunch of other papers because they are no longer required is direct behaviour, and burning a photograph to express the end of an affair is symbolic behaviour. Raising a piece of material up a pole to make a sail is direct behaviour, and raising a flag to demonstrate and arouse nationalistic loyalty is symbolic. Ducking to tease or annoy is direct behaviour, baptising to signify repentance and new life is symbolic.

The word "ritual" I shall, again in line with normal usage, use for repeated symbolic acts, but not, as some modern usage does, imply that at the same time it necessarily has no practical efficiency.

Individual, social and communal behaviour

Social behaviour is, usually, behaviour that has to do with individuals living in an organized community. It is behaviour that gets its motivation, sense and character from interaction with others. It can, in this sense, be contrasted with individual behaviour. Using the word in this way it is clear that much of the behaviour of animals, birds and insects of all kinds is social. E. O. Wilson says that thousands of the over three million species that have been identified are "highly social". He mentions particularly colony forming invertebrates such as corals, social insects, fish, birds and mammals [43].

When however we are talking about human behaviour we again find the distinction unsatisfactory, for there is an important sense in which all human behaviour is undertaken by individuals and at the same time there is no human behaviour that does not have a social dimension [44].

Two things can be drawn from these remarks. Firstly, much social behaviour is, according to our first distinction, natural. The intricate communication system to be observed in a bee hive for instance is undeniably social behaviour and it is generally understood to be determined and transmitted entirely genetically.

Secondly the distinction between individual and social behaviour is not an appropriate or useful distinction to be drawn between specific pieces of human behaviour. As we have already seen this is particularly true of symbolic behaviour, which is essentially based in social life. All symbolic behaviour arises out of a shared life.

But again we can draw out a distinction that will be useful, by introducing the category of communal behaviour. "Communal behaviour" will be used for behaviour that is shared by members of a particular community. Plausible candidates for the category of individual human behaviour can now be put forward. It can be mostly innate, as in the case of behaviour caused by a unique genetic mutation, or mostly established as in the case of an alien. We can also see the relevance of the concept of private ritual in for example an obsessional neurosis, that rather than cementing individuals into their community, separates and alienates them

134

from it.

It is in fact possible for symbolic behaviour to be communal in a number of different ways. For individuals may or may not understand the representative rules of a form of symbolic behaviour; they may or may not appreciate what it is used for, what beliefs it implies or what effect it has on the participants, and they still may or may not "see the point" of joining in. The varied reasons people might have for declining to say a Latin grace, could illuminate this at a number of different levels. On the other hand, people may join in a ritual without understanding it, or they might may value it for quite idiosyncratic reasons. An atheistic Englishman walking to participate in a Greek Orthodox service in order to keep fit makes the point. Sharing in behaviour is, therefore, in this context, a relative rather than a distinct, concept.

Three ways of talking about human behaviour have been discussed. We now have three useful distinctions, natural as opposed to established activities, direct as opposed to symbolic (or ritual) behaviour, and individual as opposed to communal behaviour. It would however be unfortunate if the impression had been given that these distinctions are clear or easy to apply. On the contrary, as we have seen in our discussion, human behaviour merges from one to the other in each case. My aim is that these categories will help us to characterize institutions, which, it will be argued, are established, communal, rituals.

Notes

1. Ted Benton, "Biological Ideas and their Cultural Uses", pp. 122-123.
2. Jean Piaget, *The Principles of Genetic Epistemology.*
3. Raymond Williams, *Culture*, p. 210.
4. Edward O. Wilson, *On Human Nature*, p. 19.
5. Michael Ruse and Edward O Wilson, "Moral Philosophy as Applied Science", p. 185.
6. Raymond Williams, *Culture*, pp. 10-12.
7. Edward O. Wilson, *On Human Nature*, pp. 29-31.
8. Ted Benton, "Biological Ideas and their Cultural Uses", pp. 122.
9. Ibid., p. 125.
10. Ibid., pp. 131-2.

11. See e.g. Emile Durkheim, *The Rules of Sociological Method.*
12. Edward O. Wilson, *On Human Nature*, p. 187.
13. I. Eibl-Eibesfeldt, "The Ethology of Man", p. 72.
14. Ibid., p. 73.
15. Peter Winch, *The Idea of a Social Science*, pp. 50-52.
16. Ibid., p. 116.
17. Ludwig Wittgenstein, *Philosophical Investigations*, I para. 217.
18. I. Eibl-Eibesfeldt, "The Ethnoloqy of Man", pp. 69-70.
19. Dan Sperber, *Rethinking Symbolism*, p. 84.
20. Evans Pritchard, *Nuer Religion*, pp. 321-322. This extract is used by permission of Oxford University Press.
21. D. Z. Phillips, *Religions Without Explanation*, pp. 40-41.
22. Mary Douglas, *Evans Pritchard*, p. 123.
23. Alasdair MacIntyre, "Is Understanding Religion Compatible with Believing", p. 122.
24. Ernest Gellner, "Concepts and Society", p. 68.
25. Peter Winch, "Understanding a Primitive Society", p. 40.
26. Ludwig Wittgenstein, "Remarks on Frazer's Golden Bough", p. 31.
27. Ludwig Wittgenstein, *Lectures and Conversations*, I para. 6.
28. Peter Winch, "Meaning and Religious Language", p. 195-6.
29. See Chapter 9.
30. Alasdair MacIntyre, "A Mistake about Causality in Social Science", p. 48-49.
30. Ibid., p. 52.
32. Peter Winch, "Understanding a Primitive Society", p. 37.
33. J. H. M. Beattie, "Objectivity and Social Anthropology", p. 8.
34. Bernard Levin, *The Times*, November 26 1980.
35. J. M. H. Beattie, "Objectivity and Social Objectivity", p. 13.
36. E.g. R. B. Braithwaite, "The Nature of Believing", p. 28.
37. Mary Douglas, *Evans Pritchard*, p. 59.
38. Peter Winch, "Understanding a Primitive Society", p. 16.
39. Ibid., p. 34.
40. See e.g. Don Cupitt, *Taking Leave of God.*
41. J. M. H. Beattie, "Objectivity and Social Anthropology", pp. 8-9.

42. Alasdair MacIntyre in, "A Mistake about Causality in Social Science", p. 60, says, "The limits of what I can do are set by the limits of the descriptions *available* to me...   And the descriptions available to me are those current in the social group to which I belong".

43. Edward O. Wilson, *On Human Nature*, p. 16.

44. Ted Benton in "Biological Ideas and their Cultural Uses", pp. 121-122, says, "I take it as established since the time of Adam Ferguson (1767), that the social state is the natural state for human kind, such that not only the greater part of human activity but even sustained existence itself is not possible independently of some sort of cultural context."

14 The nature of institutions

The nature of institutions can now be explored more closely. Institutions, it will be argued, are forms of behaviour that have the three characteristics of being established, ritual and communal, in the senses of those terms outlined in the previous chapter.

Institutions as established forms of behaviour

Institutions are forms of behaviour that have become established in a particular community and can only be defined in relation to their use in that community. They can be distinguished from natural forms of behaviour that can be identified prior to, and defined independently of, a particular social community.

The use of the word "community", implying a social rather than a genetic grouping, is intended to exclude forms of behaviour that are both ritual and shared but have been established in genetic groups by natural selection (or whatever other mechanism). It gives the word "established" the special meaning of established by social interaction rather than established by genetic selection. This restricts institutions to human communities (and possibly in a limited way to some forms of behaviour in the higher primates). In line with normal usage it associates the word "institution" with the word "culture".

Innate, species-wide ritual behaviour, such as the courtship rituals of birds or the communication system of the honey bee are therefore, in line with normal usage, not institutions. The innate symbolic behaviour of infants, as we saw in the previous section, never survives in its original form beyond infanthood, but rapidly develops into cultural forms which are specific to a particular community. They become, albeit gradually, institutionalized. For instance, innate human greeting behaviour - the smile, the open hand is developed in all human communities into specific established cultural forms of greeting, such as the institutions of hand shakes, salutes and verbal greeting rituals.

According to this definition, marriage is an institution, for, although almost all human communities have something we might recognize as marriage, what *counts* as getting married can only be determined by reference to an established practice in a particular community. Taking a mate is, in this sense, a natural form of behaviour (even if it involves a shared ritual); it is an activity we can recognize, and a concept we can confidently use, across many social and genetic groups.

Making a contract is an institutional activity; grasping hands is a natural one. Baptising is an institutional activity; washing is a natural one. Performing a ballet is an institutional activity; jumping and twirling are natural ones.

It should be obvious at this point that what we are distinguishing are not forms of behaviour *per se* but descriptions of activities. For there is a sort of identity between the pairs of actions. The handshake is the ratification of the contract. When we describe an action as baptism, it is an act of washing we are describing. When we call a period of jumping and twirling a ballet, we are giving the same activity another name. It is however not a simple identity. Both descriptions refer to the same activity but they are not interchangeable and each brings into play the possibility of a quite different set of evaluations, properties, specifications and reactions.

We can now express another characteristic of institutions. They are *grounded in nature*, for they emerge out of and are expressed by, natural activities. They are founded on the fact that people respond to similar situations in similar ways and that they agree, as Wittgenstein says, not, "in opinions, but in form of life" [1].

The relationship between the signifying activity of an institution and its established meaning can fall anywhere on a scale between the almost natural and the almost arbitrary. Crying is a natural signal of distress. That people cry when in distress is a universal biological and psychological fact of the human condition. It is not an institution because it is not an established form of behaviour. As children develop, however, their cries become moulded by interaction with others into specific cultural forms. An example of such a form is the calling of the English word "help". Crying, we might call the root of the institution of calling for help.

Richard Wollheim describes this point graphically in the case of art: "It has been said, with reason, that the crux or core of art may be recognized in some effect as simple as the completely satisfying progression from a cobbled street to the smooth base of a building that grows upward from it. Here, then, we have the dependence of art on life" [2].

As institutions move further away from their roots the relationship between the signifying activity and its established meaning comes to depend less on nature and more on convention. For an example at the other end of the scale we could look at the activity of sending a semaphore message - a thoroughly institutionalized cry for help. The activity of sending a semaphore message clearly has its roots in such natural activities as waving to attract attention, but a semaphore message can neither be identified nor evaluated without an acquaintance with the established practices and conventions of a particular culture. Unless we have been trained in semaphore by the community that uses it, we do not know what counts as an authentic semaphore message and we cannot say if a particular message is relieving or alarming, technically correct, kind or cruel, true or false.

Institutions as ritual (symbolic) forms of behaviour

Institutions are activities that are characterized by a sort of duality. They have both a natural and an institutional name. Under their natural description they can be identified and defined without reference to any particular culture. Under their institutional description they cannot be identified or evaluated without reference to a special meaning or significance that the activity has been given by a particular group of people.

Seen thus as activities which have been embedded with special meaning or significance, institutions can be seen to have similarities with words, works of art [3] and people [4], in that they can be described, perceived and responded to on at least two levels - on a physical level as the thing that signifies and on another level as the thing that is signified.

They have therefore two sets of properties - one set of natural properties and one set of culturally emergent properties. In this sense we can say that institutions are symbolic - they are activities with a meaning.

We have already seen that people use symbolic activities in at least two different ways - to represent and to express. If we want to understand the expressive component of a form of symbolic behaviour we have to ask what emotion or mood this behaviour expresses or arouses. If we want to understand the meaning of the representational component of a form of symbolic behaviour we have to ask what this person, object or action represents.

Symbolic actions can be done once, like kissing a photograph or removing a wedding ring. Pontius Pilate washing his hands before sentencing Jesus Christ is an example of a symbolic action that is not an institution because, as far as we know, it was done on one particular occasion. If someone kisses their lover's photograph every night before bed, or touches each lamp post when they walk down a particular road, their symbolic actions become rituals.

Institutions are therefore regularly repeated forms of behaviour that have a special meaning because they are representative or expressive of something in the life of the person performing them.

Institutions as communal forms of behaviour

By saying that institutions are communal forms of behaviour we mean that institutions are forms of behaviour that are shared by the members of a community.

As was said in the previous section, in order to clarify this deceptively simple looking statement it is necessary to give some sense to the idea of ritual forms of behaviour that are not shared among members of a community - the idea of a private ritual.

Ritual behaviour is meaningful behaviour and is, as Peter Winch has powerfully argued, rule-following, and therefore necessarily social. His argument rests on two points:

1. Following rules involves the idea that it must in principle be possible for other people to grasp the rule and judge when it is being correctly followed;
2. It makes no sense to suggest anyone capable of establishing a purely personal standard of behaviour *if* they had never

had any experience of human society with its socially established rules [5].

Established rules are, then, a logically necessary prerequisite of the use of symbols.

Peter Winch makes no mention of innate rule-following behaviour such as we find in animal communication, where the rule is established by natural selection. Nor does he mention unconsciously motivated and constructed rule-following behaviour such as we find in dreams and neuroses, where the rule is not necessarily "grasped" by anyone.

Neither of these cases invalidates either of his basic points or his insistence that all meaningful behaviour is social. Consider Lady Macbeth; burdened by guilt she wanders in her sleep performing endless washing movements with her hands. Is this a ritual? Is it meaningful or symbolic behaviour? Does it involve following a rule? Is it socially established behaviour? Yes, all these seem to be true and yet it is, in an important sense, not communal behaviour. It is a private ritual.

The connection between the washing action and the idea of removing guilt probably has some roots deep in the human species. (Lady Macbeth's, like Pontious Pilate's, action makes sense to us all.) It is at the same time culturally moulded into the particular form it takes. However we believe the connection to be established, it clearly involves a rule; it involves the idea of other people being able to grasp the connection, and of making a mistake - thinking for example that washing is connected with revenge rather than guilt. For these reasons Winch is correct when he says that it can only make sense in a social setting.

By labelling behaviour as neurotic we are conceding that there is a rule involved, even if no-one can quite get to the bottom of it. If we give up the idea of there being a rule we, at the same time, abandon the idea that it is neurotic behaviour and consign it to the category of the randomly bizarre.

We can now imagine a scale of ritual behaviour that stretches from the individual to the communal. At one end we have idiosyncratic obsessional neuroses that no one completely understands. Then there are neuroses which most people understand but few exhibit, such as Lady Macbeth's. At the other end of the scale we have rituals like baptism, where the same washing/guilt motif, culturally adapted in another way, is understood, valued and practised by a whole community. (Not by

142

the British but, theoretically at least, by the Christian Church.)

Winch is therefore correct in saying that no one is capable of establishing an individual rule unless they have behind them the experience of human society. But individuals, because of idiosyncratic elements in their genetic make-up or cultural training, can establish personal symbolic rules that are either not understood, not valued, or not put into practise by the rest of the community in which they are living.

In his novels William Golding frequently returns to the subject of symbolic behaviour. In *Darkness Visible* [6] he shows how it can isolate people, rather than integrate them into a community. Just as individuals within a community can use noises without it constituting a language, so they can use rituals without it constitutinq an institution.

The subject of the story, Matty, is already isolated by his strange beginnings and appearance; as a child he appears mysteriously out of a fire, deformed by the burns he has sustained. Throughout his life he increasingly rejects spoken language, only uttering rare sentences. Golding recounts a period of Matty's life spent in Australia:

> A happy year, all things considered! Only there were things... moving about under the surface. If things moved about *on* the surface there was something to be done... But how if the thing that moves beneath the surface is not to be defined but stays there, a *must* without any instructions? *Must* drove him to things he could not explain but only accept as a bit of easing when to do nothing was intolerable. Such was the placing of stones in a pattern, the making of gestures over them. Such was the slow trickling of dust from the hand and the pouring of good water into a hole [6].

After Matty's return to England an inner compulsion leads him to build matchboxes into a pile and blow on them:

> After seven days Matty added to his game. He bought a clay pot and gathered twigs; and this time when everybody started laughing at his matchboxes, Matty put the twigs together into the pot on top and tried to light them with the matches, but could not.

Matty continues his "game", day after day and eventually sets light to the parking lot and is arrested. The authorities jump to the wrong conclusions about his activity. "You are wrong in supposing that people can't read your message, translate your language," a kindly official tells him, "Of course we can. The irony is - the irony always was - that predictions of calamity have always been understood by the informed, the educated. They have not been understood by the very people who suffer most from them."

He asks Matty, "Do you have some kind of perception, some extra-sensory perception, some second-sight - in a word do you - see?.. I only mean, my dear fellow, this information you feel called to press on a unheeding world - Two words came out of Matty's mouth like two golf balls, "I feel!"" [7].

Matty's behaviour is not understood or shared. The decision to put it in the category of a ritual depends upon the decision that it has a symbolic meaning. The compulsion Matty feels suggests to us that it is not random behaviour. There is a rule there somewhere even if it is an expressive rather than a representative one and even if no-one, including Matty, understands what it is.

This action of Matty's is not an institution because it is private rather than shared by a community. The trouble with this distinction as with the others is that it is a relative rather than an absolute one. There are no answers to questions about how many people make a community, or what counts as *using* a ritual.

Defining institutions

Institutions are repetitive forms of behaviour that have a special representative or expressive meaning to their participants and are shared by members of a human community. While having roots in biological and psychological facts of the human condition, they are governed by conventions that have become established by a particular community.

Before continuing to a discussion of institutions and religion it will be helpful to draw together some further characteristics of institutions, that have to some extent already been suggested.

Institutions attract theoretical justifications and thus fall into groups or categories in respect of the sort of justification that seems relevant to the community that uses them.

As we saw from our short discussion of the relationship between

144

concepts and institutions, it is individuals who think and act, that stand between beliefs and practices, individuals armed with their own meanings and values, intentions and purposes. *It is individuals that both are made by and make institutions.*

During the training of children, institutions and their associated beliefs and values are internalized and used to interpret the world. On the other hand, as experiences change in changing historical circumstances, *institutions can come under pressure.* New meanings can be found for them, new categories proposed, changes made in the way they are practised. They may spread through a community, wane in significance, become marginalized or be abandoned.

Institutions are characterized by being open. Just as in language meanings, definitions, popularity, grammar and spelling are open to change and do change, sometimes in spite of opposition. So the use of an institution is always in principle under review and remains responsive to shifting patterns of historical experience, social behaviour and authority structures.

The concept of an institution is essentially linked with the concept of authority. When human communities agree in the use of a ritual, give it an institutional description and imbue it with culturally emergent properties, there arises a sense in which a certain procedure becomes the way the thing *ought* to be done. Those who do it in significantly different ways can be reprimanded for doing it incorrectly. The activity has acquired its own authority. *This* and not *that* is the established way of doing it.

The force of this authority is sharpened if we consider the functions institutions have for communities. It seems to me, although this is not intended as a definitive statement, that *the general function of institutions* is recalling, sharing, encouraging, reproducing and enforcing experiences and ways of living that are valued; and forgetting, diminishing, discouraging and prohibiting experiences and ways of living that are devalued. They are for and about living together. Thus to dance before battle decreases fear and cowardice and increases courage and persistence; worshipping a totem increases social identity and solidarity; marking the choosing of a mate with vows and prayers increases faithfulness and discourages promiscuity.

Institutions can thus be seen in this sense *to embody and perpetuate the values of a society.* They therefore not only

145

have an authority of their own but can be used by those in authority.

We are now in a position to distinguish four ways in which human activities can be related to institutions, although it should be noted at this point firstly that it is *descriptions* of activities that we are considering and that several descriptions may relate to the same activity. Secondly the distinction between the categories can, in real examples, be changeable, indistinct and confused.

A human activity may be:

1. a natural activity in which an institution has its roots;
2. a natural activity which is the signifier of an institution;
3. part of the traditions and expectations which surround an institution;
4. an institution, which is defined by the conventions of the community.

If we apply these distinctions to the institution of marriage - marriage can be seen to have its roots in the natural activity of taking a mate and building a home and family, but it is not defined by these activities. In Britain the basic signifying activities of marriage are the voluntary exchanging of vows and rings before legitimate witnesses and subsequent consummation in sexual union. Many other varied customs, expectations and traditions surround these basic activities, such as the stag night party, religious service, honeymoon etc. These are connected with, not definitive of, the concept of marriage. The institution is "marriage". That making vows and exchanging rings counts as getting married is a (not entirely arbitrary) connection made by a particular human community. To be able to answer such questions as: were they married when we met them last year? Do you have to be married to get this sort of tax relief? Will you marry me? - in other words, to be able to use the concept of marriage in Britain - one must be trained in the conventions of this community. One must know that for a marriage to be valid, the vows must be taken voluntarily, the person conducting the ceremony must be properly legitimated and sexual union must follow. Even if people reject the concept of marriage and opt for an alternative way of organizing their lives, they know what it is they are rejecting, and would still know what was meant by the question: but are you *really married*?

146

In most communities mates are taken and families and homes are built, and in most human communities some sort of institution has grown up to control, encourage, enjoy and mark the beginning of this activity. When we see such activities in communities other than our own we can see that it is an institution with common roots and so we call it marriage. But their concept of marriage is not ours; we do not understand what counts as a valid marriage in their community, and we do not know what rules govern the use of their concept, until we receive some training in their conventions.

And if we go on and ask; yes, but apart from the conventions of any particular community, what *really* counts as getting married? we demonstrate that we have failed to appreciate the institutional nature of the activity.

Notes

1. Ludwig Wittgenstein, *Philosophical Investigations*, I para. 241.
2. Richard Wollheim, *Art and its Objects*, pp. 117-118.
3. Joseph Margolis, "Works of Art as Physically Embodied and Culturally Emergent Entities", p. 187.
4. Frances Berenson, "Understanding Art and Understanding Persons", p. 43.
5. For a convincing recent defence of this view see Norman Malcolm, "Wittgenstein on Language and Rules", p. 5.
6. William Golding, *Darkness Visible*, p. 55.
7. Ibid., p. 68-71.

Part 3
TOWARDS AN INSTITUTIONAL THEORY OF RELIGION

15 Religious objects

Introduction

Stated most simply an institutional theory of religion says that religions are most helpfully seen as aspects of culture. It says, in other words, that what is to be considered authentic and significant in religion is substantially determined, in each community, by its institutions. According to such a theory questions about which objects are sacred, which activities have religious value, which experiences are religiously significant and where religious authority lies - are substantially determined by the institutions of particular communities and cannot be answered by reference to universal qualities or properties of physical objects, experiences, instincts or activities.

An institutional theory is incompatible with theories based on the priority of experience because it denies that there is any quality or property of anything that can consistently be used to identify what is religious independently of, or prior to, cultural institutions. It also goes beyond theories based on the priority of language because it points not only to what is said, but also, and perhaps more significantly, to what is done.

I aim to demonstrate that such a theory can be expressed in a way that avoids the unnecessary tangles of essentialist theories and highlights some important characteristics of religion, that it can become a useful tool for analysing religious phenomena and that it does not necessarily lead to unacceptable forms of relativism or naturalism.

The essentialist question: what is religion?, asked with the primary aim of reaching a rigorous definition of the concept (and necessarily focusing on borderline cases) is in my opinion largely an unprofitable one [1]. But the same question can be asked in a different spirit, the primary aim being to reach a better understanding of the way the concept is used. This sort of enquiry focuses on standard or central cases.

Having established a clearer view of the nature of institutions and seen that they have roots in unchanging biological and psychological facts of the human condition and a lively interactive relationship with the experiences and beliefs of individuals in changing social situations, the central concepts of religions - a religious object, a religious activity, and a religious experience will now be examined. The focus will be on the rules for the use of these concepts - how people decide to what they apply.

I aim to demonstrate that their use is substantially determined, in each community, by its social institutions, and that there is nothing prior to, or independent of, the development of human communities that has a significant role in regulating their use; that they are in fact institutional concepts.

In order for a word to have a use it must be regulated. There must be some things it can be used for and some things it can't, otherwise the word is useless. These rules vary from being vague and inclusive ("nice" or "that") to being precise and exclusive ("arachnid" or "metre"). Words can have diverse, metaphorically extended or arbitrarily connected rules of use; they may be used creatively, idiosyncratically or in a specialized way by different groups or individuals within any particular language community.

However looking at the way language is used and seeing what rules regulate the use of particular words is both a possible and a useful exercise (even if it only leads to seeing what can not regulate the use of a particular word [2].)

The noun "religion" is used to describe mutually exclusive sets of beliefs and activities - ways of talking and living that, taken as a whole set, are connected with a family of characteristics that are difficult to specify. They include beliefs in "transcendent" or "spiritual" beings (although exactly how these two words are used varies, not all religions contain such beliefs, and not all beliefs in spirits are considered to be religious.) They usually include activities that seem to imply such beliefs such as worship, prayer and burial rituals. They also specify sources of authority on, or answers to, questions about the ultimate nature or meaning of existence and about how people ought to live (but so do many secular thought systems).

152

Such a definition is not inconsistent with, and in fact seems to indicate, that religions are aspects of culture, but in order to establish this it is necessary to examine more closely the objects, activities and experiences that people call religious.

Institutional objects

How do we decide which objects are religious? How far are the rules by which we apply the word "religious" to objects dependent upon our knowledge of institutions rather than our knowledge of natural qualities? Are religious objects in this sense institutional objects?

If we take as a definition of an institutional object: an object as described by a word that is regulated by an institution, we see clearly that wedding rings, voting papers, crowns and flags are institutional objects. They each have a natural description; they are metal rings, pieces of paper or cloth. Under this description they have natural properties, functions and values. But they also have an institutional description which brings with it additional, culturally emergent, properties, functions and values.

We can in general distinguish five distinct ways of applying a description to an object:

1. by way of its function (what it is used for - e.g. a table);
2. by way of its properties (what it is like - e.g. a triangle);
3. by way of its value (how desirable it is, or how much I want it - e.g. a reward);
4. by way of its status (what social position it has been given - e.g. a president);
5. by way of a derivation or metaphorical extension. (We may for instance speak lyrically of a forest clearing as a green cathedral; we may, to a child, refer to a duck's mate as her husband; we may, for effect, call the weather funereal. But if pressed we would agree that it isn't really a cathedral, the drake isn't really her husband and there wasn't a funeral.)

Now it is clear that these ways of applying words are very closely intertwined. We use objects for certain functions because of their properties; we value them because of their uses; we give them a status because of their function; metaphorical uses slide into normal ones. But this does not mean that the rules of use of words are necessarily similarly intertwined. We call an object educational or refer to it as a bed because we know what it is used for; we call an object heavy or a triangle because we know its properties; we refer to an object as cheap or a pound because we know its value; we call an object reputable or a contract because we know its status.

An object is an institutional object if:

1. we know it is correctly described because we know of its function in relation to an institution (e.g. a wedding ring or a voting paper);
2. we know it is correctly described because we know of a social status that has been ascribed to it (e.g. a National Park or a mayor);
3. the value, properties or functions that are relevant to its description derive from its relation to an institution or an ascribed status.

It is relatively easy to see how the value of an object can derive from its use in an institution, or from a status that has been ascribed to it, but it is also the case that properties can derive from both function and status. Giving a new function or status to an object means that a whole new range of things can be said about it. A succession of sounds has several natural properties (e.g. it is loud, irritating or high pitched). If the sounds have the function of communicating a message (e.g. they are a morse code signal), they have several other, culturally emergent, properties (e.g. the message is unkind, untrue, presumptuous or belated). And if the message is given the status of being a promise, it gains another set of properties (e.g. it is foolhardy, improbable or reassuring).

An ascriptive declaration is the process by which objects acquire a new social status, an institutional description and a new set of functions, values, properties. It is a type of J. L. Austin's "performative utterances" [3]. Turning something into an institutional object is one of the things you can do with words, although, as it will become clear, it is rarely done with words alone and can equally well be done without them.

It is a complicated and confusing process which I shall try to untangle by looking at some examples. The first example is of a process which might appear to be an ascription but is not: a community are looking for a new source of food. Various things are put forward as possible candidates. They are tested for their properties (taste, nutritional value etc.). The experts reach an agreement and make a declaration; X is good to eat. Why this is not an ascriptive declaration will become clear when we consider the following processes which are:

A colour card becomes a standard

A group of decorators need a standard colour card for "orange". Several candidates are suggested and discussed. "We all agree then," one of them says at the end of the discussion, "We'll make this card our standard."

A man becomes a leader

A group of scientists are engaged on a research task. Over a period of time it becomes obvious to all the team that one member is taking, and being given, the leadership role - its tasks, its responsibilities and its privileges. Nothing is said.

A woman becomes President

A club needs a new president. The qualities of the various eligible members are considered. Voting papers are passed around among those eligible to vote, collected up and counted. "Mrs. X has won the vote," the secretary declares, "She shall become our President at the ceremony next week."

An assertion becomes a promise

"I'll probably come tomorrow at around six," the boy says to his girl friend. She pouts. "Well, all right, I promise I will."

A gold band becomes a wedding ring

A couple get engaged and go to buy a wedding ring. They look under the label, "wedding rings" and choose one. Before the wedding she wears it to pretend, at an interview, that she is already married, but on the day, the best man looses it. So they use a spare ring that the vicar produces and buy a replacement after the honeymoon.

Several things can be drawn out of these examples about the nature of ascriptive declarations:

It is the declaration that makes the new name applicable and provides the object with a new set of properties

This is not the case in the example regarding the food. The food always was good to eat; the testing discovered it to be so; the declaration made no difference. In contrast the colour card was not the standard sample until the declaration. The discussion led only to an agreement that it was eligible.

The motivation for making the declaration can usually be seen in terms of the need for an institution to continue

If people are to get married they have to have rings. If a club is to continue it needs a president.

The choice of objects eligible for an ascriptive declaration is often made on the basis of the natural properties, values and functions of the candidates

It was the colour of the card and the qualities of Mrs. X that made them suitable choices for the ascriptive declaration.

An ascriptive declaration always involves established practices (or institutions)

Which properties, values and functions are appropriate in candidates for ascription, and the way in which it must be done, are determined by convention. This was not the case with the food, but the boy's decision that his statement was a suitable one to make into a promise depended upon his acquaintance with the socially established practice of promising.

The declaration need not be formal

The president was installed at a public ceremony. (The stated declaration, "Mrs. X has won the election," was not ascriptive. It stated what was the case), but the decorators just said informally, "We'll make it our standard."

The declaration can be implicit and not articulated at all

The researchers never said, "X shall be our leader," but they all behaved as though they had. An object can attract an institutional description merely by being used in the context of an institution. The papers were passed out. No one said, "These shall be our voting papers". Being used for that purpose was sufficient to make them so.

The declaration can be an individual decision and can be made privately

The boy told his girl friend that his statement was a promise but (if we allow that it is possible to promise to yourself) he could have merely decided to treat it as such without telling her. (He could not of course have established the institution of promising on his own.)

The relationship between an object and an ascription need not be direct

The actual rings the couple called their wedding rings were not the ones blessed by the vicar at their wedding ceremony. The use of the word in general, rather than in particular, is regulated by the institution of marriage. Nevertheless if they had been asked of either of the rings used before or after the wedding, "But is this really your wedding ring?" they would probably have added some explanation.

Ascriptive declaration are bounded by conventions and they can fail if these are not complied with

It seems in each of these diverse cases that declarations can go wrong and people can be mistaken about them. The decorators can discover that, having elected a card to be their sample, it is too difficult or expensive a colour to produce, or a colour that people don't like. It would not, in this case be the declaration that went wrong but the choice of candidate. The ascription worked and the card became their standard, but they later regretted having done it. They might then say, "This is our standard colour, but we don't use it." In the case of the researchers, one member of the group might have begun to take a leadership role which was resented and resisted by others in the group, who preferred not to have a specific leader, or to have someone else. Here a claim to be a suitable candidate for an ascriptive declaration is rejected; the ascription never takes place. In the case of the president, agreement might be reached but something go wrong with the ceremony. The Immediate Past President, who is meant to perform the ceremony, may be taken ill, or the chain of office be mislaid. Abortive attempts at a ceremony without such essential equipment may be considered inadequate and a decision made to repeat it on another occasion. Here the formal expression of the declaration has gone wrong and has not been effective. But something else can go wrong here too. The club might find out after the ceremony, that Mrs X was not entitled to stand for the election in the first place because she did not satisfy some prescribed condition. She had perhaps not been a member for the required number of years. They could then decide that even a correctly performed ceremony had not made her into the President.

In the case of the promise, there are again candidates that fall so far short of the requirements for making promises that just saying it is a promise cannot make it one [4]. If, for example, we promise something that does not make sense, that has already failed to happen or that we could not for some other reason, possibly bring about; if, from the tone and context, we are clearly being ironical, joking, or acting a part, the declaration does not turn the statement into a promise.

In every case ascriptive declarations are bounded by conventional rules, but, as we have seen, different rules apply in different situations. Sometimes different levels of agreement are necessary; sometimes detailed procedures have to be followed.

It seems also that there is always some requirement that has to be met by candidates, although these are probably more often in the nature of defeating conditions rather than prescriptions. In each case acquaintance with the relevant institution and its traditions and rules is required and must be complied with if the declaration is to work.

These observations about how objects acquire institutional descriptions can be used to discover whether a specific description of an object is an institutional one. We can ask of an object; does this object have two sets of properties, functions and values, one natural set and one set derived from its relation to an institution? Has this object acquired its description by an ascriptive declaration (even it is not formal or explicit) or has it acquired it by the discovery of a natural property? Is it a matter of convention which properties make the description applicable and can failure to keep within the conventions make the declaration fail? Is there a natural function or property which could regulate the use of the description?

Before turning to look at religious objects this set of questions will be applied to the concept of a leader. When we call something or somebody a leader are we giving them a natural or an institutional description? We shall consider two cases:

1. Three tortoises leave their hutch and move towards their drinking bowl; one moves faster than the others so we refer to her as the leader.

2. The Labour Party goes through a complicated and long-winded election process to choose between several candidates certified as eligible to lead the party. Mr. Y the man considered by the majority to have the most impressive list of personal achievements, impeccable socialist beliefs and charismatic personality, wins the election and is ceremonially installed as the Leader of the Party.

How do we know that the tortoise and Mr. Y are leaders? The tortoise has acquired a new description; we know that it applies because of a natural property - her relative speed of travel. She could also have acquired a new function (If anyone has a use for fast tortoises). But neither of these are derived from the tortoise's relation to an institution and she has not acquired any new properties. It does not therefore appear that the declaration that she is the leader is an ascriptive one.

Mr. Y has acquired a new description which is derived from a socially established set of practices involving political parties and their organization. He now has at least two descriptions and two sets of functions, values and properties, one natural and one

159

deriving from his relation to an institution. His new name is conferred by an ascriptive declaration. Winning the election does not, on its own, make him the leader. The status of Leader is conferred in a formal ceremony. Until that time it did not apply. Although there are natural properties that make him eligible, the process by which the title is conferred is established by convention and there is, in this particular use, no natural function or property that could regulate the use of the word.

The conclusion must be that the way language is used is complex, variable and imprecise. The word "leader" can be used as both a natural and an institutional description in different contexts. Between these two examples are spread many other uses where institutional and natural factors play more or less important roles. The concept of leadership is firmly rooted in nature, but has, in some contexts, acquired an institutional use. We should take this as a warning as we turn to look at religious objects and not expect to find any less ambiguity and complexity in our results.

Religious objects

Considering some things sacred is central to the concept of religion. Asking someone if there is anything they consider sacred (asking them if they use the concept) is very much like asking them if they are religious. Asking them which objects they take to be sacred, is very much like asking them which religion they follow. Having said that we should bear in mind that attitudes towards objects in religions are invariably enigmatic [5], and that major strands of the world's religions have prohibitions about making images of divinity and reservations about the division of material things into the sacred and the secular.

What objects are held sacred? Starting with a typical village Hindu family [6], *devata* or images of gods will be found in their home. (They may say these are images of the Supreme Spirit.) They make offerings to these images to appease, ingratiate, and obtain requests. An individual worshipper is free to choose which *devata* to worship from an almost infinite list, and how such devotions shall be carried out. But, as Ursula Sharma points out, the general pattern which these rites follow is fairly constant. She describes a typical ritual act of a Tarkan woman worshipping *Baba Balak Nath* in thanksgiving for a good harvest and hope of another. She rises early, begins a fast, baths and puts on clean clothes. She re-plasters her kitchen floor with cow dung and prepares some *karah* or sweet pudding. She takes out her image of *Baba Balak Nath*, puts new cow dung on the floor of her veranda and places the image on a stool. No one in the household now approaches this area unless they have removed their shoes. She bathes the image with fresh water and offers flowers and incense before it. She takes red powder and applies it to the forehead and takes some sacred thread and ties it around the image's waist. She offers it a small quantity of *karah* by pressing it to its "mouth". The rest of the *karah* is now known as *prasad* - the transmitter of the grace of the *devata* - and it is distributed among the household. Great care is taken that none falls to the ground or is left where it might come into contact with any impure substance. Later the image is removed and put away and the area cleared. The remains of the items offered to the image are taken and thrown into a running stream.

Other objects that such a villager might consider sacred would be the Sanskritic deities in the village shrine or temple, the Brahman priest and his mandalas and texts, the wandering holy man or guru, the cow and the river Ganges.

Roman Catholic Christianity raises a remarkably similar list of sacred objects - the images of the Virgin, and of the crucified and risen Christ and the saints, might similarly be said to be aids or mediators in the Catholic's relationship with God. The equipment used in worship - rosaries, incense and holy water - are similarly revered. The wafers and wine of the Mass are consecrated before an altar, built around the relics of a saint, and thus become the Body and Blood of Christ - the means of God's grace. They are then shown the greatest respect and never allowed to fall on the ground or disposed of casually. Catholics too have their priests and holy texts, saints, relics and shrines. David Sox, in his book *Relics and Shrines*, bears witness to the continuing importance of sacred objects in the Catholic faith: "To this day, the technical definition of an altar in Roman Catholic canon law is "a tomb containing the relics of saints"... Until fairly recently when liturgical regulations have become rather lax in some parts of the Catholic world," he says, "no priest would celebrate Mass without this altar stone with its relic"[7]. He tells how in 1983 he wrote to the Pope's Vicar General at the Vatican, who is, "the day to day authority regarding most of the regulations concerning relics and their required placements in new altars." He applied for a relic of St. Rita of Cascia for his private use. It duly arrived with a certificate of authentication and a bill for five dollars to cover the cost of postage and packing [8].

In Ancient Judaism we can trace a gradual movement away from a materialistic concept of sanctity towards a more spiritual concept [9]. The idea that emerges forcibly as the Old Testament develops is that God is holy and has called out for himself a holy people. Other things, almost any other things, become holy as God, or his people, set them aside for special use. Thus the seventh day is blessed and made holy [10]. An altar is consecrated. "For seven days make atonement for the altar and consecrate it," the law demands, "Then the altar will be most holy and whatever touches it will be holy" [11]. Priests are called out from Aaron's descendants [12]. External rituals of sanctification, culminating in the sanctification of the Temple in Jerusalem, gradually give way to the call to inward holiness. The prophets go so far as to disparage the external observances of their religion when they are not accompanied by an inner practical holiness [13].

In modern Judaism [14], the scroll of the Torah is usually considered to be a holy object, as are the ruins of the Temple in Jerusalem. Other shrines, such as Hebron (the burial place of the Patriarchs), the tombs of other great Jews, and other objects such as shawls, phylacteries and mezuzas, are also seen by some to be sacred.

Muslims take the Jewish proscription against images and the sanctification of everyday life, at least as seriously as Jews [15]. Every act done with the consciousness that it fulfils the divine will is an act of worship and every created object can thus be sanctified. No images or holy objects are used in a Muslim's daily worship. Their mosques are remarkable for their emptiness and lack of representational art. Prayers are directed to an empty niche that points the worshipper towards Mecca. In Islam the sense of sacredness is centred on the words of the Qur'an and the one holy place in Mecca - the place of God's last revelation to the world. The ritual of the *Hajj* - the pilgrimage - reinforces the idea of Mecca as the "navel of the earth". Muslims purify themselves before they approach, in the allotted month and perform rituals there to fulfil the detailed requirements of God's command. However David Sox reports that two hairs from the Prophet's beard are kept in a reliquary in the Dome of the Rock in Jerusalem [16], while in certain areas *pirs* or holy men and their graves become points of pilgrimage and many Muslims wear talismans.

Muslims and Christians revere their holy books; the Sikhs have been accused of being, "blatant book worshippers" [17]. Their book of scriptures, the *Adi Granth*, is treated in a manner very similar to the way the Hindus treat their temple images - installed in a special room, elevated and kept wrapped in beautiful cloths; during worship Sikh's prostrate themselves before it, wave it with a *chowri* or fan (a sign of royalty) make offerings to it and sometimes even leave it food and drink

In the African continent [18] the connection between spiritual power and physical objects is as ubiquitous and enigmatic as anywhere. In images and natural objects of every conceivable kind, in charms and amulets, medicines and potions, kings and sorcerers, the material and the spiritual world are intimately intertwined. Objects of every kind act as the representation, the expression, the focus, the catalyst and the receptacle of all kinds of spiritual beings and forces.

Theravada Buddhist teaching [19] is probably unique in its complete rejection of the material world and its quest for transcendence and release. As the source of all deception and suffering it must, at every opportunity, be renounced [20]. However in practice Buddhists in many places revere images of the Buddha and in other places the use of sacred objects resembles that found in the African continent.

In contrast, the Eastern Orthodox cult of the icon expresses the belief that all matter is spirit-bearing and ultimately to be redeemed. The icon, usually painted on wood, of Christ, his mother or one of the saints is used specifically to remind the worshipper of the reality of the spiritual world - the divine image in man - and of man's vocation to manifest the spiritual in and through the material and thus bring harmony between spirit and matter [21].

Having brought to mind this motley collection of objects that people consider sacred we shall now ask how they decide which objects are sacred; what regulates their use of the concept? Are we looking for natural properties and functions or for institutional ones, which are conferred on objects by ascriptive declarations?   There are four different, but to some extent overlapping, categories.

Objects and places that are set apart to assist in ritual contact with the divine

This must be the basic use of the word "sacred" - something dedicated to God - and the majority of the objects we have considered fall easily into this category.   The village Hindu woman has probably made her image herself from local clay. The sweet pudding she offers it is not different from the pudding she regularly makes for her family; the act of offering changes its name, its properties, its function and its value; a completely different set of attitudes and behaviour are now appropriate.

Rosaries, chalices, church buildings, holy water and books are all mundane objects with common functions, refashioned or set apart to represent the divine to us, to focus our attention, to express some truth, to remind us of our past, to arouse the right feelings, to assist our worship.   What are sometimes considered the central objects of the Christian faith - the bread and wine of the Eucharist - are perhaps the clearest example of mundane objects being formally consecrated for a holy purpose.   The enormous range of beliefs about the mechanics or meaning of the transformation that takes place in that consecration all conform to the notion that it is effected by an ascriptive declaration that is bounded on all sides by convention.

This institutional use is the predominantly Hebrew use of the word "holy".   It is well expressed by Professor R. A. Finlayson: "In the Old Testament holiness is designated of places, things, seasons and official persons in virtue of their connection with the worship of God...   In these instances holiness signifies a relation that involves separation from common use and dedication to a sacred one" [22].

However literally or metaphorically people understand the changes that take place when something is consecrated, however real or symbolic, direct or conditional is the power it is thought to acquire, this use is clearly an institutional one.   We know which objects are sacred because we know about an institution. (We know which wafers are to be treated with respect because we know about the Eucharist).   The objects have two sets of properties, functions and values - one natural set and one set derived from its relation to an institution. (The natural properties, functions and values of a wafer are different from, although not irrelevant to, the institutional properties, functions and values of "The Body of Christ".) They acquire their new description, not by the discovery of natural properties but by ascriptive declarations, even if they are not formal or explicit, for their natural properties make them merely eligible for ascription; they do not make the description "sacred" applicable. Part of the motive for such a declaration is the continuity of the institution and it is, in every case, a matter of convention which properties make them suitable candidates, and which processes make the new description applicable. There is at the same time no natural property or function that could regulate this use.

Places or objects connected with the manifestation or revelation of the divine - places of religious experiences

People seem to have a profound sense of the significance of times and places. ("This is the very place!" "A year ago to the day!") In Genesis we read of Jacob travelling a long way from home, stopping for the night in a strange place and having his famous dream of, "a stairway resting on the earth, with its top reaching to heaven". When he woke he said, "Surely the Lord is in this place and I was not aware of it. How awesome is this place! This is none other than the house of God; this is the gate of heaven." He took the stone he had placed under his head, "set it up as a pillar and poured oil on top of it. He called the place "Bethel" (which means "house of God") though the city used to be called Luz" [23].

We see here both how places become sacred and how sacredness gets extended to cover objects connected with significant experiences. Our Coronation Stone, *The Stone of Destiny*, on which Scottish monarchs were crowned since the 13th century, is reputed to be "the very stone" that Jacob dreamed on that night. The fact that it was still in comparatively recent times regarded as, in some sense, sacred is illustrated by the fact that in 1950 when it was stolen from Westminster Abbey the BBC put a ban on jokes about it [24].

This sense of time and place is epitomized in the Islamic pilgrimage to Mecca. Kenneth Cragg, in his comments about the *Hajj*, says:

165

> Places and meanings seem so much to interdepend.
> For man expresses himself and, so to speak "locates"
> himself spiritually by the use of symbols. Symbols,
> in turn, spring from associations in space and time -
> those twin categories of the human situation. When
> space and time meet in historical event their double
> significance has, as it were, a rendezvous where the
> faithful in turn can engage with it. Geography and
> meaning then coincide in a religious focus. Place
> becomes a kind of sacrament and travel to it an
> experience of identity with the meaning, a
> participation [25].

Here in Mecca God revealed himself, and here in this holy month
the people of the revelation converge upon the holy place to
remember and to worship.

The sacredness of the time, the place and the contents of God's
revelation of himself permeates the other religions too, with
festivals, holy shrines, objects and books. G. Parrinder says of
African shrines, "The power of the natural object may be met with
at one of the shrines which are like its trysting place with men"
[26].

Devout Jews are reminded of the pinnacles of God's dealings
with his people through the annual cycle of festivals; and a visit
to the wailing wall, the only visible remains of their temple, where
God met them through the centuries, is a treasured and
emotional experience.

Similarly each Easter millions of Christian celebrate, "the day
of resurrection", and thousands visit, "the Holy Land" - the place
where it all happened. Even the place where the Buddha
received his enlightenment concerning the ultimate illusion of the
material world is visited and venerated.

Perhaps for us one of the most interesting expressions of this
sense of the holy place in modern times is the dedication of
shrines to appearances of the Virgin Mary, notably Lourdes
(where there have been over 30 episodes of reported
appearances), Fatima in Portugal, where she appeared to three
children in 1917 and Knock in Ireland where, according to David
Sox in 1985, a monsignor was, "moving mountains to attract
attention to the local shrine," where over 100 years ago, "15
parishioners saw what they believed to be the Virgin Mary in the

south gable of their church" [27].   The fact that Knock now boasts an international airport must reflect the measure of his success, and, even as I write, the newspapers report a controversy over the building of a basilica at the scene of another apparition - in Surbiton!   The local priest is, "politely sceptical," and says, "It is not impossible that these are real messages," while the Archbishop of Southwark is, "dismayed" and has, "made it quite clear that he does not approve" [28].

The question we now have to consider is - is this use of the word "sacred" to describe times, places and associated objects, where the divine is thought to have approached, an institutional one? The practice clearly has its roots in the treasuring of remarkable and valuable experiences and the desire to mark the time and place where they occurred.   Somehow the value of the experience gets transferred to the time, place and objects involved.   ("This is the day we were married."   "This is the ring he gave me." "This is where we met.")   This process makes times and places significant and valuable to individuals, but for a time or place to become valuable to a community, some sort of ascriptive declaration, based on some sort of agreement and authentication is necessary, and if we look more closely we can see that this is what happens.

What we see when we consider Marian shrines is a mixture of popular acclaim and official authentication.   The Roman Catholic Church does not investigate individual claims of appearances of the Virgin, unless they arouse popular acclaim - unless the sense of the value, the meaning and the significance of the event is shared.   They then have detailed guidelines on how to detect genuine appearances, and make official declarations on the outcome of their investigations, which are not always in accord with the sentiments of the devout public.

Do holy places then acquire their descriptions by ascription? The answer in these cases seems to be - yes.   The places acquire new sets of properties, functions and values and these are associated with the established institutions of religion.   There are conventions about which properties make them eligible and which processes make them holy.   In general we know which places and times are holy because we know which have been given either popular or official acclaim.

But are there not also cases where the use of the word is regulated by a discovery of a natural property?   It may look from the account of Jacob's dream at Bethel that he discovered the holy qualities of the place where he slept and declared its natural name - "This is none other than the house of God", just as he might have discovered that it was a cold place or a place where rattle snakes lived and called it "Windy Hill" or "Snake Ridge". But experiencing the cold, or finding rattle snakes is not like experiencing the presence of God. A religious experience is not the same sort of thing as a weird feeling, a good experience or a vivid dream; it is a feeling, an experience or a dream to which a special meaning has been attached. If this is a religious meaning it depends upon institutional practices and shared beliefs. If as we shall argue later there is no natural property of experiences that makes them religious but rather the concept of a religious experience itself is an institutional concept, transferring the value of an experience to the time and place of its occurrence is an institutional use of the word.

Objects connected with people who appear to have a special relationship with the divine

We have seen how the value of an experience can be transferred to a time, a place or an object. Similarly the value of a person can be transferred to their mortal remains and possessions. Most religions have people set apart for special religious functions - priests and imams, ministers, bishops, kings and presbyters. These are institutional roles conferred on eligible individuals. But most religions have a separate category of people, who by their lives and characters seem to display some aspects of divinity - saints, gurus and holy men and, occasionally, women. We see this supremely, in the doctrines of theophany and incarnation. Veneration of such people leads to the veneration of tombs, statues and relics, things that represent or remind, things they have used or touched.

David Sox tells us of cloths that have been made sacred by being hung down into the tombs of martyrs and oil that has been made holy by being poured into tombs and tapped off into bottles [29]. In May 1990 *The Independent* ran a story about the severed hand of a priest, martyred in 1679 which was regularly taken to parishioners, "who were ill or in need of spiritual succour". It was apparently being treated in a private laboratory, for, "a type of woodworm infestation," by a secret process that, "should preserve this hand for another few hundred years" [31].

Is this use of the word "sacred" institutional? Do we come to see someone as a saint or a guru by discovering their natural properties, or is sainthood also acquired by some sort of ascriptive declaration?

In the New Testament the apostles took on the word "saint" (*hagios*, or "holy one") to refer to the new people of God. As God had separated out Aaron's family to be dedicated as priests, so God was now calling out a new, "chosen people, a royal priesthood, a holy nation" [30]. In chapter four of his letter to the Romans, where Paul develops his theme of justification by faith, he uses the word *logid'zomai* eight times. The word is variously translated "impute", "reckon", "count", and "credit". It roughly means, "ascribe". As Paul explains, the righteousness that brings with it the status of "saint" is credited to sinners who put their faith in Christ. In chapter nine where he develops his other great doctrine of predestination, Paul quotes from Hosea, "I will call them "my people" who were not my people, and I will call her "my loved one" who is not my loved one" [32]. Thus God calls out sinners and makes them saints by his declaration. This institutional use of the word "saint" is continued in the protestant churches.

Within a few centuries however another use had arisen - an honorific title for those with an especially Christ-like character. In modern Catholicism the official use of the title "saint" is closely guarded. Candidates are proposed and examined and elaborate conventions direct the process of canonization. David Sox tells of an occasion when a declaration of sainthood by both popular and official acclaim failed. St. Philomena became popular in 1802 when an ampulla of blood and some bones were found in the catacombs of St. Priscilla bearing an inscription which was translated, "Philomena, peace be with you". A priest installed her relic in his church and made up a history for her. Several miraculous cures graced her installation and many churches were subsequently named after her. The Vatican authenticated her sainthood by permitting the composition of a Mass in her honour and naming a feast day for her. Then a Jesuit scholar discovered there had been a misreading of the inscription; "Philomena" was not a name; it just meant "beloved one". Saint Philomena ceased to exist, but her veneration continued. In 1962 she was officially taken off the books - a decision that was greeted in some quarters with anger and anguish [33].

In other areas of religion there are different relationships between popular acclaim and official declaration. The Hindu holy man, it appears, needs merely to declare himself one and start behaving like one. In fact all devout old men are expected, in the final stage of their lives to become *sannyasi*, shed their possessions and family ties and set their minds on seeking spiritual truth, and all who do are treated with the respect of a holy man [34].

If we examine more closely the varied examples of the recipients of these titles, the values and functions they acquire and the rules about eligibility and procedure, we discover they too have the characteristics of ascriptive declarations. There is no natural function or property that could regulate the use of the word, for within each religion the rules are quite different. A Catholic knows how to recognize a Catholic saint and a Hindu knows how to recognize a Hindu holy man, and it is the established practices of these different religions that make them what they are.

Objects which act as a focus of spiritual power

There is a fourth category of sacred objects that overlaps to some extent with others - objects that are not valued primarily because of associations with experiences and people but that are perceived to have special power, to charm, harm, cure or protect. Some of these also fall into other categories, like the holy water at Lourdes, a medal of St. Christopher or an African charm containing texts from the Bible or the Qur'an [35], or the bread and wine of the Eucharist. But they need a separate discussion because some objects in this category may appear to be discovered because of their natural properties rather than having a status conferred on them by an ascriptive declaration.

There is, it appears, a natural human tendency to hoard and treasure rare, beautiful or emotive objects. We can see this tendency in children who often like to possess a curious collection of objects for a curious collection of reasons. Why they are treasured (what we might call the meaning of the object to its owner) may not be clear to anyone and may be either private or shared, (although it is only possible for the notion of objects having meanings to arise in communities [36]).

William Golding's stone-age family in *The Inheritors*, for example, has a small object, found in the root of a tree and named, "the little Oa", that Lok's daughter carries around with her [37].

When such appreciation of objects is shared by a community, it becomes an institutional object and tends to attract theoretical justification - an explicit meaning - of some kind or another, which we may or may not be able to categorize as aesthetic, social, magic, scientific, religious etc. Objects that are perceived to have power in themselves to harm, cure or protect, fall, in my view, in the category of magic or, if there are consistent physical explanations of how they work, in the category of science.

Religiously powerful objects, such as relics, holy water, charms and amulets are seen to cure and protect because they focus the power of the divine by consecration, contact, similarity or representation - that is, by some sort of association. And it is just this element of association, this agreed meaning, that makes such objects institutional.

Edward Plater, in his book about the Holy Coat of Trier, has this to say about the power and value of the coat believed to have been worn by Jesus:

> The veneration paid to the Holy Coat is thus both relative and conditional: relative because it is really paid, not to the material garment, but through it to Our Blessed Lord; conditional, because it is only paid under a certain implied condition... Even supposing that this condition is not fulfilled, the ultimate honour falls none the less on its proper object, Christ Jesus our Lord [38].

In order to know which objects become sacred in this way it is necessary to know about the institutions of a particular community and to know the conventions about which objects are suitable candidates and how they become sacred. The incredible variety of natural objects that can be taken up into this category is enough to show us that there can be no natural function or property of objects that could regulate this use of the word.

Conclusion

The use of the words "sacred" and "holy" as applied to objects is mainly regulated by the idea of setting mundane things aside for special functions in relation to religious institutions - for assisting in ritual contact with the divine. Other uses are connected with the value that gets transferred to material objects from experiences and people that are seen to have special religious value, or from some other association with divine power. In each case knowing which objects are sacred involves knowing about institutions rather than knowing about natural properties.

The sacred objects in all of these categories have two sets of properties, functions and values, one arising from their natural properties, and one arising from their relationship to an institution. They acquire the description by an ascriptive declaration (even if it is not formal or explicit), not by the discovery of a natural property. It is a matter of convention which properties make candidates suitable and which processes make the description applicable, and failure to meet these requirements makes the declaration fail. There is no natural function or property which could be what regulates this use.

We need to remember however that it is not possible to define institutions rigorously (they merge into and grow out of natural, direct and individual activities); uses of concepts such as sacredness are always open to change and extension, and it is not always possible to decide if an ascriptive declaration has taken place or whether the meaning attached to an object is a religious one. Our conclusion that religious objects are institutional objects must always therefore be, to some extent, tentative.

Notes

1. This is discussed in more detail in Chapter 18.
2. See e.g. Ludwig Wittgenstein on the use of "pain", *Philosophical Investigations*, I paras. 244 ff.
4. J. L. Austin, *How to do Things with Words*.
5. The idea of, "the heathen worshipping wood and stone" is born more of misplaced cultural superiority than fact.
6. The following details are taken from Ursula Sharma, *Contribution to Indian Society*, pp. 1-21.

7. David Sox, *Relics and Shrines*, p. 8.
8. Ibid., pp. 58-9.
9. See Professor G. Walters, *The New Bible Dictionary*, J. D. Douglas (ed.) pp. 1139-1140.
10. Genesis 2 v. 3.
11. Exodus 29 v. 37.
12. Exodus 28.
13. See e.g. Isaiah 1 vs.11-17.
14. David Goldstein, *The Religion of the Jews*, pp. 59 ff.
15. Kenneth Cragg, *Islam and the Muslim*, pp. 56-63.
16. David Sox, *Relics and Shrines*, p. 212.
17. Terry Thomas, *Sikhism: the Voice of the Guru*, p. 66.
18. Geoffrey Parrinder, *African Traditional Religion*.
19. I. B. Horner, *The Concise Encyclopedia of Living Faiths*, R. C. Zaehner (ed.) pp. 263 ff.
20. *Itivuttaka*, p. 62, "Immaterial things are more peaceful than material, cessation is more peaceful than immaterial things."

21. Archimandrite Kallistos Ware, *The Orthodox Way*, pp. 62 ff.
22. R. A. Finlayson, *The New Bible Dictionary*, J. D. Douglas (ed.), p. 530.
23. Genesis 28.
24. *The Daily Telegraph*, March 21 1986.
25. Kenneth Cragg, *Islam and the Muslim*, pp. 56-57.
26. Geoffrey Parrinder, *African Traditional Religions*, p. 24.
27. David Sox, *Relics and Shrines*, p. 201.
28. *The London Standard*, March 13 1986.
29. David Sox, *Relics and Shrines*, p. 10.
30. *The Independent*, May 22 1990.
31. 1 Peter 2 v. 9.
32. Romans 9 v. 25
33. David Sox, *Relics and Shrines*, pp. 222-223.
34. A. L. Basham, *The Concise Encyclopedia of Living Faiths*, R. C. Zaehner (ed.) p. 242.
35. Geoffrey Parrinder, *African Traditional Religion*, p. 114.
36. See Peter Winch, *The Idea of a Social Science*, pp. 24 ff.

37.   William Golding, *The Inheritors*, pp. 32-33.
38.   Edward Plater, *Holy Coat of Trier*, quoted in, David Sox, *Relics and Shrines*, p. 224.

16 Religious activities

Human beings eat and sleep, they make tools and statues, and grow things, dance, sing, fight, worship, mate and die, paint pictures and tell stories, make pilgrimages, decorate themselves, write letters, vote, make gifts and promises, build and destroy... Some of the things that human beings do are described as religious activities, but what is it about a human activity that makes it a religious one?   How do we know which activities are correctly described in this way?

The answers to these questions will indicate how far the concept of a religious activity is an institutional concept, in the sense that we learn how to use it by becoming acquainted with the conventions of human communities rather than natural qualities. Paradigm examples of religious activities across all religions would include ceremonies of different kinds, dressing up, telling or acting stories, chanting, songs and prayers, moral teaching, making pilgrimages, offerings and sacrifices, images, pictures and shrines, that are visited and shown reverence.   The category also includes an individual's prayers, study and meditation, moral behaviour and service.   People who live in relatively static, homogeneous cultures have few problems deciding which of their community's activities are religious.   They are trained in the use of their language, and become aware of the coherence and continuity of sets of activities, the places where they are carried out and the people who use and control them.   They know what makes an activity religious because they know what their religious specialists (their clergy, priests or holy men and women) do and they know what goes on in their shrines, churches or temples; they are familiar with the institutions their community calls religious, and are able to extend the use of the concept in a metaphorical way. So a woman can be said to fill in her tax forms religiously.

Consider a live rendering of a Bach Mass in a cathedral. Is it a social, an aesthetic or a religious activity? The first clues come from the context, or setting, of the event. If it is organized by a musical society, advertised as being one of the finest examples of choral singing, followed by applause and evaluated by the music critics in the daily papers, we make a different judgement than if it is organized by the Cathedral staff, advertised as being in memory of a late Canon of the Cathedral, followed by quiet prayer and reported in the church press. We know how to tell which things are religious and what religious things are like, because we know about the institutions that our community calls religious.

This explanation seems straightforward and obvious, but when we consider it in more depth, especially in the context of alien cultures or mobile, pluralistic cultures, the question seems both to need more careful thought and to raise other possible answers. Does this decorated dance have a meaning? If so, is it social, magic, military or religious? By simply looking there is no way we can tell. And what if we discover that the participants have no concept of art, no way of distinguishing science from magic, social ends from religious ones, or are unable to give any reasons for the activity that make sense to us?

Are the various individuals sitting silently in rows in the cathedral, listening to the Bach Mass, engaging in a social, aesthetic or religious activity? Just by looking we are unable to tell, and what if some of them came with mixed motives or can not say clearly why they came?

There are several levels at which we attempt to answer these questions. The first has to do with whether an activity has a symbolic meaning. The others with what sort of meaning it has, for it seems clear to me that it is only by reference to established meanings that activities can be categorized as religious.

But, an antagonist will ask, is it the case that if we are to identify an activity as religious we must first establish that it is an institution? Are there no natural direct, private activities that can be recognized as religious [1]? In many, if not most religions people worship, invoke, pray and make sacrifices, tell stories, perform ceremonies, theorize and make moral rules. Are none of these activities exclusively and necessarily religious and could

176

thus have a part in regulating the concept of religion?

It seems not. There are activities that are necessarily religious - worshipping Allah, baptizing a new Christian, observing the Day of Atonement, making a pilgrimage to Mecca, taking Communion, chanting the name of Krishna. But all these activities are institutions - they are defined by convention and cannot be identified prior to, or independently of, practices that have become established in particular human communities.

If we use more general descriptions for these activities they become no longer necessarily religious; they could equally well have a secular meaning, for people express devotion, respect and praise to their fellow human beings, and even to their pets; people invoke, appease and make sacrifices and requests to things other than gods.

It might be argued that in modern usage the word "worship" is confined to religious contexts [2]. The more decisive question is: is there any natural, direct, individual, activity that can be identified as religious worship without establishing its social context - without asking the worshippers what they think they are doing, or making assumptions about what, or to whom, the activity is directed?

A tribesman falls down on his knees with his arms outstretched to the rising sun. We recognize an expression of wonder. But is it *worship* in the religious sense? Can we not imagine a modern atheist feeling exactly the same emotion, and expressing it - by writing a poem perhaps - without wanting to say that he was worshipping anything. Wonder is clearly a root activity of religion, but wonder can be expressed in a secular context. For an activity to be religious worship it would require a more complicated response - something more like the feeling William Golding puts in the mind of his stone-age character, Lok, as, with the coming of the Spring, his family returns to their summer home:

> He stood up and peered over the earth and stones down the slope. The river had not gone away either or the mountains. The overhang had waited for them. Quite suddenly he was swept up by a tide of happiness and exultation. Everything had waited for them: Oa had waited for them. Even now she was pushing up the spikes of the bulbs, fattening the grubs, reeking the smells out of the earth, bulging

177

the fat buds out of every crevice and bough.

He danced on to the terrace by the river, his arms spread wide. "Oa!" [3].

This example emphasizes what has already been noted, that institutions grow from their roots, like, "the completely satisfying progression from a cobbled street to the smooth base of a building that grows upward from it" [4]. This implies that there is no hard distinction between institutional and non-institutional activities (and therefore that institutional theories necessarily have soft edges).

Before we could confidently call a decorated dance, or an individual's visit to a cathedral a religious activity, we would have to assemble some evidence about the meaning of the activity to the participants, that they were in some sense "dancing before their god", to thank, appease or invoke him or that some of them had come, in some sense, to "meet God" rather than just to listen to the music. Without establishing something of the sort it seems to me that calling an activity religious would be speculative, and vacuous. It is the nature of the meaning given to an activity by a human community, rather than the nature of the activity itself, that takes it into the category of the religious.

Peter Winch appears to be opposing this view when he suggests that it might be possible to, "identify a set of practices as "religious" independently of any beliefs associated with them" [5]. A closer look however reveals what anyone acquainted with Winch's writing would expect, that he is not talking about non-institutional activities. He describes the sort of practice he has in mind as, "an established social practice rather than the behaviour of individuals considered separately... set apart from behaviour associated with everyday practical concerns... in the sense that it is stylized, ruled by conventional forms and perhaps thought of as stemming from long-standing traditions" [6]. What Winch is suggesting is that there are institutions that, although they have a shared meaning, in the sense of an established function in a community, have not yet attracted theoretical justifications in the minds of their users. They do not know, or can not say why they do it. He is not disputing the claim that there are no natural, direct, individual activities that are characterizable as religious.

I do still want to disagree with Winch's suggestion (although I see the disagreement as having neither any easy resolution nor serious consequence for an institutional theory). It is a fact that institutions are frequently used without the participants knowing or understanding, or being able to say, why they do so, but I still find it hard to see how religious, social, magical and aesthetic institutions can be distinguished from one another without some reference to beliefs, even if they are implicit or imputed. Some might feel attracted to the argument that all burial rituals are religious, even if they are performed by elephants. (Winch almost certainly would not.) The force in this argument is the feeling that burial rituals imply belief in life after death. It is precisely their association with beliefs that makes people want to call them religious, even when there is no question of elephants believing anything of the sort. What this example actually demonstrates is the foolishness of imputing beliefs after solely observing what people, or elephants, do.

Winch, in his remarks, emphasizes the social aspects of the practices that can be called religious. As has already been discussed in Chapter 13, symbolic, rule following behaviour can only emerge in a social context. It is for this reason that my disagreement with William James' view of religion as, "the feelings, acts, and experiences of individual men in their solitude" [7] is, in contrast to my disagreement with Winch, radical and indissoluble.

This does not however, as was discussed in Chapter 13, completely rule out the possibility of private religious actions. Having learnt from acquaintance with institutions what the features of a religious institution are, it is possible to recognize these features in rituals that are private, in the sense of not being used by a community but by an isolated individual - what in Chapter 13 were characterized as neuroses.

When we look for religious activities in unfamiliar communities we look for sets of institutions with similar sorts of *meanings* to the institutions that we call religious in our own. We can see how this is done by considering another passage from a William Golding novel.

In *Lord of the Flies* a group of English school boys are marooned on an uninhabited paradise island, but all does not go well. As they struggle with indecision and guilt they start to talk of a beast that stalks the island by night. At one stage in the story they stick the bloody head of a newly killed pig on a pole and leave it in a clearing. What are we to make of this strange action? How would we begin to judge if it is religious?

Without any reference to the shared meaning of this action to the boys we are lost. It could have a secular meaning; they could have done it out of a general playfulness, or to attract the flies away from their food store. Unless we have more clues that help us understand the shared symbolic meaning of the action we cannot recognize it as a religious one.

Golding gives us just such a clue. The boys consider the action appropriate, although perhaps not knowing why they find it so. Jack, their leader, puts it's meaning into words: "This head is for the beast," he says, "It's a gift" [8]. Immediately we recognize the religious: it is an appeasing sacrifice - not a joke, not a lure for insects, but a gift to a malevolent spirit.

When considering the institution of marriage it was noted that people could recognize institutions in other cultures by recognizing the natural roots of the now conventional activity. Can we do the same in the case of religion? Do religious institutions have their roots in any distinguishable set of natural activities or facts about the human condition?

Peter Winch suggests that worship, "is a primitive human response to certain characteristic human situations and predicaments, that it is, to use a phrase of Wittgenstein's, part of the natural history of mankind" [9]. Providing more details to this admirable answer must be speculative, but it is plausible that the roots of religion lie in a particular kind of response to the powerlessness, ignorance and wonder that human beings feel about their natural, social and personal worlds.

It is a fact of being human that, in our natural state, we don't understand where rain comes from and can't make it rain, feel exultant when it arrives after a drought and suffer when it doesn't - that we are ignorant about how best to organize our societies, can't control aggression and greed, even in ourselves, feel ecstatic when our relationships work and hurt when they fail - that we don't know what happens after death but can't avoid it, fear our own end and the loss of those we love and feel grateful when its shadow appears to have receded.

These are some of the facts of our human situation, and communities respond to them in various ways - by pursuing, for instance, scientific knowledge and magic power. The response that we associate most frequently with religions is that of looking for solutions, relief and expression, in associating or identifying with a superhuman, source of wisdom and power - and by invoking, appeasing, interceding, worshipping, serving and obeying it. It is when we see sets of institutions that seem to have meanings related to this sort of response to the biological and psychological facts of the human condition, that we feel inclined to include them in the category of the religious.

People take mates and build families but these natural activities do not regulate a community's concept of marriage. Questions such as: were they married last September?; was that a proper wedding?; is this your wedding ring?; can not be answered by reference to them. These natural activities form the roots, not a basis for the definition of, the socially established institutions of marriage. Dancing before battle increases aggression and solidarity, but the natural activities of jumping and twirling do not regulate a community's concept of the War Dance. Questions such as: did they do the war dance yesterday? do the women join in the war dance? is that the mask used in the war dance? - can not be answered by referring to them. They form the roots of, not the basis for a definition of, a socially established institution.

People find relief from the fear, guilt and suffering caused by ignorance and powerlessness and a way of expressing joy, wonder and gratitude, in natural activities such as acting, chanting, story telling, singing and dressing-up, but these natural activities do not regulate a community's concept of religion. Questions such as: is this a holy place? Was that a religious experience? Is this object sacred? - can not be answered by referring to them. They form the roots of, not a basis for, a definition of a socially established institution.

If the idea of a religious activity is, in any community, an institutional concept, if it is our institutions that regulate our use of the concept, we would expect, in changing, pluralistic societies like our own, to find the use of the concept varied, contentious and to some extent incoherent. I believe we do, and yet its use is still substantially determined by the varied institutions that cohere and continue under the label of religions. People still know what activities are religious, and what religious activities are like, because they know what goes on in the churches, mosques, synagogues and temples of their complex world.

Notes

1.   The nature of institutions as established, symbolic, communal activities, as opposed to natural, direct and

individual activities is discussed in Chapter 14. The use of these words in this section depends upon the definitions established there.

2. The words, "With my body I thee worship," are excluded from the modern Anglican wedding service. On the other hand judges, mayors and Masons still use derivations of the word in some of their titles.

3. William Golding, *The Inheritors*, pp. 31-32.

4. Richard Wollheim taking about the roots of art in, *Art and its Objects*, pp. 117-118. This passage is discussed in Chapter 14.

5. Peter Winch, "Meaning and Religious Language", p. 196.

6. Ibid., pp. 197-198. The other characteristics Winch thinks necessary for claiming some ritualistic behaviour to be religious are that it is, "associated with a sense of wonder and awe at the grandeur and beauty of aspects of the tribe's environment having particular importance in the tribe's life." These seem to me insufficient to distinguish between social, religious and aesthetic institutions.

7. William James, *The Varieties of Religious Experience*, p. 50.

8. William Golding, *Lord of the Flies*, p. 122. This title is interestingly a translation of the Hebrew *Baal Zebub* which in Greek become *Beelzebub* - The Prince of Demons (See e.g. Matthew 12 v.24).

9. Peter Winch, "Meaning and Religious Language", p. 202.

17 Religious experiences

In order to ask questions about how far the concept of a religious experience is an institutional one it is necessary to begin by raising some other questions, for unlike the subject of the last chapters, there is a considerable philosophical literature concerning religious experience. There has been debate about what sort of thing an experience is, as well as what sort of thing a religious experience is. This debate is largely covered in Chapter 8 where the empiricist view of experiences as, "conscious mental goings on", and of religious experiences as the, "private perceptions of spiritual objects", is criticized. In non-philosophical contexts when people speak of religious experiences they do not confine their talk to mental events nor to private perceptions. They refer to a wide variety of events and feelings, insights and encounters.

This chapter will begin by asking: what sorts of things do people call religious experiences? Carole Mayhall, in her book, *From the Heart of a Woman*, asks herself the question: *When* do I experience the Lord as my shepherd? Most often, she decides, in the way he guides and protects her. She tells this story:

> A cloudburst had deluged our area just as I delivered Lynn to a church party about 30 minutes from our home. Starting back, I prayed for guidance whether to go the way I had come - the freeway - or to go back a longer way. God seemed to indicate that the freeway should be avoided.
>
> That was one of the scariest drives of my life. Streets were flooded. My brakes got wet, making it difficult to stop the car; lawns were on fire from

downed power lines, sending sparks crackling into the streets... Because many streets were completely blocked by flooding, I had to go miles out of my way to get home. I finally arrived, exhausted and teary, two hours later...

A news item on the front page of the paper the next day told of a woman and her 12 year old daughter who had attempted the very underpass which led on to the freeway that I would have taken - *at the exact time I would have taken it.* They had driven into 12 feet of water and a passing motorist had to rescue them from their submerged vehicle.

Yes, I had experienced God as my guiding Shepherd, caring for me in very specific ways, on many occasions [1].

This is an account of an event. No seeing, hearing or feeling of anything "spiritual" or out of the ordinary is recounted (except perhaps that she believed God had influenced her decision to avoid the freeway). She had a scary drive, but she saw the event as an experience of answered prayer and of the guidance and protection of God. It was a powerful confirmation of her faith.

In William James' book, *The Varieties of Religious Experience*, we read the following account:

Shall I ever again have any of those prodigious reveries which sometimes came to me in former days? One day, in youth, at sunrise... and again in the mountains under the noonday sun... once more at night upon the shingly shore of the Northern Ocean, my back upon the sand and my vision ranging through the milky way; - such grand and spacious, immortal, cosmogonic reveries, when one reaches to the stars, when one owns the infinite! Moments divine, ecstatic hours; in which our thought flies from world to world, pierces the great enigma, breathes with a respiration broad, tranquil and deep as the respiration of the ocean... instants of irresistible intuition in which one feels one's self great as the universe, and calm as a god... The vestiges they leave behind are enough to fill us with belief and enthusiasm, as if they were visits of the

184

Holy Ghost [2].

In this account the writer does not retell an event but describes a feeling of a certain quality that he has had on several occasions - a feeling that is difficult to describe but that inclines him towards using language with a religious flavour, and inclines him towards believing in God.

Leslie Weatherhead recounts the following experience in his autobiography, *The Christian Agnostic*:

> I could not call myself a mystic, but on half-a-dozen occasions I have had experiences which *for me* made me certain of the reality of some supernatural Entity which, or whom, I label "God"... Vauxhall Station on a murky November Saturday evening is not the setting one would choose for a revelation of God! The third-class compartment was full. I cannot remember any particular thought processes which may have led up to the great moment... But the great moment came... For a few seconds only, I suppose, the whole compartment was filled with light. This is the only way I know in which to describe the moment, for there was nothing to *see* at all. I felt caught up into some tremendous sense of being within a loving, triumphant and shining purpose... A most curious, but overwhelming sense possessed me and filled me with ecstasy. I felt that all was well for mankind... All men were shining and glorious beings who in the end would enter incredible joy... My puny message, if I passed my exams and qualified as a minister, would contribute only an infinitesimal drop to the ocean of love and truth which God wanted men to enjoy, but my message was of the same *nature* as that ocean... In that hour I knew the ministry was the right path for me... An indescribable joy possessed me [3].

This account includes what we might call a *quasi* perception, for although he speaks of light he admits that there was nothing to see. It also includes a powerful feeling of well-being, but the aspect of the experience I want to highlight is the insight Dr. Weatherhead received. He became aware of a truth about the world that gave a new significance to his future work - a new way of looking at and feeling about it. It made him certain of the reality of God and of his vocation.

This last account comes from Alister Hardy's book, *The Spiritual Nature of Man* [4].

> At one time I reached utter despair and went and prayed God for mercy instinctively and without faith in reply. That night I stood with other patients in the grounds waiting to be let into our ward. It was a very cold night with many stars. Suddenly someone stood beside me in a dusty brown robe and a voice said, "Mad or sane you are one of My sheep." I never spoke to anyone of this but ever since it has been the pivot of my life. I realize that the form of the vision and the words I heard were the result of my education and cultural background but the voice though closer than my own heartbeat was entirely separate from me [5].

This account is of a certain sort of perception - a vision. A robed figure is "seen" and a voice is "heard", although there is no suggestion that the *quasi* perception could have been confused with a "real" one. Although distancing themself from the interpretation, the person recounting the story admits that the form of the vision was associated in their mind with a religious figure.

These few examples do not start to encompass the variety of things that people call religious experiences, but they do illustrate some recurring features and suggest some categories.

Experiences of events

These can be immense and communal like the Exodus of the Children of Israel from Egypt. They can cover the whole of a life-time; one of Hardys' contributors says: "As I look back it seems that my whole life has been a religious experience, in the sense that my religious consciousness has grown and developed as inevitably as my body and mind" [6]. They can, on the other hand, be mundane and fleeting. In his novel, *The Idiot*, Dostoevsky tells how his Prince emerged from a religious depression, "I completely recovered from this depression, I remember, one evening at Basel, and the thing that roused me was the braying of a donkey in the market place. I was quite extraordinarily struck with the donkey and for some reason very pleased with it and at once everything in my head seemed to clear up" [7]. They can, on the other hand, be so bizarre as to be frankly incredible [8]. In fact there hardly seems to be any sort of event in which someone, in the context of the feelings it engendered or its result, could not see a special sort of significance that made religious language seem appropriate. A child's recovery from fever is seen as an answered prayer; a cheque in the post as God's providence [9], an enemy's downfall as God's vindication [10], a failed exam as guidance into another career.

Experiences of feelings

Other accounts do not primarily describe events so much as feelings, sometimes of a general, and sometimes of a very specific nature - feelings that have a special significance for the raconteur. James mentions, in the course of his book, the feelings of ecstasy, guilt, release from guilt, joy, happiness, delight, fear, unity with nature, "loss of the self", conflict, power, serenity, safety, rest and freedom. In Alister Hardy's analysis of religious experience he has 20 separate headings under the title of cognitive and affective elements, that include 47 different words describing feelings. These include excitement, nostalgia, indifference and detachment [11]. From the prick of conscience to the depths of moral despair, from the warm glow of a still evening to the ineffable ecstasy of the mystic, it seems that no feeling is too bizarre or too mundane to be seen by someone, in the context of its setting or its result, to have the sort of significance that makes religious language appropriate.

Experiences of insight

People recount, as religious experiences, what we might call sudden knowledge or understanding; problems resolve, things take on a new look, a new meaning, and life takes off in a different direction. Some people claim to receive factual information through mystical experience. James for example states: "It was given to Saint Teresa to see and understand in what wise the Mother of God had been assumed into her place in Heaven" [12]. (This was timely. It is thought Teresa was canonized largely because her visions provided confirmation of the newly declared papal dogma of The Assumption.) James also quotes from Bartoli-Michel who in a quarter-hour of mystical experience claimed that he, "saw and knew more than if I had been many years together at an university. For I saw and knew the being of all things" [13].

However, since one of the characteristics of mystical experiences is their ineffability, it is hard for such claims to be substantiated in practice. It seems more likely that what is generally acquired during mystical experience is a *feeling* of knowing, that either cashes out in terms of things already known, or fails to cash out at all when the experience is over. What endures then, is a changed attitude or intention. Brian Carter worked at the Hardy Institute on reports of, "sudden apprehension or knowledge". He gives two examples:

> (While meditating during a time of emotional stress) I had - for how long I do not know - an intense feeling of having slipped out of time and of knowing in a quite different way from intellectual knowledge. Knowing with all my being what is meant by the concept God is Love. I felt that I had experienced divine love in all its reality and immediacy [14].

> A great inward light seemed to illuminate my thoughts, I experienced a magnificent sensation of arrival, I was filled with joy as though I had just discovered the secret of world peace. I suddenly *knew*. The odd thing was that I did not know what I knew. From then I set out to define it [15].

Carter goes on to suggest that the accounts he studied fell into two groups - those from people who were, "essentially either Christians or theists, whose particular experiences provides them with affirmation of belief and/or supports hope or expectation," and those who, "had little or no time for organized religion or any traditional theistic or Christian beliefs." These latter had, "much greater difficulty in describing the knowledge content of the experience, or could not do so at all" [16].

These examples do not of course give us evidence to rule as false all claims of supernatural knowledge, whether from telepathy, precognition, dreams, or messages from angels. I just note here that, more common than claims of receiving divine information through mystical experiences, is the reporting of old facts arranging themselves in new patterns so that they come to have new meanings.

Experiences of perceptions

The sorts of perceptions that people recount as religious experiences cover all the senses. They range between the normal perceptions of everyday things, that for some reason take on a special meaning, to the admittedly inadequate use of perceptual language for experiences that the raconteur acknowledges contained no normal perceptual objects. In Edward Robinson's anthology of religious experiences, *Living the Questions*, a woman tells how she saw a dead pansy:

> When I was about 37 years old there was another experience which I felt was very much of a religious nature. I was deeply moved by it and have never forgotten it. It was a midsummer afternoon... As I came up the front walk of our house, my eyes wandered over the flower bed... My discontented thoughts were stopped short. I stared for a moment at what I saw... and then I saw it. My whole attention was fixed on it as if nothing else was there. It was a pansy which had gone to seed. It stood there, kind of stiff and dry, its seed pod had opened... It was tilted downwards, so that the seed would fall to the ground. I saw it as a living thing, and for a moment I experienced the law it was so gracefully obeying. I was deeply moved by this. The feeling was of a religious nature. The thoughts were of grateful obedience, of confidence, of faith and of the supreme intelligence which operated in the law I was observing [17].

Others tell of evocative smells when flowers are absent [18], the

189

touch of friends in which is felt the touch of God, and the sensation of being touched when no-one is present [19].

Probably one of the most common types of experience in this category is an indefinable feeling of presence, and whether this really counts as a feeling or a perception is not important; the fact is that some people chose to use perceptual language in retelling such experiences. One of William James' contributors reflects upon such an experience:

> In this ecstasy of mine God had neither form, colour, odour not taste; moreover... the feeling of his presence was accompanied with no determinate localization... The more I seek words to express this intimate intercourse, the more I feel the impossibility of describing the thing by any of our usual images. At bottom the expression most apt to render what I felt is this: God was present, though invisible; he fell under no one of my senses, yet my consciousness perceived him [20].

The answer to our first question: what sorts of things do people call religious experiences?, is therefore: events of every kind, an immense range of feelings and emotions, insights, perceptions involving all the senses and *quasi* perceptions ranging in each case from the quite ordinary and trivial to the unbelievably strange and portentous. In fact it seems to be the case that there is nothing that can be called an experience that can not, by someone, in some context, be described as a religious experience.

What is it about these experiences that make people want to use religious language to describe them? It is in the answer to this question that we shall discover how far the concept of a religious experience is an institutional one - how far people need to be acquainted with the conventions of religious institutions in order to use the concept - how far what counts as a religious experiences is decided by the conventions of particular communities. For an institutional theory of religion to stand it is necessary to demonstrate that the use of the word "religious" is substantially determined by institutions - that there is nothing prior to and independent of the conventions of particular human communities that can have a determining role in regulating its use. I have divided this discussion under three headings.

Standard use

By far the most common use of the adjective "religious" as applied to experience is one in which it is connected with a religion. (In much the same way as we might adapt the word for a set of activities such as "nursing" or "politics" into an adjective - my nursing (or political) experiences.) While the adjective "religious" is notoriously slippery, almost every user of English can name an example of a religion and knows what sort of activities (institutions) are associated with it. Experiences are most commonly called "religious" because they are seen to connect in some way with one of these systems of belief and practice. We could, in these cases, substitute the adjective "Christian" or "Buddhist" or the name of another religion, without changing the meaning.

There are of course many different ways in which this connection can be made. Experiences can be what we might call second-hand, that is we can watch and listen to others engaging in the practices of a religion. This may not be what we immediately think of as a religious experience but we must have some of these second-hand religious experience before we can use the word to name any first-hand religious experiences.

As part of the Alister Hardy research programme, Edward Robinson investigated religious experiences in childhood and several come into this category [21].

A slightly different way of making the connection is to call "religious" some of the things we experience while participating in the practices of a religion. In these cases it is the context or setting of the experience that is decisive in the understanding of it:

> A friend persuaded me to go to Ely Cathedral to hear a performance of Bach's B Minor Mass... I was sitting towards the back of the nave. The Cathedral seemed to be very cold. The music thrilled me... until we got to the great Sanctus. I find this experience difficult to define. It was primarily a warning. I was frightened. I was trembling from head to foot, and wanted to cry... I heard no "voice" except the music; I saw nothing; but the warning was very definite... I was before the Judgement Seat. I was being, "weighed in the balance and

191

found wanting" [22].

Although judgement is a recurring feature in religions, one wonders if the same feeling of sudden fear, experienced in the supermarket, would have been so interpreted, or offered to the research unit as a religious experience.

Thirdly we can connect our experiences with institutional religions by choosing to interpret or describe them in the symbols of such a religion. We can see events in our lives as examples of the providence, guidance or judgement of the Christian God, see our feelings or insights as being directed towards, received from, or being about, the God of the Qur'an, we can interpret our dreams or visions as visions of Krishna or the Virgin Mary.

Hardy recounts the experiences of a man who was alone in a lake-side cottage, agonizing about whether or not to be confirmed in the Anglican Church.

> Everyday throughout the week I prayed and thought. My major prayer was, "Dear Lord, what do you want me to do?" It was a week of coldness and darkness with no indication of any kind - UNTIL on the evening before I was due to return to London I spent several hours by myself sitting on a sofa. I was unaware of time. I then saw with great vividness THE FEET OF OUR LORD some twelve feet from the floor and with that vision was the overwhelming thought of ORDINATION which hitherto had never entered my head.
>   That was the answer to my prayer and in consequence I was ordained... The clarity of this "vision" was to me unmistakable and I owe my vocation to it [23].

How would a vision of floating feet be interpreted by an atheist or Hindu, one wonders [24].

The last connection is with the result of the experience. The accounts that began this section had as a common thread the idea that the experiences led to a confirmation or renewed commitment to a religious faith. In recounting religious experiences people often tell of the events that led to their conversion, or the things that happened during a period of considering, doubting or testing the practices or teachings of a religion. What is it about a feeling of guilt or acceptance that makes it a religious feeling? The fact that it moved someone to seek God, to join the Church or to believe in the Christian gospel are all plausible answers and ones that depend upon the presence of institutional religion.

Interestingly experiences that lead to loss of faith are sometimes put in this category too. William James recounts the, "transition from orthodoxy to infidelity", of the French Philosopher Jouffroy, couched in language so similar to his accounts of conversion to faith that only the result seems to be at variance [25].

Cosmic use

This second group of ways of using the concept of a religious experience is well described by Tim Miles:

> There are three strands of meaning in the word "religion" which I want to distinguish. In the first place a religious person may be thought of as one who believes in God or in some more-than-human power; secondly, he may be thought of as one who performs certain rituals, including participating in particular acts of worship; thirdly, he may be thought of a one who holds certain "cosmic views", i.e. views about the nature and destiny of man [26].

It is this sense of the word "cosmic" that is intended here. Miles says:

> Once the mystifying verbiage is cleared, however, the notion of "religious experience" becomes perfectly intelligible. A person can describe his *religious* experiences - that is, his experiences when he tries to come to terms with cosmic issues - in the same way logically as he can describe, for instance, the experiences which he had last summer in Norway; in neither case does it make sense to ask if his experiences were mental events or if they made him aware of something non-material [27].

People call experiences religious that are connected in some way, not with an institutional religion, but with their personal search for answers to questions about the nature and destiny of human life. It might be thought that this quest is a natural (even individual) activity that occurs prior to human institutions. (It has already been suggested that it is one of the root activities from which religious institutions grow.)

One argument against this thought is that not all the experiences that are connected with this "activity" are considered religious, while many experiences that are not connected with it are. In modern times the "cosmic quest" can lead to Materialism, Scientism, Communism, Humanism etc., and it is only when the quest is connected with some specifically religious answers that an experience is appropriately categorized as religious.

A stronger argument against it is that the search for answers to cosmic questions is always a continuing, communal activity, never a purely personal one.

Quality use

David Hay investigated the religious experiences of post graduate students at Nottingham University in 1972. He records these two accounts: "I believe there is something there, and it is very important to me that it is there, but this has no relation with official Christianity... (it's) something I feel inside me, which I feel seems to be guiding me" [28]. Another contributor talks about an, "immensely powerful benign force" and continues: "I'd say it was an intoxication with the sights, sounds and forces of nature. A feeling of power coming through my body from internal and external sources... I can't distinguish what is divine and what is temporal. It's nothing to do with the Christian God" [29].

These experiences have not been recounted as examples of religious experiences because they have a connection with any orthodox religion. That connection is explicitly denied. Some argue they are put into this category because a recognized quality of the experience seems to make the adjective "religious" appropriate. But is it the case that there is a common quality to the experiences people call religious, and that it is by recognizing this quality that people know that the adjective is appropriate?

This is something that has been quite widely claimed from William James onwards [30]. In his book, *Religion, Values and*

Peak Experiences, Abraham Maslow says:

> The very beginning, the intrinsic core, the essence, the universal nucleus of every known high religion... has been the private, lonely, personal illumination, revelation or ecstasy of some acutely sensitive prophet or seer... It is very likely, indeed almost certain, that these reports, phrased in terms of supernatural revelation, were, in fact, perfectly natural, human peak experiences of the kind that can easily be examined today... to the extent that all mystical or peak experiences are the same in their essence and have always been the same, all religions are the same in their essence and have always been the same... Whatever is different about these illumination can fairly be taken to be localisms both in time and space, and are, therefore peripheral, expendable, not essential [31].

Maslow runs into the same problem as Hardy when he tries to investigate the nature of this experience. He complains: "Many people see organized religion as *the* locus, *the* source, *the* custodian and guardian and teacher of the spiritual life", and adds in a footnote:

> As a matter of fact this identity is so profoundly built into the English language that it is almost impossible to speak of the "spiritual life"... without using the vocabulary of traditional religion. There just isn't any other satisfactory language yet... This makes an almost insuperable problem for the writer who is intent on demonstrating that the common base of all religions is human, natural, empirical and that so-called spiritual values are also naturally derivable. But I have available only a theistic language for this "scientific" job [32].

Hardy says: "Just as science is science in any country of the world, so the fundamental nature of religious experience may be recognized as universal and as the basis of all the world's faiths" [33].

He talks of this universal experience as "spiritual awareness",

awareness of a benevolent "non-physical power", the feeling that there is, "another dimension to life" [34], that there is a spiritual reality, "with which the individual can have communion" [35].

Hardy's book contains reports of precognition, telepathy and clairvoyance, supposed contact with the dead, ghosts and moving Ouija boards. 16 out of the first 3,000 replies Hardy received describe the experience often called "deja vu". Hardy sees this as rather odd: "These experiences cannot usually be considered as in any way religious... They are generally thought, I believe, to have a simple psychological explanation." But, he explains, "Some of those who experience them, however, seem to feel that, like the out-of-the body experiences, they may indicate a non-material side of the everyday world, and so, for them at least, have religious significance" [36]. These experiences we might categorize as weird, in the sense that they are not, to the person recalling them, explicable in terms of scientific theory.

Some people also include in the category of religious experiences, experiences that can be described as mystical states of consciousness.

So we have this family of experiences that people see as having, for them, a religious significance, but do they, as Maslow and Hardy claim, have a recognizable quality by which they can be categorized as religious prior to and independently of, human institutions? R. C. Zaehner takes up the challenge that he sees thrown down by Aldhous Huxley, "and by many more who think like him... that religion is a matter of experience, almost of sensation; that religious experience means "mystical" experience, and that mystical experiences are everywhere and always the same" [37]. He continues:

> There seem to be two very strong objections to such a theory. The first is that few of these authors can or will define what precisely constitutes a mystical experience, and until that is done, we do not really know what we are talking about. The second is that to assert that all mystics speak the same language and convey the same message does not seem to be true even within one particular religious tradition [38].

He examines the radical differences between the Hindu and Christian ways of defining "the unitive experience", and Huxley's descriptions of his experiences under the influence of mescaline, and concludes: "To state, then, or imply, as Huxley does, that his own experience is either identical with or comparable to, either the Christian Beatific Vision or to what Hindus call *sat-cit-ananda*... is to state or to imply an obvious untruth" [39]. He then looks at nature mysticism and finds that the experiences recorded for example by Wordsworth and Tennyson have a quite different quality and meaning from the religious mystics. He concludes: "The mystical state at which the religious man aims is the reverse of the natural mystical experience" [40].

His analysis of the types of mystical experience leads him to conclude that, "there appear to be at least three distinct mystical states which cannot be identical" [41]. He claims there is, "an unbridgeable gulf (between monistic and theistic mysticism) between those who seek God as incomparably greater than oneself... and those who maintain that soul and God are one and the same and all else is pure illusion" [42].

James Bakalar considers the modern phenomena of drug induced religious experience which he says, "raises the difficult question of what is definably religious about personal experiences before they are given form by a doctrine, ritual and community" [43]. The conclusion he comes to is that, "experiences alone, especially individual experiences, do not constitute religion" [44]. Referring to Rudolf Otto's idea of the experience of "the numinous" [45] he notes that Otto says that to make the numinous into religion requires, "schematization by morality and reason," and adds, "It also requires tradition, a discipline, some practice or ritual, and a community or fellowship that allows the sense of the holy to be communicated and transmitted" [46].

Bakalar illustrates his thesis by noting two legal decisions in the United States. Firstly the approval of the use of peyote in the Native American Church (N.A.C.) on the basis of the First Amendment and secondly the decision that the use of marijuana was not part of Leary's religious practice as a Hindu. He comments:

> The rationale is that the N.A.C. is an organized traditional religion in which the use of the drug is essential to the form of worship... If religion reduced to individual feelings and ideas tends to lose its specifically religious character, the tendency becomes particularly noticeable when drugs are

197

involved.   So the courts have pronounced that at least this one form of religious or numinous experience will not be legally permitted except within a traditional community and discipline.   Although the courts expressly refuse to define what qualifies as religious, the practical effect of their decisions is that as long as drugs are involved, religion will be defined by institutions and a shared way of life, not by any individual experience or conviction [47].

The various altered states of consciousness that people call mystical, as well as not being uniform, are not necessarily interpreted in religious terms.   Many accounts of mystical experience are retold in the language of agnosticism or atheism. Zaehner, for example, quotes the following account from Richard Jefferies.   From his, "intense communion with nature" he concludes, "There is no god in nature... It is a force without a mind. I wish to indicate something more subtle than electricity, but absolutely devoid of consciousness and with no more feeling than the force which lifts the tides" [48]. Zaehner concludes that the only method we have of judging between divine and natural mysticism, between the ecstatic conviction of St. Teresa and that of a lunatic, is from the results - the experiences of the lunatic have no permanence while that of St. Teresa, "effected a total transformation and sanctification of character" [49].   Teresa became a saintly Christian.
   The fact is that the experiences mentioned in this category can be, and frequently are, experienced in a purely secular context and interpreted in purely secular terms, while many experiences widely accepted as genuinely religious are neither scientifically inexplicable, nor do they involve unusual states of consciousness.
   To say that people know which of their experiences are religious by recognizing a mystical or weird quality about them makes nonsense of the way the expression is used by ordinary believers, who see God in the whole of his natural creation, interpret day by day events as examples of his providence, find his grace in bread and wine and meet him in the simple kindness of another.   It implies that these mundane experiences are not *really* religious, while water-divining, telepathy, lunacy and drug induced experiences are.
   The Hardy research team is unperturbed by these facts; they overlook the way language works and the role it plays in making

sense of, categorizing, remembering and recalling experiences. They do not ask why or how people chose which experiences to send them. They are trying to elicit accounts of a sort of experience recognizable by its quality - an awareness of a spiritual world - but the nature of that quality is indeterminate - as is evident from the miscellany of accounts they receive. Some tell of unusual states of consciousness; some of weird experiences the teller cannot understand or explain; some tell of experiences that occurred in a religious setting or led to, or from, allegiance to orthodox religious beliefs or practices, or to some answers to cosmic questions that have some religious characteristics; some are mundane experiences interpreted by means of the symbols of a religion, or retold using religious language. The variety of the *quality* of these experiences is almost infinite. They can be intense, momentous, mundane or fleeting; they are experiences of power or gentleness, feelings of fear or guilt, joy, confidence, courage, serenity or dependence; they bring peace in anxiety, harmony in conflict, challenge in torpor. They do not by any stretch of the imagination have a common quality or a sufficiently coherent family of qualities [50] for the use to which these empiricists wish to put them.

If a belief in a spiritual world that can be perceived by a special sort of perception is rejected, as the criticism of the empiricist position in Chapter 8 advocated, any coherence in the quality of this set of experiences disappears. If there are any common themes (light, love, mercy, justice, righteousness) these reflect not the nature of the spiritual world, but people's understanding of the nature of divinity, which may not correspond to any orthodox beliefs, but is necessarily continuous with and substantially determined by the institutions of their culture. If we imagine a community with a very different divinity (capricious, dark, immoral and cruel), we can imagine a very different selection of experiences being recounted to their version of the Religious Experience Research Unit.

Our conclusion must be that there is no experience which, by its quality alone, is necessarily religious. Any experience of any quality can be retold either in religious or in secular language. The Religious Experience Research Unit want to hear about a certain kind of experience, whatever sort of language the raconteur chooses to use; the results of this incoherent quest turn out to illustrate very clearly the institutional nature of the concept of religious experience.

Conclusions

Within a religious tradition there are guidelines as to what counts as an authentic religious experience. Alasdair MacIntyre asks how people know their vision is a vision of the Virgin Mary [51]. Devout Catholics do not have problems in recognizing her; they are aware of these guidelines and if the authenticity of their vision is questioned, there are further tests that can be applied and questions that can be asked. The R.E.R.U. received many accounts from people within such religious traditions (almost all Christian so far but it is trying to widen its net).

In Britain in the 1980s and 90s, however, most people are not committed to a religious tradition in this way, nor use its ways of understanding and talking about their experiences. What for them counts as a religious experience? This is a form of the question: yes, but apart from the rules of any particular community, what *really* counts as a religious experience? The question, if the concept is an institutional one, has no answer. It is like asking: yes, but apart from the rules of particular communities what really counts as getting married, or being made president? We only can learn how to use these sorts of concepts from acquaintance with particular institutions and beyond them, the concept of a marriage or a president has no definite or coherent use.

The miscellany of experiences that arrive at the R.E.R.U. shows that, for many people in our society, the concept of a religious experience has no definite or coherent use. Outside religious communities there are no explicit rules about how the concept is to be used. But even the most secular of people are acquainted with the beliefs and practices of religious institutions; they know the sorts of things religious people do and say. We could say they have a concept of divinity, or perhaps of spirituality, derived from the religious institutions they are acquainted with.

This is the common thread that runs through the R.E.R.U. material. Recognizing an experience as religious requires the possession of a concept of divinity; seeing, hearing or feeling the presence of God are things that can only be experienced by people who know what a communication from God is like. And people can only learn what God is like and how he interacts with people, from their acquaintance with religious institutions. In societies like this people have varied, individual, even idiosyncratic ideas about religious matters, but these are substantially determined by religious institutions. People also call religious, experiences that they connect with the quest to find answers about the nature and destiny of human life, but this quest does not necessarily terminate in religious answers and is always part of an ongoing communal activity.

But does an institutional analysis of religious experience reflect what religious believers themselves say about their experiences? I believe that it accords better with orthodox Christianity than an empiricist analysis. An institutional analysis does not imply that God does not *really* communicate with people, but that it is only possible to hear God speaking if we have first heard about him - as Paul says in the letter to the Romans, "How can they believe in the one of whom they have not heard? And how can they hear without someone preaching to them?" [52]. Neither does it raise difficulties for innovative religious experiences, for aspects of culture are not isolated from one another. Although substantially determined by our experiences of religious institutions, a wide range of experiences can affect our understanding of the concept of divinity. (See for example the effect of the feminist movement on modern theology.) Thus changing social and historical situations can change our view of God and our views about which experiences count as communications from him. (See e.g. the case study on George Fox in Chapter 6.)

An orthodox (and institutional) Christian view of religious experience is well expressed in George Herbert's hymn:

> Teach me, my God and King,
> In all things Thee to see;
> And what I do in anything,
> To do it as for Thee.
>
> A man that looks on glass,
> On it may stay his eye;
> Or, if he pleaseth, through it pass,
> And then the heaven espy [53].

Notes

1.   Carole Mayhall, *From the Heart of a Woman*, pp. 28-29.

This extract is used by permission of Nav Press.

2.   William James, *The Varieties of Religious Experience*, pp. 380-381, (Taken from Ameil's, *Journal In Time*, i. 43-44.)

3.   Alister Hardy, *The Spiritual Nature of Man*, p. 53, (Taken from Leslie Weatherhead, *The Christian Agnostic*.) This and the other extacts from *The Spiritual Nature of Man* in this chapter are by permission of Oxford University Press.

4.   Chapter 8 contains a critical discussion of Hardy's philosophical assumptions and the use he makes of the accounts of experience the Religious Experience Research Institute (R.E.R.U.) in Oxford gathers. These accounts are nevertheless a useful source of examples of the sort of experiences that people choose to put into this category - of the way they use the concept of religious experience.

5.   Alister Hardy, *The Spiritual Nature of Man*, p. 91.

6.   Ibid., p. 70.

7.   Dostoevsky, *The Idiot*, p. 82.

8.   Alister Hardy, *The Spiritual Nature of Man*, p. 151 has, for example, an account of an experience of, "a beam passing between our eyes and also a third eye in the middle of our foreheads," that apparently lasted for, "about two hours".

9.   Ibid., p. 66.

10.   See, *Journals of George Fox*, John Nickalls (ed.) pp. 504-505. Fox lists the ill fortunes which overtook his enemies. He concludes, "When I came into the county again all these aforesaid were dead and ruined in their estates and several others of our persecutors whom the Lord blasted and ruined; and though I did not seek to execute the law upon them for their acting contrary to their own laws against me, yet the Lord had executed his vengeance upon them."

11.   Alister Hardy, *The Spiritual Nature of Man*, p. 27.

12.   William James, *The Varieties of Religious Experience*, p. 397.

13.   Ibid., p. 396 fn.

14.   Alister Hardy, *The Spiritual Nature of Man*, p. 109.

15.   Ibid., p. 110.

16.   Ibid., pp. 109-110. These comments of Carter's display his

unfounded assumptions both that there is a "knowledge content" in this kind of experience and that something comparable is going on in both these groups of people.

17. Edward Robinson (ed.), *Living the Questions*, pp. 106-107.
18. Alister Hardy, *The Spiritual Nature of Man*, p. 43.
19. Ibid., p. 42.
20. William James, *The Varieties of Religious Experience*, p. 83.
21. See, for example, Edward Robinson, *The Original Vision*, pp. 97-99. "I was certainly influenced by the services in the Synagogue... there was an excellent choir; the music they sang in Hebrew used to stir me deeply."
22. Alister Hardy, *The Spiritual Nature of Man*, p. 85.
23. Ibid., pp. 33-34.
24. One wonders too if they would have such a vision at all, for it is not the case that Protestants and Hindus have visions of Mary and think it is some other woman.
25. William James, *The Varieties of Religious Experience*, pp. 181-182.
26. T. Miles, *Religious Experience*, p. 18.
27. Ibid., p. 23. These extracts from *Religious Experience* are used by permission of Macmillan Ltd.
28. Alister Hardy, *The Spiritual Nature of Man*, p. 147.
29. Ibid., p. 149.
30. See, for example, William James, *The Varieties of Religious Experience*, pp. 480-481.
31. Abraham Maslow, *Religion, Values, and Peak-Experiences*, pp. 19-20.
32. Ibid., p. 4.
33. Alister Hardy, *Science, Religion and World Unity*, p. 1.
34. Alister Hardy, *The Spiritual Nature of Man*, p. 1.
35. Ibid., p. 132. For a book length, but still unconvincing, exposition of this thesis see Daniel Goleman, *The Varieties of the Meditative Experience*.
36. Alister Hardy, *The Spiritual Nature of Man*, p. 38.
37. R. C. Zaehner, *Mysticism Sacred and Profane*, pp. 26-27.
38. Ibid., p. 27. This extract is used by permission of Oxford University Press.

39. Ibid., p. 33.
40. Ibid., p. 149.
41. Ibid., p. 168.
42. Ibid., p. 204.
43. James Bakalar, "Social and Intellectual Attitudes towards Drug Induced Religious Experience", p. 45.
44. Ibid., p. 57.
45. See Rudolf Otto, *The Idea of the Holy*.
46. James Bakalar, "Social and Intellectual Attitudes towards Drug Induced Religious Experiences", p. 57.
47. Ibid pp. 62-63. Several papers in Steven T. Katz (ed.), *Mysticism and Philosophical Analysis*, add to the argument that mystical experiences are not of a uniform quality.
48. Richard Jefferies, *The Story of my Heart*, pp. 81-82, quoted in R. C. Zaehner, *Mysticism Sacred and Profane*, p. 48.
49. R. C. Zaehner, *Mysticism Sacred and Profane*, p. 105.
50. Ludwig Wittgenstein pointed out that phenomena do not have to have one thing in common to make the use of the same word for all of them coherent. *Philosophical Investigations*, I paras. 65. ff. The use of the expression "religious experience" is perfectly in order in normal, common usage. This demonstration that there is no common quality merely establishes the incoherence of the empiricist's claim that its use *is* substantially determined by a common quality.
51. Alasdair MacIntyre, "Visions", p. 259.
52. Romans 10 v. 14.
53. George Herbert (1593-1633), *The Elixir*.

18 Objections and replies 1: Essentialism and understanding

Introduction

An institutional theory of religion, by seeking to say something about the nature of religion, and by giving precedence to cultural processes and the products of human communities, may attract a variety of, sometimes incompatible, criticisms.

Such a theory may seem to imply an essentialist approach, or a strong form of naturalism, or a strong form of relativism. If these inferences are well-founded, an institutional theory is either open to criticism or in need of further defence. If it implies that we can give an essentialist definition of religion, it is open to the criticism that the terms in which religion is understood in an institutional theory are not sufficiently rigorous to be used in this way. If it implies that religious believers do not believe in absolute truth and divine revelation or that such beliefs have no meaning for them, it is made false by facts that are too obvious to need rehearsing. If it implies that believers are wrong to hold such beliefs it is necessary philosophically to defend a strong form of naturalism and a strong relativism about religion.

This chapter will argue that all these inferences are unfounded.

Essentialism and understanding

Institutional theories in general seem to attract the criticism of essentialism. One of the strongest and most frequently voiced denunciations of institutional theories of art is that the question they appear to answer is one that is not worth asking [1]. Since the things we regard as art do not make up a natural class, trying to define art in term of what is essential to it is, as Kendall L. Walton put it, "a useless and uninteresting" task [2].

Such a charge has never had the same impact in relation to religion and, even in the case of art, the charge of essentialism has been somewhat misdirected and the term "institutional theory" somewhat abused.

In some senses the quest for an institutional theory of either art or religion can be seen as a response to the bankruptcy of the essentialist project - a turn away from a quest for a common nature towards a quest for greater understanding. Richard Wollheim's essay, *Art and its Objects*, for instance, which he vigorously insists is not an attempt to set up an institutional theory [3] (in order to avoid the charge of essentialism), undeniably is an attempt to see how an examination of the institutional character of art illuminates its nature and its processes [4].

As far as this project is concerned it has been stated [5] that both the characteristics of institutions and the way language works, make any of the essentialist's aims pointless and misleading. The empiricist's emphasis on the priority of experience in religion and others' emphasis on the priority of language, have not traditionally been interpreted as exercises in creating essentialist definitions, but as exercises in understanding. A theory, therefore, that emphasizes the role of institutions in religion, and rather than distinguish religion from everything else, stresses what it has in common with other human activities, can with little difficulty it is hoped, be interpreted in the same spirit.

Notes

1. For a discussion of these criticisms of institutional theories of art see Chapter 12.
2. Kendall L. Walton, A review of George Dickie's, "Art and the Aesthetic: an Institutional Analysis", p. 100.
3. Richard Wollheim, "The Institutional Theory of Art", *Art and its Objects*, p. 157.
4. See Richard Wollheim, *Art and its Objects*. Paras. 45. ff. discuss art as, "a form of life".
5. See Chapter 14.

19 Objections and replies 2: Relativism and truth

The subject of relativism is a minefield of misunderstanding. There are so many different kinds of relativism, and words like "relative", "truth", "fact", "reality" etc. are open to such a variety of different uses that great care needs to be taken in defining how they are being used on each particular occasion.

I shall start by asking what sort of relativism an institutional theory of religion implies and then go on to ask whether it is compatible with the absolute truth claims that are so characteristic of religious belief systems.

An institutional theory of religion states that religions are aspects of culture, that what is to be considered authentic and significant in religion is substantially determined, in each community, by its institutions. The fact that religious institutions can be radically different from one community to another suggests, and experience confirms, that the set of propositions held to be true by one religious community can be radically different from, and mutually incompatible with, those held by another.

Religions involve, as well as other things, language systems, ways of thinking and speaking, rules for constructing arguments, assessing evidence, interpreting and describing experiences and giving reasons, along with rules for the use of such words as "genuine", "real", "good", "true", "objective", "proved", etc. These systems substantially determine both how experiences are to be interpreted and how arguments are to be constructed (what is to be believed, on what grounds). They determine what counts as a true proposition within the system.

A Christian wants to know if her sins are truly forgiven. She is pointed to Jesus' promises, and demonstrations of his power to forgive sins in the Gospels, to Paul's arguments about the effectiveness of Christ's atoning sacrifice and ways of appropriating its effects and to evidence of the presence of the Holy Spirit in her life.

A Hindu wants to know if it is true that his recent experience of Krishna's help was genuine. He is pointed to the *Bhagavad Gita* and other Hindu scriptures and asked to compare his experience and its effects in his life with these authentic appearances of Krishna.

This sort of evidence and these sorts of reasons and arguments are not part of the cognitive resources of a non-believer. They just would not use those words in that way. They can see that they may be reasons for *her*, as a Christian, to believe that her sins are forgiven, or for *him*, as a Hindu, to believe that his experience of Krishna was genuine, but not that either statement is *true* in any way that they want to use the word in relation to themselves.

If our institutions substantially determine how we experience the world, what we can say about it and how we construct reasons for believing which propositions are true, truth in religion is, in this sense, relative; what are reasons and arguments for the Christian are not reasons and arguments for the Hindu, or the Muslim.

But religious believers and non-believers use the word "true" in another way. They claim that what they believe is not relatively, but absolutely true - that it corresponds in some way to the way things stand, independently of what anyone sees, thinks or believes. Monotheistic religions characteristically contain just such beliefs.

If an institutional theory of religion implies that such beliefs are not held or have no meaning to those who hold them, then it implies something that is false. If it implies that such beliefs are necessarily false, or in some other way intellectually unreasonable, then this needs to be philosophically defended.

But nothing that has been said in the setting up of this theory has suggested any such implications. That people's religious beliefs are substantially determined by the religious institutions in their culture implies nothing about the content nor the legitimacy of such beliefs. It therefore remains to argue that the sort of cognitive relativism of religious truth that it does imply (as described above) is not incompatible with the making of absolute truth claims.

I shall begin by asking what is relative to the cognitive systems we inherit from our culture? And the answer is - our perception, our experiences and our interpretations and descriptions of them, our concepts, our thinking and feeling, our ways of arguing, our ways of constructing reasons, what we count as genuine and objective, as evidence and proof, our sense of what is possible and what is real, our apprehension of facts - all these are substantially determined by the cognitive system we inherit from our culture and share with our community. They are culturally relative.

What then is not relative to our cognitive systems? The world that is not relative to our ways of thinking and talking is difficult to think or speak of, but it is a mistake to think that it is, therefore, non-existent. A useful word for it is the technical word "noumenal" (as opposed to "phenomenal"). The noumenal world is the world as it is in itself, independent of any human beings' perception, thought, or reasoning system. It is the absolutely real; facts about it are absolute facts. Absolute truth claims, like those we find in monotheistic religions, purport to be claims about this world. But can such claims have any meaning and can we ever be justified in making them?

There are basically two problems about absolute truth claims. Firstly there is the problem of whether propositions expressed in human language systems can identify possible facts in the noumenal world. For a proposition to identify an absolute fact its words must correspond in some way to objects and relationships in the noumenal world, but we have no guarantee that they do so, since our perception of objects and relationships is determined by our cognitive systems. Propositions are, on the whole, not even very good at identifying possible facts in the phenomenal world, although utterances (propositions in use) do this better. Since God is not, in most traditions, even considered to be an object, there are special difficulties in attempting, with our words and sentences, to identify God as he is in himself, rather than God as we experience him.

Secondly, if we think we have successfully identified a possible absolute fact with our proposition, we still have the problem of having access to the noumenal world to check what is the case. For, as we have seen, our access to absolute facts is curtailed and distorted by our cognitive systems.

These two problems do not, however, combine to make absolute truth claims meaningless. We know what an absolute truth claim entails even if we do not know whether this particular proposition identifies a possible or an actual fact in the noumenal world. The difficulty of access does not rule out the possibility that it does both, only that we could never know for certain that it does. Absolute truth claims, therefore, make perfect sense.

It is also easy to overstate the difficulty of access to the noumenal world, for it is a factor in our perception and it does have a causal effect on our cognitive systems. The purpose of a cognitive system is to help us understand, organize and live successfully in our world, and cognitive systems are constructed, compared and chosen in relation to their effectiveness in these respects. One might for example compare the success of the belief that pain can and should be alleviated by medical treatment with the failure of the belief that it is an illusion.

Absolute truth claims are not meaningless, but can we ever be justified in making them? In order for a rational life to be pursued it is necessary that some propositions are held to be absolutely true. Joseph Runzo (in his book *Reason, Relativism and God*) although committed to a strong cognitive relativism concedes that, because the nature of truth, meaning and knowledge acquisition are so fundamental to rational enquiry, what he calls epistemological relativism, "would seem to undermine rational discourse itself" [1]. He continues by saying that rational discourse depends on the assumption that fundamental canons of rationality are not mere relative truths, and comments: "Since the whole purpose of talking about the relativity of truth and knowledge... is to arrive at a rational understanding of one's universe, the very concerns which give rise to and undergird relativism presuppose that not all truth is relative" [2].

He suggests that, "At least the law of non-contradiction must hold in all possible worlds, irrespective of particular conceptual schemes, for it is itself a necessary condition of there being any conceptual schema and any possible worlds" [3]. It is not only rational but, "only coherent... to *treat* one's own view of the nature and criteria of truth, of semantic meaning, and of knowledge acquisition as being, if true, absolutely true" [4].

This principle of treating some propositions as absolutely true for the sake of continuing to pursue a rational life needs to be extended beyond the fundamental canons of rationality [5]. For any cognitive system there are some propositions which so undergird the system that they must be held to be absolutely true if the system is not to be effectively annihilated. To submit them to serious and prolonged questioning is to give up that way of thinking and, unless one's cognitive life is to disintegrate entirely, to take up another way of thinking, undergirded by a different set of absolutely held propositions.

Cognitive commitment is then an essential part of functioning as a rational being. The choices we make as to where to put that commitment, since they cannot be made on a strictly rational level, have to be made on pragmatic grounds, guided by our, albeit distorted, interaction with the noumenal world.

It is good at this point to be able to return to William James. Entwined with the empiricism that I have rejected is James' suggestion of a reasonable form of epistemological pragmatism. "Our passional nature not only lawfully may, but must decide," he says, to take action towards believing one of several options open to us, if the option we take is living (in the sense of meaningful and tempting), forced (in the sense that we cannot avoid making some choice) and momentous (as opposed to trivial), and if it cannot be decided on intellectual grounds, "for to say under such circumstances, "Do not decide but leave the question open" is itself a passional decision just like the decision yes or no, and is attended with the same risk of losing the truth" [6].

There is, I would suggest, nothing special about religious truth claims. Some of them are relative, (Taking communion on Sunday gives you strength for the whole week); some are absolute, (There is no god but Allah and Muhammad is his prophet.) Both of these sorts of truth claims make sense in exactly the same way as secular truth claims, which can also be either relative or absolute. For all truth claims are expressed by means of a human language system and all reasons for believing are internal to some system of reasons; while in all systems, religious or secular, absolute truth claims are held out of grammatical rather than logical necessity.

But this does not mean that it is equally reasonable to make any truth claim or to commit oneself to any belief system. We use a variety of reason-systems at once and they overlap and can be assessed and compared in terms of each other, in terms of how wide a range of social activities and experiences they help us understand and control, and in terms of what we see to be the general demands of rationality. As long as some of our beliefs are held absolutely at any time, others can be questioned as we follow the pull towards cognitive integrity.

Some belief systems - because they are consistent with the basic canons of rationality and with a number of the other reason-systems we currently use, because they are wide ranging in application and seem useful in making sense of our phenomenal world, and because they give us answers to the questions and problems that present themselves as the most pressing - are more reasonable to hold than others, that are narrow in application, distant from logic, incompatible with the other systems we use and irrelevant to the problems of our daily lives.

Religious beliefs do, however, have a characteristic feature, although it is by no means a necessary or an exclusive feature. They tend to become central to a person's life and so to dominate their thinking and behaviour. They become then not just a part of their total reasoning system, that can be rearranged and repositioned without a great deal of energy, but the foundation of a whole life. They are, however, still the focus of faith rather than knowledge, as Runzo says, "The risk of faith is that our human truth claims do not correctly refer to the noumenal God. The commitment of faith includes the trust that they do" [7].

Notes

1. Joseph Runzo, *Reason, Relativism and God*, p. 40.
2. Ibid., p. 43.
3. Ibid., p. 44.
4. Ibid., p. 46.
5. Joseph Runzo goes on to make this point, pp. 155 ff.
6. William James, *The Will to Believe*, p. 19.
7. Joseph Runzo, *Reason, Relativism and God*, p. 258.

20 Objections and replies 3: Naturalism and revelation

There are again a great many forms and varieties of naturalism and of criticisms naturalist philosophers make against religions. I will begin by asking what sort of naturalism an institutional theory of religion implies, and then ask if it is in any way compatible with the concept of divine revelation, which is characteristic of the world's most successful religions and inimical to a strong form of naturalism.

An institutional theory of religion states that religions are aspects of culture - that what is to be considered authentic and significant in religions is substantially determined in each community by its institutions. This supplies what is, in one use of the word, a naturalistic explanation for the phenomena of religions, that is, an explanation that depends on reasoning from evidence derived from people's experience of the natural world. Religious activities, beliefs and institutions are generated and develop in human communities as they respond to their natural and social environment.

The concept of revelation, prevalent in a major section of the world's religions, implies that there is a source of knowledge that, in some ways, transcends the natural world. The creator, or sustainer, of the natural world reveals himself - communicates with human beings in ways that make it possible for them to respond. If the possibility of people holding such beliefs and finding some meaning in them, is ruled out by the sort of naturalism that an institutional theory implies, it is made false by the facts. If an institutional theory implies that such beliefs are necessarily false or inherently unreasonable such a strong form of naturalism needs a philosophical defence.

The institutional theory suggested in this thesis, however, contains no implications about the content or legitimacy of people's religious beliefs. The fact that an institutional theory provides a naturalistic explanation for the phenomenon of religions may seem, on its own, to imply that there can be no external reality beyond the lives and minds which figure in this explanation or beyond the natural world, which inspires and shapes these activities, beliefs and institutions; but it does no such thing. It does not simply follow from the fact that there are naturalistic explanations of a phenomenon that are satisfactory in their own terms, that there are not, in addition, true, non-naturalistic explanations.

Some naturalists, however, have another charge against religions, for they demand not only that acceptable explanations must depend on reasoning from experience of the natural world, but also that they must be expressed in terms of categories and concepts that refer to objects and events that we can observe, or perceive, in the natural world. They insist, for example, that we may not infer beyond the world to a supernatural cause, creator, sustainer, redeemer etc. on the ground that such an inference is logically unjustifiable [1]. An institutional theory implies that religious believers do make just this kind of inference, but on the question of whether such inferring is or is not philosophically justifiable it has nothing to say. It implies neither that it is nor that it is not.

An institutional theory thus defends a kind of methodological naturalism without prejudicing the terms of further understanding. The advantage of this is that it thereby avoids the impasse between believers and unbelievers created by the theories it rejects.

An institutional theory of religion in fact saves religions from the charge that they are unacceptably non-naturalistic in the sense that they are responses to quasi-sensory experiences of another, "spiritual", world. Our investigation of religious experiences showed that it was neither necessary nor correct to view religious experience in this way. If there is a God who reveals himself, he does it through, or in, the natural world of sensory experience. Religious activities and beliefs are naturalistic in the sense that they are attempts to find explanations for the course of our normal sensory experience. The only God we could know is the God self-revealed in the only world we know.

What then are the implications of an institutional theory of religion for an understanding of the concept of revelation? It does not imply that there is no possibility of a source of revelation that is, in a sense, beyond the natural world, but it rejects the idea that such communication characteristically comes in a form of private mysticism - the quasi-perception of another, spiritual, world. If God reveals himself it is in, or through, our normal sensory experience of the only world we know. An institutional theory also emphasizes the fact that cultural training is an essential precursor to recognizing and responding to divine revelation.

These implications may cause problems for a traditional philosophical understanding of how God could, or could not, communicate with his creatures; but the gods of philosophy are not always the same as the gods of religion. The biblical, rather than the patristic or medieval deity, is not, for instance, the utterly transcendent, impassive, immutable, timeless God that Kai Nielsen finds so difficult to comprehend [2]; he is intimately involved with, and affected by, his people's actions and decisions, and communicates with them, not in moments of private mysticism, but through the events of history, interpreted to the community by the prophets.

The idea of the physical embodiment of cultural entities explored by J. Margolis [3] in relation to works of art (and applied to religious experiences in Chapter 17) will help us here. People and works of art can, Margolis says, be recognized as having two sets of properties - one set is identified as the properties of a physical object, the other is recognized as the properties of a culturally emergent entity. The relationship between the two sets of properties he characterizes as embodiment. Margolis draws an analogy with signalling. To recognize a signal within a bodily movement we must be conversant with the conventions of a particular culture that we share with the signaller, for signalling can only occur only in a cultural context (like works of art and persons). To identify an act of signalling we need to identify a suitable event that by reference to an appropriate tradition or rule or custom, may be taken as embodying it. Cultural aliens are puzzled, seeing only the physical event and not the culturally emergent one embedded in it.

This idea illumines not only the concept of a religious experience but also the concept of revelation. For the acts and the words of God are culturally emergent entities, that people find embedded in historical events.

This institutional analysis of revelation is again more in line with a biblical view of revelation, and with usual Christian practice than the empiricist analysis. Billy Graham, in his evangelistic methods, may seem to assume that cultural training can be short-cut and people step from unbelief to belief in the instant of "a decision". But a closer scrutiny of the methods of his organization and the way it has developed over the years in response to its results, shows that it has moved more and more towards an emphasis on pre- and post-decision enculturization as the most effective means of making Christians [4].

The Bible does not represent God as revealing himself in a cultural vacuum. Revelation is progressive and to a community. The knowledge of God's nature and plan for mankind grows step by step, like an ongoing dialogue between God and the community of Israel. God is characteristically introduced as, "the God of your fathers" [5]. In the New Testament the revelation has the same continuity with the past; who Jesus was, had to be understood in terms of past revelations, and then spread by God's new community - the Church.

The view of revelation that is incompatible with an institutional theory of religion is the one already rejected, that God reveals himself to isolated individuals in a cultural vacuum via a sort of private mysticism - a view much discussed by philosophers [6] but hard to find in the Bible.

The biblical view of revelation - that God leaves trails of signals through nature and history (through the normal sensory experiences of individuals) that must be recognized and interpreted within the framework of a community's growing understanding (its scriptures) [7] - is characteristic of the world's revealed religions. It accords well with an institutional theory, and its implication that religious experiences are culturally emergent entities embedded in the normal experiences of encountering objects and events in the natural world.

Whether an institutional theory of religion is or is not seriously in error, does not seem materially to affect the debate about the preference for naturalistic or non-naturalistic explanations. It seems to me there remains the same freedom to prefer the more intellectually rigorous, but narrow and drab, explanations of the naturalist [8] or the more satisfying and comprehensive, but perhaps mysterious, explanations of the religious believer, or even

216

the hybrid explanations that try, not altogether satisfactory, to hold the two together [9].

Each position requires taking a metaphysical position of some sort. And this can be seen as the result of attempting to decide, which explanations seem best to fit our varied sensory experiences, including the ones which seem, even to the most convinced naturalist [10] to be pleading for some concept of transcendence of the world.

Notes

1. For an example of this sort of argument see Kai Nielsen, *An Introduction to the Philosophy of Religion.*
2. Ibid.
3. J. Margolis, "Works of art as physically embodied and culturally emergent entities", p. 187.
4. See Peter Brierley, *What Happened at Mission '89?*
5. See, for example, Exodus 3 v.6.
6. Probably best expressed by Alister Hardy in, *The Spiritual Nature of Man*, but also found in Anthony O'Hear, *Experience, Explanation and Faith* and Alasdair MacIntyre "Visions", *New Essays in Philosophical Theology.*
7. As expressed in, for example, Psalm 19 vs.1-4, Acts 14 v.17, Romans 1 v.18 and 2 v.14 and 15.
8. For example, Kai Nielsen, *An Introduction to the Philosophy of Religion.*
9. For example, P. F. Strawson, *Skepticism and Naturalism*, S. Alexander, *Space, Time and Deity*, or even Paul Tillich, *Systematic Theology.*
10. Nielsen does not deny that such experiences exist. See, *An Introduction to the Philosophy of Religion*, p. 151, but adds (with prejudice?) that we make, "a deliberate category mistake" if we seek non-naturalistic explanations, "to express what we antecedently feel". p. 153.

21 A summary of the argument and some conclusions

A summary of the argument

This book opened with an observation - that the proposers of two incompatible theories of religion (William James and Alasdair MacIntyre), when confronting the phenomenon of innovation in religion, invoke the same historical character as an exemplar.

A closer examination of both the theories and their implications for innovation in religion immediately raise problems, which are only reinforced by viewing contributions to the debate from other people working from an empiricist base and other people who stress the priority of language in religion.

MacIntyre's argument against the principle of religious experiences being the source of religious concepts, based on Wittgenstein's work, is disastrous to James. But his characterization of religions as isolated and arbitrary rule-following systems also leads him into problems with radical innovation. His own solution - that innovators make one of their own experiences a criterion by which further experiences can be tested - fails to resolve the problems.

Richard Swinburne, who attempts to refute MacIntyre's position with talk of private perceptions and private objects fails in his project. Because of the special nature of religious concepts it is necessary that people are already acquainted with a concept of divinity if they are to recognize the divine in their experiences. The problems Alister Hardy's research unit in Oxford meets when it tries to apply empiricist assumptions to an investigation into the nature of religious experiences serves to support this conclusion.

Peter Winch also enters into debate with Alasdair MacIntyre about the possibility of radical innovation in religion. He talks about internal development within rule-following systems, the open character of rules and the two-way relationship between practice (socially established rituals) and theory in religion, but continues to press the isolated and arbitrary aspects of rule-following behaviour.

In his early work, D. Z. Phillips' emphasis on the exclusively internal role of theology, the exclusively expressive role of religious language and the isolation of religious beliefs from external justifications, does nothing to resolve any of the problems. However in later writing Phillips moves towards a resolution by proposing that we see religious rites and practices themselves as "language-games", that can interact with religious discourse and that can change in response to changing events and activities.

An historical case study of George Fox, the chosen exemplar of both William James and Alasdair MacIntyre, throws some light on the problems related to innovation in religion. The story quite dramatically fails to exemplify either James' or MacIntyre's theory of innovation. Fox was trained in the use of religious concepts, which he did not reject as a result of private experiences of a "spiritual world", nor did he coin new concepts to name the things he had experienced. He rejected the religious authorities of his day, in the company of many of his contemporaries, as an intelligible response to the general crisis of authority thrown up by their historical circumstances. His lasting contribution to the history of religions was not the setting up any of his own experiences as a criterion of authenticity or value, but the setting up of a new institution - the Quaker Meeting - a new source of authority in religion based on the democratic ideas emerging in the current political milieu.

The theoretical problems of explaining radical innovation in religion from an empiricist position and from a position based on the priority of language are considered. The empiricist's anomalous use of the concepts of private perception and private objects is indefensible; the idea that experiences can be recognized as religious prior to the possession of the appropriate concepts cannot be made to work; experiences cannot be used as evidence for the existence of a supernatural world, and there are serious problems involved in their role in the criticism and change of religious concepts and institutions.

219

Theories of religion based on the priority of language have problems explaining radical innovation because they see religions primarily as socially-established, rule-following systems of beliefs. They emphasize their arbitrary nature and their isolation from justification or criticism from external sources, such as independent rational deliberation or experiences of an independently perceived world. The implications of this position seem to be that: changes in allegiance from one set of beliefs to another cannot be seen as conclusions from evidence, or any sort of rational inference from experience; theology has an exclusively internal role within the language-system that substantially constitutes the religion; the construction of new religious belief systems is arbitrary. These apparent implications however all appear, from acquaintance with the way innovation occurs in religions, to be false. MacIntyre's, Winch's and Phillips' attempts to resolve this dilemma are examined and criticized. Although hints are obtained as to how a resolution might be effected, no satisfactory explanation of radical innovation in religion is found.

The clues suggested by the case study and by this theoretical analysis are brought together in the suggestion that these problems might be resolved by considering religions not primarily as a sort of experience, nor primarily as a sort of language, but as an aspect of culture, open to the influence of people's changing natural and social environment - in other words, by setting up an institutional theory of religion. A satisfactory explanation of innovation in religion must be based on sound philosophical assumptions and correspond in a satisfying way to plausible accounts of instances of the phenomenon. This is taken to mean that it must begin with the assumption that there is no source of criteria for giving intelligibility or credibility to our talk or experiences that is independent of culture. On the other hand, to be credible, accounts need to accommodate the facts that: many religions are committed to the idea of absolute truth and to explanations of the meaning and destiny of human life in terms of concepts that transcend, in some way, the natural world; religions can act as a base for the criticism and change of culture; innovators can criticize and change religions in ways that can be seen to be intelligibly related to changing historical situations; the reception or rejection of new religious practices and ideas by individuals is not detached from their experiences nor from intelligible reasons; the role of theology includes relating religious ideas and practices to other aspects of a community's intellectual and social milieu.

Attempts to set up institutional theories of art and their copious critics are examined. The majority of these attempts largely fail because of the historical association of institutional theories with rigorous essentialist theories, and because they tend to interpret "institutions" in terms of socially-established bodies of people, rather than socially established activities.

The religious concept of consecration sheds some light on the idea of making objects into works of art. An institutional approach also promises to illuminate the concept of revelation, the social functions of ritual activities and their relationship to belief systems and to the beliefs and experiences of individuals, the role of experiences and of tradition and authority in religion, as well as the central concern of the book - the process of innovation in religion.

The nature of institutions is investigated. Institutions are defined as socially established (rather than natural) repeated, symbolic activities (i.e. rituals) that are shared by a community (rather than being private). This definition is not a tight one. In each case the distinctions being made are imprecise. An institutional theory can not therefore be used to construct a rigorous essentialist definition of religion, only as an aid to understanding.

Other characteristics of institutions are that they have roots in biological and psychological facts of the human condition (and in natural activities), but come to be governed and defined by conventions that are established in particular communities. They do not always have explicit meanings for their participants but tend to attract theoretical justifications. Although they are the property of communities and although, in some senses, they determine the way individuals perceive and think, and mould their actions and beliefs, institutions are made by people who feel, think, intend and act. Institutions are necessarily linked with the concept of authority - the inherent authority of tradition (of rule following activities), and the power of people who use and control them. They are, nevertheless, also characterized by being open to change - responsive to shifting patterns of experiences, behaviour and authority structures.

The idea of an institutional concept is clarified; a concept is institutional if its use is regulated by institutions - if decisions about the correct application of a word are substantially determined by acquaintance with institutional, rather than natural, functions, properties and values. The question is put: how far are the concepts of a religious object, a religious activity and a religious experience institutional concepts?

The chapter on religious objects begins with a discussion of institutional objects and ascriptive declarations - the process by which objects acquire institutional descriptions, functions, values and properties. This process is seen to be complex and imprecise. Objects are considered sacred in all religions because they have been set apart to assist in ritual contact with the divine, because they are connected either with places where significant religious experiences have taken place or with people who appear to have a special relationship with the divine, or because they are objects which seem to act as a focus of spiritual power. But in each of these cases the use is institutional, for the choice of experiences, people and objects and the process of acquiring the new status is regulated by conventions. In each case knowing which objects are sacred involves knowing about institutions, rather than distinguishing natural properties. Sacred objects acquire their status by the process of ascriptive declaration, even if it is not formal or explicit (as it is in the case of consecration, canonization etc.).

Human activities are generally recognized as religious by their connection with the cohering and continuing set of institutions recognized as religious by an individual's community. People know what makes an activity religious because they know what their religious specialists do and what goes on in their religious buildings. In alien or pluralistic cultures the process is more complicated. Human activities can there be recognized as religious (rather than, for instance, aesthetic, military or political) by making reference to the supposed meaning of the activity for its participants (whether or not the meaning is made explicit by the community). There are no natural, direct, private activities that can be recognized as religious without reference to such a meaning. All such activities can have a secular meaning to their participants; religious worship, for example, is a complicated activity that cannot be equated with the expression of wonder or respect.

Institutions can sometimes be recognized from their natural roots. (Marriage, for instance, can be recognized from its roots in taking mates.) But institutional activities are defined by the particular conventions that regulate them. There is no answer to questions such as: Yes, but apart from the conventions of a particular community, what counts as marrying? A religious activity is, in this sense, an institutional concept.

The experiences which people class as religious are investigated. They are expressed in the language of events, feelings, insights and perceptions. In each category the range is immense, covering almost everything that could be called an experience.
There appear to be three main ways in which people use the adjective "religious" to apply to experiences. The standard use is one in which the experience is directly connected with a religious tradition, either because of the setting or context, the choice of symbols in which it is expressed, or its result in leading someone towards or away from religious belief and practice.
What is called the "cosmic" use is one in which experiences are connected with the "cosmic quest" - the search for answers to questions about the nature and destiny of human life. This quest can, however, terminate in mundane, secular, naturalistic or atheistic beliefs. It is also, in some senses, necessarily a communal, rather than a personal, activity.

Some people claim that experiences can be classed as religious by the recognition of a certain quality, which includes the weird and inexplicable, and various unusual states of consciousness. This use was shown to be incoherent; there is no quality, or family of qualities, that identifies the experiences regarded as religiously significant and valuable by the religions of the world. Experiences of any quality whatsoever can be described in religious or in secular language. Any coherence in the experiences chosen to be recounted in religious terms is more plausibly explained in terms of currently available concepts of divinity. In each case therefore the use of the concept of a religious experience is an institutional one.

Some possible philosophical criticisms are faced, namely, that an institutional theory of religion necessarily implies or leads to unacceptable forms of essentialism, relativism and naturalism.
It is argued that an institutional theory of religion can reasonably be seen as a quest for understanding, rather than a quest for an essentialist definition of religion; and that the kind of relativism an institutional theory implies is not inconsistent with the absolute truth claims that are characteristic of many religious belief systems. The fairly strong cognitive relativism it implies does not mean that absolute truth claims are necessarily meaningless, nor that there is no justification for making them,

223

nor intelligible reasons for choosing between them. It is also argued that the kind of naturalism an institutional theory of religion implies is not inconsistent with the most common religious concept of revelation, for while it implies a kind of methodological naturalism it does not prejudice the terms of further understanding.

Towards an institutional theory of religion

An institutional theory of religion denies that there is any property of objects, or quality of experiences, or kinds of activity, attitude or instinct (that is any brute fact) that can be identified as, or used to identify what counts as, religious, independently of, or prior to, cultural institutions; rather, that it is the historical continuity of these institutions (that is a set of institutional facts) that substantially determines what is, and what is not, to be valued and considered authentic in religion in each community. Institutions are seen, in this context, not as bodies of people (a view which contributed much to the failure of institutional theories of art), but as activities or practices that have acquired special significance and authority within a particular community (like opera, elections or baptism). More specifically they are socially established (rather than natural), repeated, symbolic (i.e. ritual) activities that are shared (rather than being private).

Activities, objects and experiences are, therefore, correctly described as religious by virtue of their position in relation to an institutional framework - a set of culturally established practices - rather than by virtue of any natural property or quality or relationship. People who use the concepts of a religious activity, a religious object and a religious experience, do so (and can only do so) against the background of such sets of practices, even if they do not engage in them themselves.

In general there are, therefore, no constraints on which activities, objects and experiences can be designated religious. But individuals, from within their own social context, are constrained by history - by the activities, objects and experiences which have been so designated by their community (or other communities with which they are familiar) in the past. Religions are not the product, nor the property, of individuals; they grow in, and belong to, communities. Individuals within a community encounter and participate in religious institutions to a different extent and in various ways, but it is from their acquaintance with them that they learn how to use religious concepts, to recognize and interpret religious experiences and, in some cases, to build up a personal set of religious beliefs and patterns of behaviour.

These institutions - not as isolated spheres of influence, but as aspects of a whole culture - form and determine the way people understand, interpret and reason about all their experiences, serving specific functions in the community and in the lives of individuals within it that are related to and interact with their psychology and life histories. As aspects of a wider culture, they can be compared with, and assessed in terms of, other aspects of that culture, and they can act as a base for its criticism and change. If they are going to survive and flourish they must continue to relate in some way to the wider culture in which those who use them live.

The advantages of an institutional theory of religion

The philosophy of religion has in the past tended to be preoccupied with the justification of religious beliefs - with questions about whether the creeds espoused by religious believers can, in any sense of the word, be true, whether they can be rationally assessed and if so how, and with what results. An institutional theory disconnects understanding and justification. It directs attention away from religions as systems of cognitive beliefs which can or cannot be justified, towards religions as they are practised, within the wider cultures in which they are embedded.

Understanding is quite as legitimate a philosophical interest as justification. (It has always been a central concern of aesthetics for example.) And seeing religions as institutions, embedded in other aspects of culture, makes a major contribution towards our understanding of them.

Particularly it highlights the importance of the tension between tradition and innovation within religions. Religions, in order to survive and flourish in changing historical circumstances, have to change. Rituals related exclusively to the harvest serve little function in an urban society; a theology based on feudal relationships and male chauvinism cannot flourish in a society transformed by self-determination and feminist activity; missionary strategy based on a colonial mind-set is doomed in a

225

developing world.

But, on the other hand, religions must, if they are to survive, hold onto their traditions. As institutions, in the sense outlined in this thesis, the central core of their authority is their nature as established practices. Discussions within religious traditions about possible changes in their practices, and subsidiary questions about who has the authority to make changes, threaten the feeling of coherence and security produced by the inherent authority of a tradition.

This explains to some extent why changes in practice (such as the introduction of an alternative prayer book, or the ordination of women) are so rigorously resisted (and not only by the members of the community in question; it is interesting to speculate on why philosophers so frequently seem to back the conservatives in these debates). But tradition is not the only source of authority in religions and what frequently happens in these sorts of situations is that religious communities look to other sources of authority to back the need for change against the authority of tradition. Thus George Fox appealed to the authority of the Meeting, led by the Inner Light, Martin Luther appealed to St Paul's theology and Christian feminists go back to try and re-interpret the teaching of the New Testament.

This internal tension is of course not only a problem for the Church of England, or European Christianity; in any situation where social relationships are changing, or where communities with different traditions live side-by side, there is a tension between the policy of retreating into an isolated sub-culture, and that of allowing one's tradition to become so changed that the sense of continuity is lost. Both policies, if pursued too rigorously, lead to the impoverishment, or the demise, of the tradition, with the risk of emotional upheaval and social dislocation.

An institutional theory not only helps us understand the tensions within religions, but also the tensions between different religions, and religions and the wider culture, for changes in the secular aspects of a culture can insidiously erode the authority of a religion which is embedded in it. Religious traditions that are transposed by immigration into cultures very different from the ones in which they arose and flourished have special difficulties here. The case study of George Fox showed how the rise of individualism and democracy in the political sphere eroded the authority of the established church in the seventeenth century.

The same point could have been made by pointing to the way literary and historical scholarship was seen to erode the authority of the Bible in a later century, or to the way Asian immigrant communities struggle to relate their religious traditions to their new cultural situation.

On the other hand, this book has been written during the spectacular collapse of the authority of Communism in Eastern Europe, the seeds of which can be seen to have been nurtured within the Christian communities of those countries, whose very presence provided an alternative focus of authority.

It is becoming clear that religions are not going to die out in Western society (as philosophers have from time to time suggested) nor does it at the moment seem likely that syncretism will come up with any lasting answers. Religious pluralism is here to stay. It therefore becomes increasingly important to understand the factors involved in the relationship between different religious traditions and the wider culture in which they seek to flourish, so that the tensions that arise within and between them might be directed into creative, rather than destructive channels.

The advantages of an institutional theory in accounting for radical innovation in religion

A theory of innovation in religion based on an institutional theory would look like this: institutions, as they have been described in this book, serve social functions. They are used by groups of people, who may come to find them inadequate or irrelevant for all sorts of reasons probably best described as changes in their historical situation. Invasion, emigration, failure of the harvest, intellectual or technological revolution, a change in geographical location, in power, economic and social structures and relationships, contact with other cultures etc. change people's life histories, their social and psychological needs, their ways of thinking and their views about what is significant or important. It is these sorts of changes that put pressure on people to abandon or change institutions which no longer seem to be necessary or satisfactory. At the same time the internal authority of rule-following activities, and the power of the people who have an interest in their continued existence, produce resistance to change.

227

Changes in the use of institutions can occur gradually. They can lose their significance, be moved to the edges of a society and linger there, or die out. Alternatively they can be revitalized by being gradually changed in a way that is seen as an intelligible development in the rules controlling their use - the idea of, "going on in the same way" - being interpreted in a different, but recognizably similar way (whether it is the activity that is changed or its meaning to its participants).

Sometimes, however, in situations of tension like these, an individual innovator comes up with a radical idea - a proposal for a major change in a particular religious institution, or for the introduction of a completely new one. If the proposal seems appropriate to, and is accepted by, a sufficient number of people, a new religious tradition is formed, but for this to happen the new institution has to be intelligibly related both to the institutions it replaces (in order to be recognized as a religious institution) and to the historical situation that provoked it (in order to satisfy the needs of its participants).

An institutional theory of religion appears to be a fruitful base for further work in a wide variety of fields. The theory itself needs refining and developing, particularly in relation to the roles of tradition and experience, and different sources of authority, in determining the religious beliefs and practices of communities and individuals. Further case studies of innovation and change in different cultural settings could be helpful here, such as the development of Jewish theology during the exile in Babylon, Guru Nanak and the founding of the Sikh religion in early 16th century India, the development of the Christian Eucharist from the Passover and its subsequent development in practice and meaning through different periods of history, or the tensions and changes experienced in the religious traditions of Asian immigrants to Britain. The social function of ritual activities could be further investigated, as well as the relationship between such activities and the belief systems that accompany them.

The attempt to find an analysis of religion that (unlike empiricist theories) recognizes the place of tradition without (like theories based on the priority of language) denying the possibility of radical innovation, has thus led towards an institutional theory of religion that is based on sound philosophical assumptions, corresponds in a satisfactory way to plausible accounts of how radical innovation takes place in religions and is a fruitful base for further work towards a better understanding of religion.

228

Bibliography

Aagaard-Mogensen, Lars (ed.) (1976), *Culture and Art*,
   Humanities Press, New Jersey.
Alexander, S. (1927), *Space, Time and Deity,* (Gifford
   Lectures 1916-18), Macmillan, London.
Anscombe, Elizabeth (1958), "On Brute Facts", *Analysis*, 18.
Austin, J. L. (1962), *How to do things with Words*, (The
   William James Lecture 1955), The Clarendon Press, Oxford.
Ayer, A. J. (1968), *The Origins of Pragmatism*, Macmillan,
   London.
Aylmer, G. E. (ed.) (1975), *The Levellers in the English
   Revolution*, Thames-Hudson, London.
Bakalar, James (1985), "Social and Intellectual Attitudes towards
   Drug Induced Religious Experience", *Journal of Humanistic
   Psychology*, Vol. 25, No. 4.
Basham, A. L. (1959), *The Concise Encyclopedia of Living
   Faiths*, R. C. Zaehner (ed.)
Beardsley, Monroe C. (1976) "Is Art Essentially Institutional?",
   Culture and Art, Lars Aagaard-Mogenson (ed.)
Beattie, J. H. M. (1984), "Objectivity and Social Anthropology",
   Objectivity and Cultural Divergence, S. C. Brown (ed.)
Benton, Ted (1984), "Biological Ideas and their Cultural Uses",
   Objectivity and Cultural Divergence, S. C. Brown (ed.)
Berenson, Frances (1984), "Understanding Art and Understanding
   Persons", *Objectivity and Cultural Divergence,* S. C. Brown
   (ed.)
Betjeman, John (1984), *Collected Poems*, Guild publishing,
   London.

Biblical references are from the *New International Version* (1987), Hodder and Stoughton, London.

Blizek, William (1974), "An Institutional Theory of Art", *British Journal of Aesthetics*, Vol. 14.

Braithwaite, R. B. (1967), "The Nature of Believing", *Knowledge and Belief*, A. Phillips Griffiths (ed.)

Brierley, Peter (1990), *What Happened at Mission '89?*, (Research Monograph), Marc Europe, London.

Brinton, Howard (1955), *Guide to Quaker Practice*, Pendle Hill Publications, Wallingford, Penn.

Brown, Hedy and Stevens, Richard (eds.) (1975), *Social Behaviour and Experience*, Open University/Hodder and Stoughton, London.

Brown, Stuart C. (1969), *Do Religious Claims make Sense?* SCM, London.

-- (ed.) (1977), *Reason and Religion*, Royal Institute of Philosophy/Cornell University Press, Ithaca.

-- (ed.) (1984), *Objectivity and Cultural Divergence*, Royal Institute of Philosophy/Cambridge University Press, Cambridge.

Cohen, Ted (1973), "The Possibility of Art: Remarks on a Proposal by Dickie", *Philosophical Reviews*, Vol. 82.

Cragg, Kenneth (1978), *Islam and the Muslim*, Units 20-21 Open University Course 208, Open University Press.

Cupitt, Don (1980), *Taking Leave of God*, SCM, London.

Danto, Arthur C. (1964), "The Artworld", reprinted in *Culture and Art*, Lars Aagaard-Mogensen (ed.)

-- (1973), "Artworks and Real Things", *Theoria*, Vol. 39.

Dickie, George (1974), *Art and the Aesthetic: An Institutional Analysis*, Cornell University Press, Ithaca.

-- (1976), "What is Art?", *Culture and Art*, Lars Aagaard-Mogensen (ed.)

-- (1984), *The Art Circle*, Haven Publications, New York.

Diffey, T. J. (1969), "The Republic of Art", *British Journal of Aesthetics*, Vol. 9.

-- (1979), "On Defining Art", *British Journal of Aesthetics*, Vol. 19.

Dillistone, F. W. (1981), *Religious Experience and Christian Faith*, SCM, London.

Dilman, Ilman and Phillips, D. Z. (1971), *Sense and Delusion*, Routledge and Kegan Paul, London.

Dostoevski, Fyodor (1913), *The Idiot*, Constance Garnett (trs.),

Heineman, London.

-- (1953), *The Devils*, David Magarshack (trs.), Penguin, London.

Douglas, J. D. (ed.) (1962), *The New Bible Dictionary*, Inter-Varsity Fellowship, London.

Douglas, Mary (1980), *Evans Prichard*, Harvester Press, Brighton.

Durkheim, Emile (1982), *The Rules of Sociological Method*, W. D. Halls (trs.), Free Press, New York.

Eibl-eibesfeldt, I. (1975), "The Ethology of Man", *Social Behaviour and Experience*, Hedy Brown and Richard Stevens (eds.)

Finlayson, R. A. (1962), *The New Bible Dictionary*, J. D. Douglas (ed.)

Flew, A. and MacIntyre, A. (eds.), (1955), *New Essays in Philosophical Theology*, SCM, London.

Frazer, James (1922), *The Golden Bough*, Macmillan, London.

Fried, Michael (1965), Catalogue Essay for *Three American Painters*, an exhibition of Noland, Olitski and Stells, Fog Art Museum, Harvard University.

Gellner, Ernest (1970), "Concepts and Society", *Rationality*, Bryan Wilson (ed.), Blackwell, Oxford.

Golding, William (1954), *Lord of the Flies*, Faber and Faber (1984), London.

-- (1955), *The Inheritors*, Faber and Faber (1961), London.

-- (1979), *Darkness Visible*, Faber and Faber (1988), London.

Goleman, Daniel (1977), *The Varieties of the Meditative Experience*, Irvington, New York.

Goulder, Michael and John Hick (1983), *Why Believe in God?*, SCM, London.

Goldstein, David (1978), *The Religion of the Jews*, Units 16-17 OU course 208, Open University Press.

Griffiths, A. Phillips (ed.) (1967), *Knowledge and Belief*, Oxford University Press, London.

Haack, Robin (1982), "Wittgenstein's Pragmatism", *American Philosophical Quarterly*, Vol. 19, No. 2.

Hardy, Alister (1979), *Science, Religion and World Unity*, Religious Experience Research Unit, Oxford.

-- (1979), *The Spiritual Nature of Man*, Oxford University Press, Oxford.

Heelas, Paul (1984), "Emotions Across Cultures", *Objectivity and Cultural Divergence*, S. C. Brown (ed.)

Hick, John (ed.) (1964), *Faith and the Philosophers*, St Martin's Press, New York.

-- (ed) (1964), *The Existence of God*, Macmillan, London.

-- (1967), *Faith and Knowledge*, Macmillan, London.

-- (1969), "Religious faith as experiencing-as", *Talk of God*, G. N. A. Vesey (ed.)

Hill, Christopher et. al. (1982), *Seventeenth Century England: a Changing Culture 1618-1689*, Block 1 Open University Course 203, Open University.

Horner, I. B. (1977), *The Concise Encylopedia of Living Faiths*, R. C. Zaehner (ed.)

Hoskins, Anne and Sharman, Alison (eds.) (1980), *Quakers in the Eighties*, Quaker Home Service, London.

Hudson, W. D. (1968), *Ludwig Wittgenstein*, Lutterworth Press, London.

-- (1975), *Wittgenstein and Religious Belief*, Macmillan, London.

Hughs, Ann (ed.) (1980), *Seventeenth Century England: A Changing Culture, Vol. 1 Primary Sources*, Open University.

James, William (1888), *What the Will Effects*, Scribeners Magazine III.

-- (1890), *The Principles of Psychology*, Harvard University Press (1981), Cambridge, Mass.

-- (1897), "The Sentiment of Rationality", *The Will to Believe*, Fred Burkhardt (ed.), Harvard University Press (1979), Cambridge, Mass.

-- (1898), "Philosophical Conceptions and Practical Results", *The Writings of William James*, John J. McDermott, (ed.) University of Chicago Press (1977), Chigago.

-- (1901-1902), *The Varieties of Religious Experience*, (The Modern Library, New York 1936) Fontana (1977), Glasgow.

Jenkins, David (1987), An interview with Walter Schwarz, *Guardian Weekly*, November 15th.

Katz, Steven T. (ed.) (1978), *Mysticism and Philosophical Analysis*, Sheldon Press, London.

Keightley, Alan (1976), *Wittgenstein, Grammar and God*, Epworth, London.

Kennick, William (1965), "Comments on the Artworld", *Journal of Philosophy*, Vol, 63.

Kierkegaard, Soren (1941), *The Sickness unto Death*, Walter
Lowrie (trs.), Princeton University Press, Princeton.

Lampen, John (1981), *Wait in the Light*, Quaker Home Service,
London.

Lash, Nicholas (1986), *Theology on the Way to Emmaus*, SCM,
London.

Laslet and Runciman (eds.) (1972), *Philosophy, Politics and
Society*, Second Series, Blackwell, Oxford.

Levin, Bernard (1980), *The Times*, November 26th.

Levinson, Jerrold (1979), "Defining Art Historically", *British
Journal of Aesthetics*, Vol. 19.

Lewis, C. S. (1959), *Surprised by Joy*, Fontana, London.

Lyas, Colin (1977), "The Groundlessness of Religious Belief",
Reason and Religion, Stuart C. Brown (ed.)

Macfague, Sallie (1983), *Metaphorical Theology*, SCM,
London.

Macintyre, Alasdair (1955), "Visions", *New Essays in
Philosophical Theology*, A. Flew, and A. MacIntyre (eds.)
-- (1957), "The Logical Status of Religious Belief",
Metaphysical Belief: Three Essays, Stephen E. Toulmin,
Ronald W. Hepburn and Alasdair MacIntyre (eds.)
-- (1964), "Is Understanding Religion Compatible with
Believing?" *Faith and the Philosophers*, John Hick (ed.)
-- (1972) "A Mistake about Causality in Social Science",
Philosophy, Politics and Society, Second Series, Laslett and
Runciman (eds.)

Malcolm, Norman (1964), "A Contemporary Discussion", *The
Existence of God*, John Hick (ed.)
-- (1989), "Wittgenstein on Language and Rules", *Philosophy*,
Vol. 64, No. 246.

Margolis, J (1974), "Works of Art as Physically Embodied and
Culturally Emergent Entities", *British Journal of Aesthetics*,
Vol. 14.

Maslow, Abraham (1970), *Religion, Values, and Peak-
Experiences*, Kappa Delta Pi - an international Honor Society
in Education, Lafayette.

Mayhall, Carole (1976), *From the Heart of a Woman*,
Navpress, Colorado.

McFee, Graham (1985), "Wollheim and the Institutional Theory
of Art", *Philosophical Quarterly*, Vol. 35, No. 139.

Miles, T. R. (1972), *Religious Experiences*, Macmillan, London.

Mitchell, Basil (1973), *The Justification of Religious Belief*, Macmillan, London.

Morton, Bruce N. (1973), "A Review of George Dickie's Aesthetics: an Introduction", *Journal of Aesthetics and Art Criticism*, Vol. 32.

Mullen, John Douglas (1988), *Kierkegaard's Philosophy*, New American Library, New York.

Nielsen, Kai (1982), *An Introduction of the Philosophy of Religion*, Macmillan, London.

Nickalls John (ed.) (1975), *Journal of George Fox*, Religious Society of Friends, London.

O'Hear, Anthony (1984), *Experience, Explanation and Faith*, Routhledge and Kegan Paul, London.

-- (1989), "Wittgenstein and the Transmission of Tradition", From the text of a lecture delivered at the Royal Institute of Philosophy. The course of lectures was later published as *Wittgenstein Centenary Essays*, Royal Institute of Philosophy and Cambridge University Press (1990), Cambridge.

Osborne, Harold (1974), "Primitive Art and Society", *British Journal of Aesthetics*, Vol. 14.

Otto, Rudolf (1923), *The Idea of the Holy*, Oxford University Press (1958), London.

Parrinder, Geoffrey (1954), *African Traditional Religion*, Sheldon Press (1974), London.

Perry, Ralph Barton (1935), *The Thought and Character of William James*, Harvard University Press, Cambridge, Mass.

Phillips, D. Z. (ed.) (1967), *Religion and Understanding*, Blackwell, Oxford.

-- (1970), *Faith and Philosophical Enquiry*, Routledge and Kegan Paul, London.

-- (1971) "Philosophizing and Reading a Story", *Sense and Delusion*, Ilman Dilman and D. Z. Phillips (eds.)

-- (1976), *Religion without Explanation*, Blackwell, Oxford.

-- (1986), *Belief, Change and Forms of Life*, Macmillan Press, London.

Piaget, Jean (1976), *The Principles of Genetic Epistemology*, Wolfe Mays (trs.), Routledge and Kegan Paul, London.

Plato, *The Republic*, A. D. Lindsay (trs.), Dent (1976), London.

Pritchard, Evans (1956), *Nuer Religion*, The Clarendon Press, Oxford.

Quinton, Anthony (ed.) (1967), *Political Philosophy*, Oxford

University Press, London.

Rader, Melvin (1974), "Dickie and Socrates on Definition", *Journal of Aesthetics and Art Criticism*, Vol. 32.

Ramsey, Ian T. (1957), *Religious Language*, SCM, London.

Robinson, Edward (ed.) (1977), *The Original Vision*, Religious Experience Research Unit, Oxford.

-- (1978), *Living the Questions*, Religious Experience Research Unit, Oxford.

Runzo, Joseph (1986), *Reason, Relativism and God*, Macmillan, London.

Ruse, Michael and Wilson, Edward O. (1986), "Moral Philosophy as Applied Science", *Philosophy*, Vol. 61, No. 236.

Sclafani, Richard J. (1973), "Artworks, Art Theory and the Artworld", *Theoria*, Vol. 39.

-- (1973), "Art as a Social Institution: Dickie's New Definition", *Journal of Aesthetics and Art Criticism*, Vol. 32.

Sharma, Ursula (1973), *Contributions to Indian Sociology*, Vikas Publishing House.

Sharrock, W. W. and Anderson, R. J. (1985), "Criticizing Forms of Life", *Philosophy*, Vol. 60, No. 233.

Silvers, Anita (1976), "The Artworld Discarded", *Journal of Aesthetics and Art Criticism*, Vol. 34, No. 4.

Sox, David (1985), *Relics and Shrines*, George Allen and Unwin, London.

Sperber, Dan (1975), *Rethinking Symbolism*, Alice I. Morton (trs.), Cambridge University Press, Cambridge.

Strawson, P. F. (1985), *Skepticism and Naturalism: Some Varieties*, (Woodbridge Lectures 1983), Methuen, London.

Swinburne, Richard (1979), *The Existence of God*, Clarendon Press, Oxford.

Taber, John A. (1986), "The Philosophical Evaluation of Religious Experience", *International Journal for Philosophy of Religion*, Vol. 19, Nos. 1-2.

Thomas, Terry (1978), *Sikhism: the Voice of the Guru*, Units 12-13 Open University Course AD208, Open University Press.

Tillich, Paul (1951), *Systematic Theology*, University of Chicago Press, Chicago.

Toulmin, Stephen E., Ronald W. Hepburn and Alasdair MacIntyre (eds.) (1957), *Metaphysical Belief: Three Essays*, SCM, London.

Trigg, Roger (1973), *Reason and Commitment*, Cambridge

University Press, Cambridge.

Vesey, G. N. A. (ed.) (1969), *Talk of God*, Royal Institute of Philosophy/ Macmillan, London.

Walters, Professor G. (1962), *The New Bible Dictionary*, J. D. Douglas (ed.)

Walton, Kendall L. A. (1977), A review of Dickie's, "Art and the Aesthetic: an Institutional Analysis", *Philosophical Reviews*, Vol. 86.

Ware, Archimandrite Kallistos (1979), *The Orthodox Way*, Mowbrays, London.

Weil, Simone (1970), *First and Last Notebooks*, Richard Rees (trs.), Oxford University Press, London.

Weitz, Morris (1956), "The Role of Theory in Aesthetics", *Journal of Aesthetics and Art Criticism*, Vol. 15, pp. 27-35.

Williams, Raymond (1981), *Culture*, Fontana, London.

Wilson, Edward O. (1978), *On Human Nature*, Harvard University Press, Cambridge Mass.

Winch, Peter (1958), *The Idea of a Social Science*, Routledge and Kegan Paul, London.

-- (1967), "Understanding a Primitive Society", *Religion and Understanding*, D. Z. Phillips (ed.)

-- (1967), "Authority", *Political Philosophy*, Anthony Quinton (ed.)

-- (1977), "Meaning and Religious Language", *Reason and Religion*, Stuart C. Brown (ed.)

Wittgenstein, Ludwig (1958), *Philosophical Investigations*, Blackwell, London.

-- (1966), "Lectures on Religious Belief", *Lectures and Conversations*, Cyril Barnett (ed.), Basil Blackwell, Oxford.

-- (1967), *Zettel*, G. E. M. Anscombe and G. H. von Wright (eds.), Basil Blackwell, Oxford.

-- (1969), *On Certainty*, G. E. M. Anscombe and G. H. von Wright (eds.), Basil Blackwell, Oxford.

-- (1971), "Remarks on Frazer's Golden Bough", *The Human World*, No. 3.

Wollheim, Richard (1975), *Art and its Objects*, Penguin, Harmondsworth. Originally published, Harper and Row (1968), New York.

-- (1980), "The Institutional Theory of Art", One of six essays published at the end of the 1980 edition of, *Art and its Objects*, Cambridge University Press, Cambridge.

Wragge, J. Philip (1950), *George Fox*, Friends Home Service
Committee.
Zaehner R. C. (1961), *Mysticism Sacred and Profane*, Oxford
University Press, Oxford.
-- (ed.) (1977), *The Concise Encylopedia of Living Faiths*,
Hutchinson, London.
Ziff, Paul (1953), "The Task of Defining a Work of Art",
Philosophical Reviews, 58-78.